164

GREEK FIRE, POISON ARROWS, AND SCORPION BOMBS

"Greek Fire, Poison Arrows, and Scorpion Bombs"

Biological and Chemical Warfare in the Ancient World

Adrienne Mayor

OVERLOOK DUCKWORTH
WOODSTOCK • NEW YORK • LONDON

First published in the United States in 2003 by
The Overlook Press, Peter Mayer Publishers, Inc.
Woodstock & New York

WOODSTOCK:
One Overlook Drive
Woodstock, NY 12498
www.overlookpress.com
[for individual orders, bulk and special sales, contact our Woodstock office]

NEW YORK:
141 Wooster Street
New York, NY 10012

LONDON:
Duckworth
61 Frith Street
London W1D 3JL
www.ducknet.co.uk

∞ The paper used in this book meets the requirements for paper
permanence as described in the ANSI Z39.48-1992 standard.

Cataloging-in-Publication Data is available from the Library of Congress

Book design and type formatting by Bernard Schleifer
Printed in the United States of America
ISBN 1-58567-348-X (US)
ISBN 0-7156-3257-4 (UK)
FIRST EDITION
1 3 5 7 9 8 6 4 2

For Michele and Michelle,
my sisters and friends

Contents

ACKNOWLEDGMENTS   9

HISTORICAL TIME LINE   11

MAPS   19

INTRODUCTION: War Outside the Rules   23

1 Hercules and the Hydra: The Invention of Biological Weapons   41

2 Alexander the Great and the Arrows of Doom   63

3 Poison Waters, Deadly Vapors   99

4 A Casket of Plague in the Temple of Babylon   119

5 Sweet Sabotage   145

6 Animal Allies and Scorpion Bombs   171

7 Infernal Fire   207

AFTERWORD: The Many-Headed Hydra   251

NOTES   259

BIBLIOGRAPHY   295

LIST OF ILLUSTRATIONS   307

INDEX   313

ACKNOWLEDGMENTS

MANY SCHOLARS, scientists, and friends helped this project take form. For expert knowledge, valuable references, critical support, and/or substantive comments on early versions of chapters, I thank Aaron Bauer, Steve Casey, Will Keener, John Kelsay, Milton Leitenberg, Michelle Maskiell, Josh Ober, Severo Perez, Robert Peterson, Julian Perry Robinson, Jack Sasson, Barry Strauss, Philip Thibodeau, Kathleen Vogel, and Mark Wheelis. Special thanks go to the LPG members of Princeton for clear-headed critiques and friendly support.

Sure-handed guidance in envisioning this project was provided by Kirsten Manges, my agent at Curtis Brown, Ltd. Caroline Trefler, my editor at The Overlook Press, offered enthusiastic support and made many valuable suggestions for improvement. I thank Michele Angel for creating the maps and helping to prepare illustrations, and Barbara Mayor for her proofreading acumen. John Herrmann, Charles Kline, Kenneth Lapatin, and John Oakley went out of their way to help me obtain illustrations.

I'm grateful that my interest in investigating the hidden scientific depths of classical legends received encouragement at early stages from Gerald Erickson, Mott T. Greene, William Hansen, Zeph Stewart, and Henriette Warwick. Some of the research gathered here first saw light in preliminary form thanks to Rob Cowley, former editor of *MHQ: Quarterly Journal of Military History* (Autumn 1997) and Peter Young, editor of *Archaeology* (November-December 1995 and March-April 1997).

And to Josiah Ober, my heart's companion: Long may our conversation continue.

HISTORICAL TIME LINE

1770 BC   Sumerian cuneiform tablets at Mari show understanding of contagion

1500–1200 BC Hittite plague victims sent to enemy lands

1300–1100 BC Bronze Age Greece

1300 BC   Ten Plagues in Egypt, called down by Moses

              Destruction of Jericho by Israelites, about 1350

1200 BC   Trojan War, poison arrows

              Philistine plague follows theft of Israelites' Arc of the Covenant

1000 BC   Solomon builds Temple at Jerusalem, plague spirits trapped in jars

              Chrysame's drugged-bull strategy helps Greeks conquer Ionia

900 BC   Elijah's fire trick with naphtha, about 875

              Assyrian fire arrows and "grenades" depicted on stone reliefs

800 BC   Homer, about 750, describes Odysseus poisoning arrows

700 BC   Projectile weapons banned in Lelantine War, Greece

              Sennacherib's Assyrian army struck by plague in Egypt/Jerusalem

              Deuteronomy rules of war written

600 BC Kirrha, Greece, defeated by poison in water supply, about 590

Nebuchadnezzar sacks Jerusalem temple, releasing plague, 586

Baba Gurgur, eternal petroleum fire worshipped in Babylonia

Alyattes vs Cimmerians, using war dogs

Queen Tomyris of the Massagetae, army defeated with wine

Cyrus of Persia, d. 530

Cambyses of Persia, defeats Egypt with phalanx of sacred animals

500 BC Sun Tzu, *Art of War,* fire weapons

Scythian culture flourishes until about AD 300

Battle of Marathon, Greece, 490

Persian land invasion of Greece, 480

Herodotus, about 450

Peloponnesian War, 431–404

Plague of Athens, 430

Sparta vs Plataia, 429, sulphur conflagration

Boeotians vs Delium, 424, flamethrower

Thucydides, about 425

Sophocles

Euripides

Ctesias, describes oil weapon of India

Thessalos

Empedocles drains malarial swamps in Sicily

Sicilian disaster (Athens), 415–413

400 BC

Xenophon, about 400

Carthage invades Sicily, 409–396

Himlico and Maharbal poison enemy wine with mandrake

Clearchus, destroys army by forcing it to camp in swamps, 360

Alexander the Great, 356–323

Fire ship at Tyre, Phoenicians vs Alexander, 332

Porus's Indian war elephants defeated by Alexander, 326

King Chandragupta, Mauryan Empire, India, 326

Laws of Manu ban poison-tipped and fire arrows, India

Kautilya, *Arthashastra* advises poison and fire strategies, India

Chinese recipes for poison gas and toxic arrows

Battle of Harmatelia, India, poison arrows

Aeneas the Tactician, about 350

Theophrastus

Demetrius Poliorcetes vs Rhodes, fire weapons, 304

300 BC

Pyrrhus invades Italy with war elephants, 280

Antigonus Gonatus vs Megara, elephants routed by pigs, 270

First Punic War, 264–241

Hamilcar Barca

Hannibal crosses Alps with war elephants, 218

Second Punic War, 218–201

Hasdrubal's head catapulted into Carthaginian camp

Archimedes uses mirrors to burn Roman navy, Syracuse, 212

Susruta Samhita, India, written sometime between 500–100

Berossus

Antiochus vs Galatians, war elephants

200 BC   Hannibal catapults vipers, about 190

Marius, b. 157

Third Punic War, 149–146

Aquillius poisons wells in Asia, 131–129

Varro, 127–116

100 BC   Mithridates VI of Pontus, d. 63

Mithridatic Wars, 90–63

Cicero, d. 43

Sertorius vs Characitani, Spain, choking dust, about 80

Virgil, b. 70

Strabo, b. 64

Lucullus's campaigns vs Mithridates, 74–66

Pompey's army decimated by toxic honey, 65

Tigranocerta, flaming naphtha vs Romans, 69–68

Samosata, burning mud vs Romans, 69–68

Lucretius

Livy

Julius Caesar, b. 100

Diodorus of Sicily, 30

AD 1   Ovid, d. 17

Arminius's revolt in Germany

Germanicus

Dioscorides

Celsus

Frontinus

Pliny the Elder, d. 79

Tacitus, b. 56

Psylli, snake charmers of North Africa

Josephus, b. 38

Rufus of Ephesus

Lucan, b. 39

Seneca, d. 65

Domitian, b. 51

Silius Italicus

Apollonius of Tyana

Cato

Titus destroys Temple in Jerusalem, 70

"Man-made plague," Rome, 90–91

Nitishastra, by Shukra (India)

AD 100   Plutarch, about 100

Nicander, about 130

Florus

Pausanias, about 150

Galen

Appian, about 130

Polyaenus, about 161

Dio Cassius, b. 164

Commodus, b. 161

Apollodorus of Damascus

Julius Africanus

Plague of 165–180, released from Temple of Apollo, Babylonia

Marcus Aurelius, d. 180

Lucius Verus, d. 169

"Man-made plague," Rome, 189

Testament of Solomon

Septimius Severus, 145–211

Hatra, scorpion bombs and naphtha vs Romans, 198–99

AD 200   Aelian, d. 230

Chinese surgeon Hua T'o treats poison-arrow wounds

Persians vs Romans, Dura-Europos (Syria)

Plague of Cyprian

Constantine, b. 272

AD 300   Quintus of Smyrna, about 350

Vegetius, about 390

Ammianus Marcellinus, about 350

AD 400   Nag Hammadi library

AD 500   Justinian vs Chosroes of Persia

Byzantine naphtha "squirt guns"

AD 600   Koran written

Muhammad's siege of Ta'if, 630

Muhammad, d. 632

Kallinikos invents Greek Fire, 668

Greek Fire saves Constantinople, 673

Ummayad Muslims besiege Mecca with naphtha, 683

AD 700	Greek Fire saves Constantinople, 718
AD 800	Baghdad destroyed by naphtha, 813
	Naphtha troops in Islamic armies
	Gunpowder invented in China, about 850
AD 900	Russians vs Olga of Kiev, defeated by toxic honey
	Chinese battle on Yangtze, naphtha disaster, 975
	Firdawsi, Persian poet, describes Alexander as inventor of fire weapons
AD 1000	Poison Maiden lore, India
	Mahmud of Ahazna catapults snakes at Sistan, Afghanistan
AD 1100	Second Lateran Council bans Greek Fire
	Cairo destroyed by naphtha, 1167
AD 1200	Genghis Khan's conquest of China, using fire-carrying animals, 1211
	Gunpowder known to Arabs and Europeans
AD 1300	Mongols catapult plague corpses at Kaffa, 1346
	Tamerlane sacks Delhi, routing elephants with burning camels

THE MAPS

Map 1. Italy, Greece, and the Aegean.　　　　　　　　　　(Map by Michele Angel)

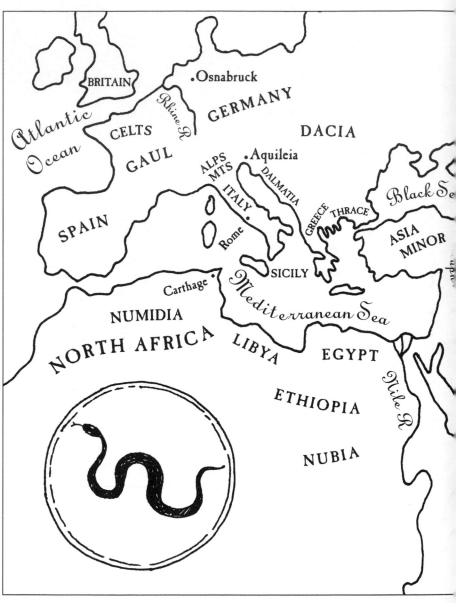

Map 2. The ancient world. (Map by Michele Angel)

SCYTHIA

Caspian Sea

Aral Sea

MASSAGETAE

CHINA

MATIA

Tigris R

PARTHIA

Khyber Pass

PERSIA

Indus River

Hydapses R

HIMALAYA MTS

LONIA

GEDROSIA

Ganges R

.Harmatelia

MAURYA

INDIA

Indian Ocean

Map 3. Asia Minor, Near East, Mesopotamia, and Parthia.

(Map by Michele Angel)

INTRODUCTION:
WAR OUTSIDE THE RULES

> In times of peace, individuals and states
> follow higher standards. . . .
> But war is a stern teacher.
>
> —THUCYDIDES,
> *History of the Peloponnesian War*

A PHALANX OF warriors armed with swords and spears advances across an open plain to confront a force of similarly armed men. Following the rules of fair combat, the fighting is hand to hand and grimly predictable. After the battle, the dead are retrieved, and victory is clear and honorable.

This stark picture has been widely assumed to sum up the ancient experience of armed conflict. Images of a long-lost era of heroic combat by brave men wielding simple weapons continue to inspire us: the Trojan War of Homeric myth, the historic Battle of Marathon, the Spartans facing Persian hordes at Thermopylae, the outnumbered Athenian triremes defeating the Persian fleet at Salamis, the Romans resisting Hannibal. But behind these glorious vignettes lurks a darker military reality, and terrifying options that rendered the courage of warriors meaningless. This book chronicles how the genie of biochemical warfare first escaped.

Germ warfare? Chemical weapons? Most people assume these terrors are recent innovations. Surely the ability to manipulate pathogens, toxins, and chemicals into tools of war requires modern scientific understanding of epidemiology, biology, and chemistry, as well as advanced delivery systems. Besides, wasn't warfare in antiquity based on honor, valor, and skill? Outside of a few well poisonings, the odd plague victim catapulted over walls in the Middle Ages, and the fabled Byzantine recipe for Greek Fire, no one really waged deliberate biological or chemical warfare until the modern era. Or did they?

Ways of turning nature's armory into weapons of war were practiced—and documented—much earlier and more extensively in pre-modern eras than has been commonly realized. Even when the practice of ancient biowar is acknowledged, modern historians have lacked convincing evidence for it. In their 1992 article "History of Biological Warfare," for example, the microbiologists Poupard and Miller mentioned that early civilizations used crude forms of biological warfare, but they alluded to only two vague examples before the eighteenth century. "Historical documentation [of] the use of biological warfare has always been sparse," they write. "The murkiness of the historical record may discourage academic pursuit of the subject but does add a certain mystique to attempts to chronicle the history of biological warfare."

Why has the ancient world remained uncharted territory in the history of chemical and biological warfare? In the first place, many historians, like the general public, have assumed that biochemical weaponry required scientific knowledge not yet developed in antiquity. Second is the assumption that even if cultures of the past *knew* how to make war with toxins and combustibles, they generally refrained from such strategies out of respect for traditional rules of war. The third reason is the difficulty of systematically collecting widely scattered and little-known ancient accounts of biochemical weapons and their forerunners in the ancient world.[1]

That evidence is gathered and analyzed for the first time in this book, and it far exceeds what we have been led to expect for pre-scientific societies. The evidence also reveals that despite the ancient literature expressing deep-seated aversion to the use of poison in war, toxic weapons were deployed by many ancient peoples. The sheer number of legendary narratives and historically verifiable incidents invites us to revise assumptions about the origins of biological and chemical warfare and its moral and technological constraints.

The ideas of poison and incendiary weapons were first described in ancient myths about arrows dipped in serpent venom, water poisoned with drugs, plagues unleashed on armies, and secret formulas for combustible weapons. The legendary Trojan War was won with poison arrows, and the celebrated heroes of Greek myth—Hercules, Odysseus, and Achilles—deliberately treated their weapons with toxins.

But killing enemies by exploiting the lethal forces of nature was not just mythical fantasy. I have gathered accounts from more than fifty authors in the ancient world, along with numerous archaeological finds, to provide evidence that biological and chemical weapons saw action in historical battles—in Europe and the Mediterranean, North Africa, Mesopotamia, Asia Minor, the Asian steppes, India, and China. Among the historical victims and perpetrators of biochemical warfare were such prominent figures as Hannibal, Julius Caesar, and Alexander the Great.

The timeframe of this book covers almost three thousand years of antiquity, beginning with Near Eastern records of 1770 BC and archaic Greek myths written down by Homer in about 750 BC. Greek historians, from the fifth century BC through the second century AD, document many examples of warfare waged by biological and chemical means, as do Latin accounts beginning with the foundation of Rome and continuing through the late Roman Empire of the sixth century AD. Meanwhile, in China and India, weapons of poison and combustible chemicals were described in military and medical treatises from about 500 BC onward. The story continues with the development of Greek Fire and other incendiaries described in Byzantine and Islamic sources of late antiquity, from the seventh through fourteenth centuries AD.

In each chapter, I have presented modern scientific discoveries and technological developments that help illuminate the ancient accounts and show how early unconventional weapons and strategies have evolved into today's biological and chemical armaments. The range of human inventiveness in the early annals of biochemical warfare is staggering. But equally impressive is the way the ancient examples anticipated, in substance or in principle, almost every basic form of biological and chemical weapon known today, even the most scientifically advanced armaments.

Pathogens and toxins unleashed on enemies? Archers in antiquity created toxic projectiles with snake venoms, poison plants, and bacteriological substances. Other options included contaminating an enemy's water and food supplies, or forcing foes to camp in mosquito-infested marshes.

Anthrax, smallpox, and bubonic plague as weapons? Deliberate attempts to spread contagion are recorded in cuneiform tablets and biblical traditions and by Roman historians who decried "man-made pestilence." Vaccinations to protect against bio-weapons? The ancients were the first to try to seek immunity against the toxic weapons of their day.

Today, it is feared that a single "smallpox martyr" could deliver a devastating biological attack. The practice of sending infected individuals into enemy territory was already operating more than three thousand years ago among the Hittites. Later, "Poison Maidens" were sent to assassinate Alexander the Great and other military commanders.

What could be more modern than "ethnic" bio-weapons? These agents, based on genetic engineering of DNA, would target certain racial groups. Yet, the primitive roots of such weapons lie in the systematic slaughter of men and the rape of women, crude but effective blows against an enemy's reproduction. Practiced since earliest times, such strategies have been documented most recently in the ethnic wars of former Yugoslavia.

The current "war on terrorism" has launched new, so-called nonlethal weapons, such as "calmative mists," to tranquilize, disorient, or knock out enemies, rendering them incapable of defending themselves. The same principle was first applied in warfare in an ingenious plot by the ancient Greeks when they conquered Ionia (modern Turkey). Victories via intoxicants occurred in ancient military engagements in Gaul, North Africa, Asia Minor, and Mesopotamia. The biological "calmatives" of antiquity included toxic honey, drugged sacrificial bulls, barrels of alcohol, and mandrake-laced wine.[2]

What about stench warfare? Acoustic weapons? In recent years the

Pentagon has unveiled "psychologically toxic" armaments designed by bioengineers to assault the senses with unbearable odors and sound waves. More than two millennia ago, armies in Asia and Germany employed noxious smells and blaring noises to overwhelm foes.

Cyborg rats wired to deliver explosives? Sea lions as sentinels or assassins? Bees enlisted to detect the presence of enemies and chemical agents? Even these sophisticated biological operations have ancient antecedents. Live insects and animals have been drafted for war for thousands of years: wasps' nests were lobbed over walls, vipers were catapulted onto ships, and scorpion bombs were hurled at besiegers. A veritable menagerie of creatures—from mice and elephants to flaming pigs—became allies on the battlefields of antiquity. Generals even devised ways for animals to deliver combustibles and figured out how to exploit inter-species hostilities.

How about poison gas, flamethrowers, and incendiary bombs? Propelling fire and creating toxic fumes have a venerable history, too. Flaming arrows were only the beginning. The Assyrians tossed firebombs of oil, and during the Peloponnesian War, the Spartans created poison gas and a flame-blowing machine to defeat fortified positions. Recipes for toxic smoke were secret weapons in ancient China and India, and asphyxiating gases suffocated many a tunneler in Roman-era sieges. Meanwhile, catapults shot firebolts fueled by sulphur. In the time of Alexander the Great, fire ships laden with burning chemicals destroyed navies, and foot soldiers were incinerated by incendiary shrapnel in the form of red-hot sand. During the siege of Syracuse in 212 BC, mirrors were used to ignite ships, more than two thousand years before the development of high-tech laser and microwave guns.

Napalm? Invented in the 1940s, the devastating effects of this petroleum weapon that flows like water and adheres like flaming glue were prominent in Vietnam in the 1970s. Greek Fire had similar properties and became the dreaded naval incendiary of the Byzantine era, until the formula was lost forever. But many centuries earlier, long *before* the invention of Greek Fire in AD 668, petroleum and other chemicals were combined to create harrowing weapons of unquenchable fire, used to immolate Roman soldiers in the Middle East.

What all these modern weapons and their ancient precursors have in common is the fact that they allow their creators to *weaponize nature*, according to the best understandings of the day. Not all of the ancient examples presented in the following chapters fit the strict definitions of biological or chemical weapons current today, but they do represent the earliest evidence of the intentions, principles, and practices that evolved into modern biological and chemical warfare. The parallels between the pre-scientific methods of antiquity and the most up-to-the-minute armaments suggest the need to expand definitions of biological and chemical weaponry beyond narrow categories.

Chemical warfare is the military use of poisonous gases and incendiary materials, and includes blistering, blinding, asphyxiating agents and mineral poisons. *Biological* weapons are viable, based on living organisms. They include infectious bacteria, viruses, parasites, and spores, all of which can multiply in the body to increase in effect, and can be contagious. The hostile use of plant toxins and venomous substances derived from animals, reptiles, amphibians, marine creatures, and insects constitutes another category of biological weapons. Living insects and animals turned to the service of war, and genetic strategies against adversaries, are additional types of weapons based on biology. The biological-chemical weapons arsenal also comprises disabling or harmful agents created through biology, chemistry, and physics to act on the body; these include pharmaceuticals, malodorants, light or sonic waves, electric shocks, heat rays, and the like. Using scientific knowledge to create agents that give soldiers special powers or protection can also be considered part of the biochemical armory.[3]

In essence, biochemical warfare is the manipulation of the forces or elements of nature to insidiously attack or destroy an adversary's biological functions in ways that cannot be deflected or avoided. Biological agents and chemical incendiaries intensify levels of suffering and destruction of human life far beyond what would be expected in conventional warfare. In early antiquity, conventional weapons were sharp or blunt instruments of stone, wood, and metal: rocks, arrows, spears, swords. Over time, catapults and other siege machines came to be generally accepted as conventional, but poison weapons, despite their recurrent use, continued to arouse ethical concern and condemnation.[4]

Historical texts document specific episodes of biological and chemical warfare in datable conflicts, but myths and legendary events, ideas for creating biochemical weaponry, and recipes of evil effect also demonstrate the antiquity of the search for ever more creative ways of turning nature to military use. The conscious intention to communicate infectious disease, regardless of success, is a valid criteria for analyzing biological warfare, according to the microbiologist and bio-war historian Mark Wheelis. For example, the ancient practice of entreating the gods who were believed to control plagues to attack enemies demonstrates a clear *desire* to wage biological warfare. Accusations of the deliberate spread of epidemics also belong in this history, because, as has Wheelis noted, they "attest to the fact that biological attack" was imaginable and plausible.[5]

*   *   *

After citing a few oft-repeated incidents of biochemical strategies in antiquity and the Middle Ages, typical histories of biological and chemical weaponry usually designate the gas warfare of World War I as the beginning point. Historians have assumed that biological and chemical weapons were "exceedingly rare" in antiquity because they were "inhibited by societal constraint" and expressly forbidden in codes of war. Indeed, the existence of age-old "taboos" against the use of poisons in war, many historians argue, can serve as the "moral backbone" for creating sustainable, effective biochemical arms treaties today.

But as it turns out, war with poison and chemicals was not so rare in the ancient world and reactions to it were complex. An astounding panoply of toxic substances, venomous creatures, poison plants, animals and insects, deleterious environments, virulent pathogens, infectious agents, noxious gases, and combustible chemicals were marshaled to defeat foes—and *panoply* is an apt term here, because it is the ancient Greek word for "all weapons." Many of these bio-weapons and stratagems, some crude and others quite sophisticated, were considered fair, acceptable ruses of war, while others were reviled. The ancient tension between notions of fair combat and actual practice reveals that moral questions about biochemical weapons is not a modern phenomenon, but has existed ever since the first war arrow was dipped in poison. Ethical revulsion for poison weapons did not arise in a vacuum, but developed in reaction to real practices. Edward Neufeld, a scholar of ancient Mesopotamia, has suggested that the "deep aversion to this type of warfare" stemmed not from humanitarian philosophies, but was a moral judgment that flowed directly from "feelings evoked by experience" with egregiously cruel and brutal weapons.[6]

Since antiquity it has been recognized that conventions of war are culturally and historically determined. In the first century BC, the geographer Strabo remarked: "Among all the customs of warfare and of usage of arms there neither is, nor has been, any single custom." The Greek historian Thucydides (fifth century BC) stressed that ideal standards of behavior in war were in constant conflict with expediency, ingenuity, and passion. In early antiquity, a single day's battle between equally armed warriors was often decisive, and biological weapons may have been less of a temptation. Yet, biological and chemical weapons were known from earliest times, and with the development of siegecraft and long, drawn-out wars, "unfair" secret weapons became ever more attractive. In sieges, civil wars, and rebellions, or in conflicts with exotic cultures, the whole population was considered the enemy, further lifting constraints on vicious weaponry and total-war tactics.[7]

"As fighting became more destructive," notes historian Peter Krentz, "a new, nostalgic ideology of war developed." Krentz was speaking of Greece after the savage Peloponnesian War (431–404 BC), but his words could also apply to modern historians who imagine that wars were somehow more humane and fair in antiquity. As historian Josiah Ober remarks, however, "Any argument which assumes that a universal sense of fair play and decency was an innate part of early Greek military culture is easily falsified." The tension between the "fair fight" and "winning by whatever means necessary" was evident from the very beginning.

Ordinary fighting with regular hacking and stabbing weapons was violent, and riveting descriptions of the mayhem of classical Greek combat—hand-to-hand fighting by hoplites (infantrymen armed with helmets, shields, and spears)—can be found in *The Western Way of War* (1989) by Victor Davis Hanson. The Roman historian Sallust painted a vivid picture of the aftermath of a typical, decisive battle between Roman troops and Numidian and Moorish divisions in 106 BC: "The end of it was that the enemy were everywhere defeated. The broad plain presented a ghastly spectacle of flight and pursuit, slaughter and capture. Horses and men were thrown down; many of the wounded, without the strength to escape or patience to lie still, struggled to get up only to collapse immediately. As far as the eye could reach, the battlefield was strewn with weapons, armor, and corpses, with patches of blood-stained earth showing between them."[8]

FIGURE 1. *Heroic hoplite combat, face-to-face fighting between equally matched Greek warriors using conventional weapons of spear and shield, 500–480 BC, amphora.*

(The J. Paul Getty Museum)

As dreadful as such carnage was, though, it was exactly what men and their commanders expected and prepared for. A well-armed and armored soldier trained for the fighting, steeled himself for the battle and the possibility of death, advanced into the fray and fought the enemy face-to-face to the end. Courage and skill counted for something: a soldier could win or die honorably, crucial values for ancient warrior cultures.

But clever ruses were also highly respected in warrior cultures. Odysseus, the archer-hero of Homer's *Odyssey,* was a master of deception. A complex figure who practiced both acceptable and heinous ruses, Odysseus's most celebrated trick was the Trojan Horse. It was a tempting gift that the Trojans could have rejected. Odysseus played on their pride and greed, not their biological vulnerability, therefore the ploy seems fair. But Odysseus also poisoned his arrows, and Homer makes it clear that toxic projectiles were dishonorable. Archers were admired for their marksmanship but they were not models of bravery, since they shot missiles from afar, avoiding direct confrontation.

If long-distance weapons in themselves were regarded with ambivalence by classical Greeks and Romans, then treating long-distance projectiles with poison could elicit even more disapproval. Use of a poisoned arrow meant that even a poor marksman could inflict grievous suffering and death on the mightiest warrior, because just a slight nick sent lethal toxins into his bloodstream. In cultures that valued intelligent cunning as well as physical courage in battle situations, conflicting ideas arose over which weapons and strategies were acceptable and which were questionable. Were crafty methods—what some would call underhanded, cowardly ruses—ever justified? The traditional view held that "vile tricks and treachery" should be shameful to any true warrior. Like arrows and ambush, biochemical weapons also allowed one to surprise and destroy enemies from a position of safety, without risking battle. As the toxic equivalents of arrows and ambush, therefore, poison weapons could elicit criticism, yet they were certainly not always shunned. Drawing the line between creative resourcefulness and reprehensible tactics proved difficult in practice.

What do ancient rules of war have to say about insidious weapons? For the most part one must extrapolate ideas about biowar from military practices described in ancient accounts. Very little is known about Persian and Carthaginian rules of war, for example, and we must rely on Greek and Latin historians for descriptions of war among the Gauls, Africans, and Scythians of Central Asia. These "barbarians" used poison projectiles, but they were also the victims of biological subterfuges by the Romans and Persians. Disapproval of the use of either poisons or chemicals can be found in ancient Indian, Greek, Roman, and Muslim traditions, but inconsistencies and contradictions cloud the issue of what was deemed acceptable in warfare.[9]

In ancient India, as in Greece, two kinds of warfare were recognized. There was righteous war carried out according to ethical principles with the approval of society, and there was crafty, ruthless war pursued in secret, without regard for moral standards. The tensions between these two approaches are embodied in two famous military codes of ancient India. The *Laws of Manu* are Hindu rules of conduct for Brahman rulers dating in oral form to about 500 BC, codified in Sanskrit in about AD 150. The *Laws* are commonly cited as the oldest prohibitions against biochemical warfare, because they forbade the use of arrows tipped with poison or fire. Reading further, though, one finds the *Laws* advising kings to "continually spoil the grass and water" of a besieged enemy.

The *Arthashastra* represented the nefarious side of ancient Indian warfare. This military treatise, written by the Brahman advisor to King Chandragupta in the fourth century BC, is filled with instructions for waging war with secret weapons and it urged kings to deploy poisons without qualms. The *Arthashastra*'s compilation of hundreds of recipes for toxic weapons and the unscrupulous tactics it describes foreshadow the sentiment attributed to the notorious Dr. Shiro Ishii, director of Japan's bio-weapons program in World War II: If a weapon is important enough to be prohibited, it must be worth having in one's arsenal.

Yet, even the ruthless *Arthashastra* also advised kings to win over enemy hearts with their "own excellent qualities," and exhorted victors to spare the wounded and vanquished. An example of dramatically opposite advice in the two Indian treatises applies to calmatives. The *Laws of Manu* forbade attacks on sleeping enemies, whereas the *Arthashastra* recommended intoxicants and soporifics, for the best time to attack is when foes are overcome by sleep.

Contradictions can be found among rules of war and military manuals in China, too. *The Art of War* by Sun Tzu (about 500 BC), for example, stressed *kueitao,* deceptive means, and advocated the use of fire as a terror weapon, and other Chinese treatises described myriad recipes for toxic smokes and poison incendiaries. Humanitarian codes of war of about 450–200 BC, however, forbade ruses of war, harming noncombatants, and causing unnecessary suffering.[10]

In the ancient Near East, the book of Deuteronomy (written in the seventh century BC) sets forth Yahweh's rules of war for the Israelites. The instructions include the famous law of retaliation "without pity," namely "life for life, eye for eye, tooth for tooth, hand for hand." When God's chosen people besieged cities outside the promised land that "refused to become enslaved," the Jews were to kill all males and claim women and children as booty. Cities within Palestine were to be treated mercilessly: "You shall utterly destroy them, leaving nothing alive that breathes." Only orchards were to be spared. These rules were put into practice, for example, in the total destruction of Jericho in about 1350 BC. Biological weapons would not appear to be prohibited under these harsh "holy war" principles and, notably, Exodus recounts some of the earliest intentions to carry out biological warfare, in the plagues called down on Egypt—although the motive in that case was resistance, not aggression.[11]

Many histories of biological and chemical warfare indicate that the Koran (written in the seventh century AD) forbids the use of poison and fire as weapons of war, but injunctions that might apply to biochemical strategies are vague: "Do not make mischief on the earth," "Show restraint," and "Do not transgress limits." These probably presupposed a "warrior code of honor known to its first hearers" but now lost, suggests John Kelsay, a scholar of Islamic rules of war. More specific rules have been inferred from later Islamic traditions, based on the deeds and sayings of Muhammad compiled after his death (in AD 632). According to the opinion of the modern Islamic scholar Hamza Yusef, Muhammad "clearly prohibited killing noncombatants, women and children [and] poisoning wells, which I think can be applied to biological warfare." Muhammad also "prohibited using fire as a means to kill another being," because fire belonged to Allah. But as many historians have pointed out, early Islamic scholars differed over permissible weapons.

Denying drinking water, even to enemies, was a grievous wrong in early Islamic belief. (In contrast, the Romans had no qualms about achieving victories "by thirst.") In the civil wars after Muhammad's death, however, that rule was violated by the dominant Umayyad forces, who were censured for transgressions of Islamic ideals. Fire weapons, on the other hand, were used routinely by early Islamic armies, even against other Muslims. Muhammad had lived at a time when petrochemical incendiaries were common in siege-craft, and the Koran prescribes punishment by fire for disbelievers: "For them are cut out garments of fire, boiling water shall be poured over their heads," and their skin and body "shall be melted." During the siege of Mecca in AD 683, Muslim forces catapulted burning petroleum at the rival Muslim defenders. By AD 900, Islamic armies maintained special troops to wield devastating "liquid fire," which became a favorite weapon against the Crusaders. Perhaps because of bans on poisoning water or air, however, Muslims apparently refrained from adding toxins to their incendiaries, as were common in ancient Chinese and Indian recipes.[12]

No formal set of rules of war existed in Greece. The military historian Polybius (born 204 BC) stated that the "ancients" preferred open, hand-to-hand battle to deception and ruses and followed a "convention among themselves" not to use "secret missiles or those discharged from a distance." But only two instances of sworn agreements prohibiting certain types of weapons are known in Greece. One, recounted by Strabo, was inscribed on a column in a temple in Euboea and recorded that in the Lelantine War (about 700 BC) the contending parties had agreed to ban projectile weapons. The other agreement directly applies to biological warfare. In the sixth century BC, after a Greek city was destroyed by poison during an attack by an alliance of city-states, the alliance vowed to refrain from such acts against fellow Greeks.

A dozen informal rules of war were gleaned from ancient Greek literature by Josiah Ober in 1994. They concern declarations of war and truces; prohibit the killing of messengers, noncombatants, and captives; and express a distaste for projectile weapons. As Ober notes, these rules "were certainly not always honored in practice," and during the Peloponnesian War, the "informal Greek rules of war broke down."

The main sources of information about warfare practices are histories written in antiquity, but even then, the writers rarely considered the rules of war unless some exceptional event occurred. It was only in describing unusual biological strategies that authors sometimes indicated the generally held standards of conduct in war. Herodotus, for example, a Greek historian of about 450 BC, described the moral outrage of a barbarian commander, Queen Tomyris, when the Persians set out wine to drug her unsuspecting troops and then slaughtered them. There is no soldierly honor in your victory, she declared, only shame.

During the Peloponnesian War, which brought accusations of well-poisoning and inventions of new chemical weapons, Thucydides wrote approvingly of one hoplite battle of 433 BC that was an increasingly rare instance in which "courage and sheer strength played a greater part than scientific methods." The brutality of the Peloponnesian War undermined the "general laws of humanity," despaired Thucydides. "Victory won by treachery" was equated with "superior intelligence," and "most people are ready to call villainy cleverness." Profound disapproval suffuses his descriptions of atrocities against noncombatants.

After the Peloponnesian War, Aeneas the Tactician wrote a manual on how to survive sieges. He advised defenders to poison water supplies, to throw burning materials onto attackers, and to choke them with noxious smoke. Significantly, all these biochemical tactics were intended for the *defense* of besieged cities. In antiquity, as today, biochemical weapons often seem more acceptable when used against aggressors.[13]

Roman notions of just war were articulated by the philosopher Cicero (106–43 BC), who believed that obeying rules of war and refraining from cruelty was what set men apart from beasts. But his laws concerned the legitimate grounds for going to war, rather than its conduct. Reactions to biological strategies are found in other Roman writers' remarks. The historian Florus, for example, castigated a Roman general for poisoning wells in Asia, and thereby sullying Roman honor; the poet Ovid deplored toxic arrows, and Silius Italicus declared that poisons brought "disgrace" to iron weapons. The historian Tacitus (AD 98) voiced grudging admiration for a German tribe who intensified "their savage instincts by trickery and clever" means, rather than opting for poison arrows like the Gauls and other groups. The Germans blackened their shields, dyed their bodies black, and "chose pitch dark nights for their battle," wrote Tacitus. "The appearance of such a ghoulish army inspires mortal panic, for no enemy can endure a sight so strange and hellish." This ancient example of creative psychological warfare was considered fair, whereas poisoning, Tacitus makes clear elsewhere, violated the old Roman tradition of open battle.

In contrast, by the second century AD, the Roman strategist Polyaenus wrote a military treatise for emperors that openly advocated biochemical and devious stratagems for defeating barbarians without risking battle. As the empire was increasingly forced to desperately defend all its borders, the old ideals of forthright combat and leniency were replaced by policies of maximum force and treachery. The new policies were articulated by the Roman military strategist Vegetius, writing in AD 390, "It is preferable to subdue an enemy by famine, raids, and terror, than in battle where fortune tends to have more influence than bravery."[14]

Despite a general sense in antiquity that biological weapons were cruel and dishonorable, the evidence shows they were employed in certain situations. So, when might the rules of war be overridden? Self-defense, mentioned earlier, was a time-honored rationale. Besieged cities resorted to all manner of resistance, including biochemical options, and desperate populations overcome by invaders turned to bioweapons as a last resort. When one's forces were outnumbered or facing troops superior in courage, skill, or technology, biological strategies were a real advantage. But the perils and loss of lives in a fair fight could be avoided altogether by deploying toxic weapons, an approach that appealed to Polyaenus and other Romans who admired the Greek hero Odysseus as the model strategist.

When opponents are identified as barbarians or cultural outsiders, their "uncivilized nature" has long served as an excuse to use unscrupulous weapons and inhumane tactics against them. Other situations, such as holy wars or quelling rebellions, also encouraged the indiscriminate use of bio-weapons, targeting noncombatants as well as warriors. Some commanders used poison in frustration when losing a war, or to break a stalemate or a long, drawn-out siege. The threat of horrifying weapons might discourage would-be attackers, or could be used by aggressors to bring quick capitulation. And then there were those ruthless generals who had no compunctions about using any strategy or weapon at hand to win victory, and in many of the cultures encountered by the Greeks and Romans, poison arrows and ambush were the customary way of war.[15]

*   *   *

Although it is tempting to imagine an ancient era innocent of biochemical weaponry, in fact this Pandora's box of horrors was opened thousands of years ago. The history of making war with biological weapons begins in mythology, in ancient oral traditions that preserved records of actual events and ideas of the era before the invention of written histories. Although the evidence from ancient myth shatters the notion of a time when bio-war was unthinkable, it also suggests that profound doubts about the propriety of such weapons arose along with their earliest usage.

After describing the mythic invention of poison weapons and their use in the legendary Trojan War in the first chapter, we turn to the actual practices of biological and chemical warfare in historical times. Ancient authors reveal exactly how arrow poisons were concocted from venoms and toxins and who used them in the ancient world, and they describe the first documented cases of poisoning enemies' water supplies and maneuvering foes into deadly environments. Next, compelling evidence from Near Eastern, Greek and Latin, and Indian sources suggests how plagues and other infectious diseases may have been deliberately spread. Other chapters show that toxic honey, tainted wine, and other attractive lures have long served as secret weapons, and tell how venomous creatures and large and small animals were drafted for war duty. Chemical incendiaries have a surprisingly ancient history, too, beginning with the earliest uses of poison gases and ancient versions of napalm centuries before the invention of Greek Fire.

The difficulty of controlling the forces unleashed when nature itself is turned into a weapon means that the annals of biochemical warfare are rife with risks of self-injury, friends fired upon in error, collateral damage, and unforeseen consequences for future generations. Because secret weapons are intended to destabilize and play on the unexpected, such strategies by their very nature have cut an erratic swath through history. It is only logical, therefore, that those who use biochemical weapons should reap a "whirlwind of unintended results."[16] That bio-war is a double-edged sword is a theme that originated in myth and pervades the long history of biochemical weapons.

Hercules and the Hydra:
The Invention of
Biological Weapons

> The poison, heated by fire, coursed through his limbs.
> His blood, saturated by the burning poison,
> hissed and boiled. There was no limit
> to his agony as flames attacked his heart
> and the hidden pestilence melted his bones.
> —Death of Hercules, Ovid, *Metamorphoses*

IT WAS HERCULES, the greatest hero of Greek mythology, who invented the first biological weapon described in Western literature. When he dipped his arrows in serpent venom, he opened up a world not only of toxic warfare, but also of unanticipated consequences. Indeed, the deepest roots of the concept of biological weapons extend very far back in time, even before the Greek myths were written down by Homer in the eighth century BC. Poison and arrows were deeply intertwined in the ancient Greek language itself. The word for poison in ancient Greek, *toxicon*, derived from *toxon*, arrow. And in Latin, the word for poison, *toxica,* was said to derive from *taxus,* yew, because the first poison arrows had been daubed with deadly yew-berry juice. In antiquity, then, a "toxic" substance meant "something for the bow and arrow."

The great Greek physician of the first century AD, Dioscorides, was the first to remark on the derivation of the word "toxic" from "arrow." But Dioscorides insisted that only barbarian foreigners—never the

Greeks themselves—resorted to poisoned weapons. His assumption was widely accepted in antiquity and still holds sway today, as evident in a recent declaration about poison arrows by Guido Majno, the medical historian whose specialty is war wounds in the ancient world: "This kind of treachery never occurs in the tales about Troy."[1]

Since antiquity, the Greek legends about great heroes and the Trojan War have been celebrated for their thrilling battles and heroic deaths in the era of myth. To be sure, the typical weapons of Bronze Age warfare glorified in the myths—bow and arrow, javelin, spear, sword, and axe—unleashed enough gory mayhem and violent death on the battlefield to satisfy the most bloodthirsty audience. But most people today assume that the very idea of poisoning weapons was a barbaric practice abhorred by the ancient Greeks. Modern audiences take it for granted that heroes like Hercules and the warriors of the Trojan War must have engaged in the noblest forms of ancient combat, fighting fairly and face-to-face. They wreaked havoc, but remained honorable in their behavior.

But not always. A closer look uncovers compelling evidence of less noble, decidedly unheroic forms of warfare in these legendary roots of Western culture. Mythical conflicts teem with treachery, and secretly poisoned arrows and spears were wielded by some of the greatest champions of classical mythology. This picture of morally unsettling ways of dispatching enemies is usually overshadowed by the larger-than-life figures and their exciting adventures. But once we begin to peer into the darker reaches of the mythic tapestry, scenes of nefarious trickery and ghastly suffering from poisoned weapons emerge.

Two famous Greek myths—the story of Hercules and the Hydra, and the Trojan War—turn out to have crucial information about the origins of biological weapons and the ancient attitudes toward their use.

*   *   *

Hercules, the superhero of Greek myth, was renowned for his Twelve Labors. In his first labor, he slaughtered the fearsome Lion of Nemea. He then donned its skin and set out on his second task. His mission was to destroy an even more daunting monster, the Many-Headed Hydra. This gigantic, poisonous water-serpent lurked in the swamps of Lerna, terrorizing the people of southern Greece. The Hydra was said to have nine, ten, fifty, even a hundred heads—and worse yet, the central head was immortal.

Hercules forced the Hydra to emerge from its den by shooting fiery arrows coated with pitch—the sticky sap from pine trees. The mighty hero then seized the giant snake with his bare hands, thinking he could strangle it like the Nemean Lion. Hercules was strong, but no match for the Hydra. It coiled its huge body around his legs and poised its multiple heads to strike. Hercules began to smash the horrid snake heads with his club. When this proved futile, he drew his sword to chop them off.

The most diabolical thing about the Hydra was that it actually "thrived on its wounds," in the words of the Roman poet, Ovid. Each time Hercules cut off one head, two more instantly regenerated. Soon

FIGURE 2. *Hercules and the Hydra. Hercules (left) chops off the heads, while his companion (right) cauterizes the necks with torches. Hercules will later dip his arrows in the Hydra's venom; meanwhile, Athena, Greek goddess of war (far right), holds the conventional weapons of a hoplite warrior, eschewed by Hercules. Krater, about 525 BC, by the Kleophrades Painter.* (The J. Paul Getty Museum)

the monster was bristling with heads and fangs dripping with venom. What to do? His ordinary weapons—hands, club, sword, arrows— were useless. So Hercules resorted to fire. Taking up a burning torch, he cauterized each bloody neck as he chopped off a head, to prevent it from sprouting new ones. But the middle head was immortal. This head Hercules hacked off, and quickly buried it alive in the ground. Then he placed a heavy rock over the spot. The ancient Greeks and Romans used to point out a colossal boulder on the road to Lerna, marking the place where Hercules had entombed the Hydra's living head.

Hercules was a hunter who took trophies: he had fashioned his famous cape from the skin of the Nemean Lion. After slaying the Hydra, Hercules slashed open the body and dipped his arrows in the poisonous venom of the monstrous serpent. Ever after, Hercules' over- sized quiver carried a seemingly endless supply of arrows made super- deadly by Hydra venom.[2]

By steeping his arrows in the monster's venom, Hercules created the first biological weapon. The inspiration flowed naturally from his pre- vious idea for magnifying the power of his arrows, by coating them in pine resin to create noxious fire and fumes (in essence, a chemical weapon). Next, Hercules appropriated the Hydra's natural weapon of deadly venom to enhance his own weapons. Since myths often coa- lesced around a core of historical and scientific realities, the ancient story of the Hydra arrows suggests that projectile weapons tipped with toxic or combustible substances must have been known very early in Greek history. Notably, the descriptions of poisoned wounds in the myths of Hercules—and the Trojan War—accurately depict the very real effects of snake venom and other known arrow toxins. In historical accounts of the ancient use of poisoned projectiles, archers concocted effective arrow poisons from a variety of pernicious ingredients, includ- ing viper venom. Indeed, the Scythians, real-life nomadic horse-people of the Steppes who were dreaded for their snake-poison arrows, con- sidered Hercules to be their cultural founder.

The mythical lore that grew up around Hercules' invention of snake-venom arrows reveals the complex attitudes of the ancient Greeks toward weapons that delivered hidden poisons. Deep misgivings were expressed in the earliest myths about warriors who destroyed their enemies with toxic weapons. Many mythological characters succumbed to Hercules' arrows. Almost as soon as they were created, however, the poison weapons set in motion a relentless train of tragedies for Hercules and the Greeks—not to mention the Greeks' enemies, the Trojans. With the very first deployment of his newly discovered biological weapons, Hercules proved powerless to avoid hurting his own friends and innocent bystanders.

The first victims included some of Hercules' oldest friends. On his way to another labor—killing a gigantic boar—Hercules attended a party hosted by his Centaur friend, the half-man, half-horse, Pholus. But when Pholus opened a jug of wine, a gang of violent Centaurs invaded the party. Hercules leapt up to repel them, and in the ensuing clash many Centaurs were felled by Hercules' poisoned arrows as he pursued them over the landscape. The fleeing horde of horse-men took refuge in the cave of Chiron, a peaceful Centaur who had taught humankind the arts of medicine and who was an old friend of Hercules.

As the Centaurs cowered around Chiron, Hercules let fly a host of Hydra-venom arrows. By mischance, one struck Chiron in the knee. Hercules rushed to his old friend's side, deeply distressed. He drew the shaft out from Chiron's leg and quickly applied a special poultice, as Chiron directed. And here the mythographers explain just how terrible a wound from a venom-tipped arrow was: The pain was so horrendous that you would sell your eternal soul for a swift death! According to myth, Chiron was immortal, but the agony was so excruciating that he begged the gods to relieve him of immortality and allow him to die.

Chiron's plea was answered when Prometheus volunteered to take on Chiron's eternal life. The Centaur was released from endless pain, and expired. Prometheus was destined to regret his act, however. When

FIGURE 3. *Hercules shoots the Centaur Nessus with a Hydra-venom arrow, as he carries away Deianeira. It was the Centaur's venom-poisoned blood that ultimately destroyed Hercules himself.*

he later stole fire from the gods and gave it to humankind, Prometheus's punishment was particularly horrifying because he could not die. As every Greek knew, every day for the rest of time, Zeus's vulture came to torture the immortal Prometheus.

While Hercules was tending the grievously wounded Chiron, his other Centaur friend, Pholus, became another unintended victim. Pholus removed an arrow from one of his companions' corpses and wondered how such a little thing could have killed such a strong creature. As he examined the arrow, it slipped from his hand and dropped on his foot. He was mortally wounded, and Hercules sorrowfully buried yet another victim of "collateral damage."

The danger of self-inflicted wounds or accidents with poison projectiles was always present, since even a mere scratch could be devastating. Legendary "friendly fire" incidents, like the tragic deaths of Chiron and Pholus, were favorite subjects of Greek and Roman painters and sculptors. Another innocent victim was Hercules' own son, Telephus. During the preparations for the Trojan War, the youth tripped on a vine and fell against a spear carried by Achilles, the great Greek warrior. The point struck Telephus's thigh, causing an incurable, festering wound. The unhealing wound implies that Achilles had smeared his spearpoint with some sort of poison. And as fate would have it, a poison arrow would bring Achilles' own demise on the battle-field at Troy.[3]

In the most ironic twist of fate, Hercules himself ultimately succumbed to the Hydra venom that he had daubed on his own arrows. A wily Centaur named Nessus tricked Hercules and abducted his wife, Deianeira. Enraged, Hercules shot Nessus in the back with a Hydra arrow that pierced his heart. As the Roman poet Ovid stressed in his version of the myth, it is not fair to shoot even a rogue in the back with a poisoned arrow. And as in most mythic tales, treachery bred more treachery, and the venom multiplied in power, just like the Hydra's heads. The dying Centaur tricked Deianeira into collecting the toxic blood flowing from his wound. Advising her to keep it in an airtight container, away from heat and light, Nessus promised that if she daubed this substance on a tunic for Hercules someday, it would work as a love charm.

Years later, Deianeira, unaware of the potential for second-hand poisoning, secretly treated a beautiful tunic with the Centaur's contaminated blood and gave it as a gift to her husband. What happened next was the subject of a famous tragedy by the Athenian playwright Sophocles (written about 430 BC). Hercules put on the shirt to make a special sacrifice. As he approached the fire, the heat activated the Hydra poison. The envenomed tunic caused Hercules such fiery torture that he ran amok, bellowing like a wounded bull and uprooting trees. In desperation, he plunged into a stream. But the water only increased the poison's burning power, and that stream ran scalding-hot forever after.

Hercules struggled to tear off the garment, but it adhered to his flesh and corroded his skin like acid or some unnatural fire.

Unable to bear the pain of the burning poison, Hercules shouted for his companions to light a large funeral pyre. His arms-bearer and friend, the great archer Philoctetes, was the only one courageous enough to obey. In gratitude, Hercules bequeathed his special bow (originally a gift from Apollo, the archer-god whose arrows brought plague) and his quiver of Hydra arrows to his friend. Then the mighty hero threw himself onto the flaming pyre and was burned alive.

Hercules' agony is a poetic representation of painful death by viper venom, which was often compared to burning alive. Indeed, fire motifs pervade the early mythology of biological weapons. Flaming arrows and searing torches had destroyed the Hydra, and now the Hydra venom was activated by heat and took on the nature of unquenchable fire. In fact, a real viper much feared in Greece, called the *dipsas* in antiquity, injects a thick venom into its victims and, according to

FIG 4. *Hercules on his funeral pyre entrusting the quiver of Hydra-venom arrows to the young archer, Philoctetes. Red-figure psykter, 475–425 BC.*

(Private collection, New York)

ancient writers, it was said to "burn and corrode, setting victims on fire as if they were lying on a funeral pyre."[4]

But the tragic consequences ignited by Hercules' invention of poison arrows did not end with the hero's death. When she learned the result of her unwitting use of a poison weapon, Deianeira killed herself. And the quiver of deadly arrows went on to bring great misfortune to Philoctetes during the Trojan War.

*   *   *

"Mighty-walled Troy" of Greek epic was probably the Late Bronze Age city designated Troy VI in the series of ruined cities in northwest Turkey first excavated by Heinrich Schliemann in 1870–90. The ruins show that the citadel of Troy VI was destroyed by fire in about 1200 BC. The legendary Trojan War was most famously described by Homer in the *Iliad* in about 750 BC, but an extensive cycle of Trojan War stories circulated in Greek and Roman times, recounted by many other mythographers and playwrights, some of whose works now survive only as fragments.

Most classical scholars agree that the oral epics probably grew up around actual battles during the Bronze Age (1300–1100 BC), and that some residue of truth exists in the legends concerning the Trojan War, including many aspects of real warfare of that era. This cycle of myths and legends provides striking evidence of the two complex, parallel pictures of warfare in classical antiquity: the familiar, idealized Homeric version of clean, fair fighting, epitomized by heroes like Achilles in the *Iliad*, and other, more nefarious ways of overcoming foes, often attributed to barbarians, but admired in crafty Greek heroes like Odysseus.[5]

According to myth, Apollo's divine arrows inflicted deadly epidemics and fevers, especially during wartime. The *Iliad* opens with the god aiming his bow at the Greek army in the tenth year of their siege of Troy, cutting down King Agamemnon's troops with a devastating plague. (The gods took sides in Greek mythology: Apollo favored the Trojans while Athena helped the Greeks.) In Homer's words, Apollo let fly his "black bolts of plague" on the soldiers for nine days. The god's first targets were the pack animals and dogs, then "one by one our men came down with it and died hard as the god's arrows raked the army." Funeral pyres burned night and day, and the Greeks' hopes of completing the siege of Troy were dashed.

This opening scene is a not-so-subtle reminder of the ancient linguistic metaphor linking arrows and toxins. Several other passages in the *Iliad* hint strongly that poisoned weapons were wielded by warriors on the battlefield, although Homer never says this outright. When Menelaus was wounded by a Trojan arrow, for example, Machaon (son of the legendary god of healing, Asclepius) was summoned to suck out the "black blood." This treatment was the emergency remedy for snakebite and poisoned-arrow wounds in real life. Elsewhere, Homer described "black blood" gushing from arrow wounds, and referred to Philoctetes' "black wound from a deadly snake." Black blood, as opposed to red, always signaled a poisoned wound to ancient battlefield doctors, and in fact snake venom does cause black, oozing wounds. In the *Iliad*, Machaon also applied a special balm prepared by the Centaur Chiron, recalling the treatment for the Centaur's own poisoned-arrow wound.[6]

Only once did Homer explicitly describe a Greek hero actually searching out a poison for treating his arrows (not surprisingly, it was Odysseus, master of cunning tricks). But many other ancient mythographers make it clear that arrow poison was employed by both sides in the Trojan War.

The Trojan War began when the Greeks launched an expedition to avenge the abduction of the Spartan beauty, Helen, by the Trojan seducer, Paris. Hercules' old friend, the great archer Philoctetes, commanded seven of the twelve hundred Greek ships sailing to Troy. Homer specified that each of Philoctetes' ships was rowed by fifty expert bowmen. Did Philoctetes equip his archers with poison arrows from Hercules' quiver, which he was bringing to Troy?

Homer does not say, but an ill-omened accident involving serpent venom did occur on the voyage. Philoctetes received a hideous "black

FIGURE 5. *Archer testing shaft and point of arrow; any archer who tipped his projectiles with poison had to avoid all contact with the sharp point. Red-figure wine cup, Athens, 520–510 BC.*

(Henry Lillie Pierce Fund © Museum of Fine Arts, Boston)

wound" in the foot. According to some versions of the myth, he was accidentally struck by one of the poison arrows he had inherited from Hercules. In other versions, he was bitten by a poisonous *hydra,* a water-snake. Both versions underscore the perils of handling toxic substances used to create bio-weapons. Philoctetes' accident was an inauspicious start for launching the war. The men found the stench of his festering wound intolerable and his howls of pain a very bad omen. Agamemnon ordered his captain Odysseus to abandon Philoctetes on a tiny desert island called Chryse, near the island of Lemnos, and continue on to Troy.

For a decade, while his companions fought the Trojans, the warrior was marooned in unending pain and fever, as "a black flux of blood and matter" continued to ooze from his wound. Philoctetes, the most skilled archer after Odysseus, survived by shooting birds with Hercules' bow and poison arrows. The mythic description of Philoctetes' suppurating, never-healing wound and spreading necrosis is an accurate depiction of the aftermath of a snakebite.

Until about AD 150, Philoctetes' desert island was a popular landmark visited by Greek and Roman travelers. A small shrine there memorialized the warrior's ordeal with the poisoned arrows: the altar displayed Philoctetes' bow, his bronze armor, and a bronze water snake. Philoctetes' tragic tale was widely known: he was celebrated as a god in Italy, where he was said to have settled at the end of his life. His tribulations were illustrated in numerous art works and presented on the Athenian stage in plays by Sophocles, Aeschylus, and Euripides.

FIGURE 6. *On his way to Troy, Philoctetes was abandoned on a desert island after his accident with a poison arrow. This Athenian vase (about 420 BC) shows him with bandaged foot and the quiver of poison arrows.*

(Fletcher Fund, Metropolitan Museum of Art)

Ten years into the war with Troy, an oracle advised the Greeks that the Trojans could only be defeated by Hercules' original poison arrows. So, Odysseus led an envoy of Greeks back to Chryse, where they had stranded Philoctetes so long ago. The men were horrified to find the once-proud warrior living like an animal in a cave, whose floor was slick with the fetid pus draining from his wound. The emaciated archer, surrounded by feathers and bird bones, was still racked by pain from the arrow poison. The Greeks were filled with pity for their companion, yet they expressed no qualms about using the same nasty poison against the Trojans.

The delegation tried to persuade the long-suffering Philoctetes to bring the arrows to Troy, but he refused, embittered by their cruel treatment of him. He even threatened to shoot them with the poison arrows. So Odysseus hatched a scheme to deceive Philoctetes in order to get the bow and quiver. But Achilles' son, an honorable youth named Neoptolemus, was outraged by Odysseus's lack of principles. He insisted that "vile tricks and treachery" should be shameful to a true warrior. The scene, as described by Sophocles, is fraught with the age-old tension between war by the rules and war by devious means.[7]

Finally, after the ghost of Hercules appeared and promised he would be cured, Philoctetes agreed to rejoin the Greeks. At Troy, Philoctetes' wound was successfully treated by Machaon, the Greek army doctor, and out on the battlefield, Philoctetes became an avenging whirlwind with the Hydra arrows, destroying legions of Trojans. Then, in an archery duel with the Trojan champion Paris, Philoctetes turned the tide of the war in favor of the Greeks.

Quintus of Smyrna, a poet of the fourth century AD, described the rain of deadly arrows in his epic, *The Fall of Troy*. First he told how the mighty Greek warrior Achilles was brought down with an arrow deliberately aimed at his vulnerable heel. Achilles' mother had held the infant Achilles by the heel as she dipped him in the River Styx to make him invincible to iron weapons. Normally, a wound in the heel would be superficial—only an arrow carrying poison could render such a wound fatal. In some versions of the myth, it was Apollo who shot

Achilles from behind with one of his plague arrows. But others said that Apollo had guided Paris's arrow to the back of Achilles' foot. According to Ovid, the god "saw Paris flinging an occasional arrow at some Greek of no importance." "Why waste your shafts?" scolded Apollo, and turned Paris's bow in the direction of Achilles' heel.

Reeling with "sudden pangs of mortal sickness," Achilles toppled "like a tower." Rolling his eyes and gnashing his teeth from the pain of the "god-envenomed wound," the dying Achilles expressed the traditional Greek warrior's visceral loathing of dishonorable death. Not only had he been struck by a weapon of hidden poison, but his cowardly adversary had struck from behind, just as Hercules had shot Nessus in the back. As the doomed champion sensed the toxins racing through his veins, bringing an unheroic, "piteous death," Achilles glared about and shouted, "Who shot me with a stealthy-smiting shaft? Let him dare to meet me face-to-face! Only dastards lurk in hidden ambush. None dare meet me man-to-man. . . . Let him face me then!"

To avenge the shocking death of Achilles from a poisoned arrow in the heel, Philoctetes drew back his great bow and aimed a "merciless shaft" with its "terrible, death-hissing point" at Paris (the poet's words evoke the imagery of snakes). The first arrow grazed Paris's wrist, and the next one plunged into his side. "Torturing wounds" sent Paris into a "frenzy of pain, his liver seething as in flame." The Trojan doctors rushed onto the battlefield to apply salves and blood-sucking leeches to draw out the poison, but these means were useless against the "fierce venom which crawled through his innards with corrupting fangs." Parched with thirst, scarcely conscious, and writhing in pain, Paris desperately held onto the hope that a nymph he had once loved would bring special healing herbs. The nymph did arrive at last, but it was too late to save the Trojan warrior-lover, who finally perished in anguish.[8]

*   *   *

Despite the importance of the bow and arrow from the Bronze Age and onward in Greece, Homer and many other writers tell us that archers were disdained because they shot safely from afar: long-range missiles implied unwillingness to face the enemy at close range. And long-range missiles daubed with poison seemed even more cowardly and villainous. Ambush from behind was another military practice that, like poisoning arrows, was usually attributed to barbarians. Traditional Greek—and Roman—warfare was supposed to be hand-to-hand, up close and personal, as ranks of similarly armed and armored soldiers engaged in face-to-face combat or one-on-one duels. Yet at the same time, clever, inventive deceptions were also admirable—as long as the tricks did not cross certain bounds. The line between acceptable and reprehensible ruses was difficult to pin down, but classical authors often indicate some generally accepted attitudes.

Wounds in the back were never honorable, signaling cowardice or treachery on someone's part (the *Iliad* and the *Fall of Troy* and other poems are filled with exhortations to face the enemy and avoid getting hit in the back or being taken by surprise).[9] Individual courage, working together as a group, physical strength, military prowess, and steadfastness were key—and poisoned weapons and ambush undermined every one of those values. The mythic episodes pose a timeless question, deeply disturbing to warriors of any era: What good are bravery, skill, and strength when your enemy attacks deviously with weapons made ever more deadly with poison?

After the carnage on the battlefield cut down the best of the Greek and Trojan champions, the Greeks devised the ingenious ruse of the Trojan Horse to gain entry to the citadel of Troy. The Greeks sacked the city. Then, after a series of adventures like those recounted in Homer's *Odyssey* and other myths, the Greek victors headed home. Meanwhile, after the destruction of Troy, a party of Trojan survivors led by their hero Aeneas set off for Italy to found Rome, as described by the great Latin poet Virgil in his *Aeneid*. That epic poem, written during the reign of Augustus (first century BC), was intended to glorify Rome's legendary past and destiny. The Trojans brought their poison weapons with them to Italy, according to Virgil's description of Aeneas's fellow warrior,

Amycus: "No man was more skilled at dipping darts and arming metal with poison."

And what became of Hercules' quiver of Hydra-venom arrows after the Greek victory at Troy? According to legend, Philoctetes, like many of the other Trojan War veterans, restlessly wandered the Mediterranean after the war. After fighting various mercenary battles with his deadly bow and arrows, he finally settled in Italy. Before he died and was buried near Sybaris, in the toe of Italy, he founded a Temple to Apollo at Krimissa. There, the old warrior dedicated his poisoned weapons to the god whose own bow and arrows brought plague and pestilence.[10]

*   *   *

Ambivalence over the use of poison by Greek heroes stands out in a pair of passages in Homer's *Odyssey,* the epic poem recounting the postwar adventures of the Greek hero Odysseus. After ten years of wandering, Odysseus finally returned home to Ithaca to find his wife, Penelope, and his young son, Telemachus, besieged by a gang of swaggering suitors who had taken over his palace. The surly interlopers lay about drinking wine and idly speculating about how young Telemachus might try to roust them. Perhaps, proposed one suitor, he'll travel to Ephyra, in northwestern Greece, to obtain a poisonous plant that flourishes there (as his father once did). "He could drop the poison into our wine barrels and kill us all!"

If Hercules was the mythic inventor of arrows poisoned with snake venom, Odysseus was the first mythic character to poison arrows with plant toxins. Homer tells us that Odysseus, the archer renowned for crafty tricks, did indeed sail to Ephyra on a quest for a deadly plant to smear on his bronze arrowheads.

Ephyra in Epirus, near the River Styx and the mouth of the Acheron River of Hades, was a fitting place to gather poisons, since it was famed in antiquity as one of the "gateways" to the realm of the dead. For one of his Labors, Hercules had descended by one of these entrances into the

Underworld and dragged out Cerberus, the monstrous, three-headed hound of Hell. Foam from the beast's jaws had flecked the green grass and was transformed into the poison flowers of aconite (monkshood). Other plants with potent poisons—such as black hellebore and deadly nightshade—thrived here too, nourished by Underworld vapors so noxious that birds flying over the area dropped dead.

Odysseus had once come here to consult the pallid, embittered ghosts of the Underworld. Three centuries after Homer, in the fifth century BC, the ancient Greek historian Herodotus described a renowned *necromanteon,* an Oracle of the Dead, at Ephyra. Archaeologists have discovered the substantial ruins of an underground labyrinth, whose features match Homer's description of the Halls of Hades in the *Odyssey.* Scholars believe that local hallucinogenic plants were used in the ancient rites of the Oracle of the Dead at Ephyra.

So Ephyra was a poisoners' paradise. But King Ilus, the ruler of the territory, being "a man of virtue," refused to supply Odysseus with the "man-killing" poison (Homer's wording makes it clear that the poison would be used for war, not hunting). Odysseus did finally succeed in obtaining some arrow toxin, though, on an island south of Ephyra. But the incident with King Ilus reveals once again the conflicted emotions about using toxic weapons. Creative trickery, ruses, and deception were respected by the ancient Greeks. Should they admire Odysseus's resourcefulness? Or should they agree with the honorable King Ilus that secret poisoning of foes was never virtuous? The moral issue was further complicated when the goddess of war and wisdom, Athena, suggested that poison arrows would be a good way to dispatch the gang of suitors besieging Odysseus's family back in Ithaca. Perhaps the answer lies in the lessons to be learned from what happened to those who resorted to poison weapons.

Given Odysseus's involvement with shrewd ruses and arrow poisons, it is somehow fitting that Odysseus himself was killed with toxic spear at the hands of his other son, Telegonus. Unknown to Odysseus, Telegonus had been born to Circe, with whom Odysseus had dallied on the long way home after the Trojan War. A sorceress-goddess who knew the powers of many mysterious *pharmaka* (drugs, chemicals, and poisons), Circe had enchanted Odysseus's men with a potion that turned them into swine. This was by no means the first time Circe used drugs to obtain a desired outcome. She had also once poisoned a river with "evil herbs, whose juices contained horrid powers" in order to destroy an enemy.

With a mother like Circe and a trickster father like Odysseus, it was not surprising that Telegonus would use a poisoned weapon. The youth had journeyed to Ithaca searching for his father. When he first encountered Odysseus, however, he mistook him for an enemy and ran him through with his lance. The spear was tipped with barb of truly diabolical and ingenious design—the poisonous spine of a stingray.[11]

*　　*　　*

Awareness of the idea of biological weapons, as evident in the archaic Greek myths about Hercules, Philoctetes, Odysseus, and Apollo, existed long before the first historical reports of using poisons in warfare. One of the most remarkable features of these myths is the very early recognition of the ethical and practical questions surrounding such methods. Again and again, the ancient myths hammer home the idea that once created, weapons based on poison seem to take on a life of their own, with tragic consequences that can extend over generations. Not only are biological weapons difficult to direct with precision, but they are almost impossible to destroy once created.

If the myth of Hercules and the Hydra was a poetic account of the invention of envenomed arrows in the deep past, then Hercules was the perfect figure for the role. In his celebrated labors and exploits, Hercules impulsively used his weapons to destroy all manner of monsters and enemies. Significantly, however, Hercules always managed to leave chaos in his wake. He was a paradoxical figure for the Greeks: an admired destroyer of monsters, he also frequently brought destruction to those he hoped to protect. The playwright Sophocles made it clear that when Hercules dipped his arrows in the Hydra venom, he was creating the possibility—even the inevitability—of his own death by the same agent. And his poisoned arrows certainly left a long trail of tragedy.[12]

The image of the "Many-Headed Hydra" has come to symbolize a multifaceted, thorny dilemma that generates new obstacles each time one is overcome or solved. Indeed, the Hydra is a wonderfully apt symbol for the problems set in motion by biological weapons. The nightmarish image of infinitely replicating heads, the impossibility of ever completely destroying the monster, and the perils of unintended casualties: these are vivid details that capture the moral and practical dangers of creating and handling biochemical agents of destruction.

Like Hercules, Philoctetes was another complex, contradictory figure whose tragic story fascinated the Greeks. One of the many unintended victims of the Hydra arrows, Philoctetes survived to destroy multitudes of Trojans with the same arrows that had brought him so much suffering. Yet at the end of his life, Philoctetes decided to store the terrible bow and quiver safely in a temple of Apollo, instead of passing them on to another warrior. This conclusion to his legend suggests a mythic model for trying to contain the proliferating Hydra heads of biological warfare. The indestructible head of the Hydra monster still lurked somewhere under the earth, but at least the hellish Hydra-venom arrows could be retired from the battlefield, to be guarded by Apollo, who was also the god of healing.

The other heroes implicated in the use of bio weapons—Achilles, Paris, and Odysseus—were also ambivalent figures, fitting vehicles for provocative stories about challenging the ideals of fair combat. Homer's deep understanding of human nature allowed him to show how noble virtues vied with dishonorable impulses in these heroes' all-too-human characters. In the *Iliad*, Achilles was the brightest star of Greek warriors, but he was also a savage berserker who committed outrages against Hector and other Trojan foes. Paris, the playboy-warrior who started the Trojan War by taking up with Helen, was berated as a coward by his own brother, Hector, and by his lover, Helen. And the wily Odysseus was the quintessential trickster-warrior, never above stooping to devious weapons and ploys. All three of these heroes lived and died by poisoned weapons.

The mythic consequences of Hercules' invention convey a strong warning for those who contemplate the use of biological armaments. The fates of the ancient bio-warriors fulfill an age-old folklore motif of poetic justice known as "the poisoner poisoned," in which each hero who employed poison weapons was himself harmed or destroyed with the toxic agents, either by accident or in retaliation. There are many modern military examples that demonstrate how "poisoner poisoned" effects, as well as "friendly fire" accidents, continue to threaten those involved in biochemical arms. In 1943, for instance, in the worst Allied seaport disaster since Pearl Harbor, thousands of American soldiers and Italian townspeople in Bari, Italy, were killed by exposure to poison gas when a U.S. ship secretly carrying two thousand chemical bombs was shelled in the harbor by German aircraft. A more recent example is the cluster of health problems suffered by U.S. troops who destroyed Iraq's biochemical munitions in the Gulf War of 1991. In 2003 it transpired that many of the biological agents used to create those weapons had come from the United States during the 1980s.[13]

Another telling feature of the mythology of biochemical warfare is the way the elements of poison, contagion, and fire are intertwined. The actions of deadly toxins and images of unquenchable fires are intermingled in several myths, foreshadowing the later historical accounts of military deployments of poisons and disease vectors, and prefiguring the invention of Greek Fire and earlier petroleum-based weapons, generally considered to be among the most inhumane agents of war ever invented. Weapons based on poisons, contagion, and combustibles are, of course, the prototypes of modern biological weapons and chemical incendiaries. Amazingly, these elemental agents were already combined in the ancient imagination more than three thousand years before the invention of modern germ warfare, napalm, and nuclear conflagrations.[14]

Poisoned projectiles, created to inflict extreme suffering and bring ignominious death, were more feared than hand-to-hand combat with swords, spears, axes, and clubs. Poison arrows killed, but never cleanly. In Quintus's words, they dealt "ghastly wounds that caused the mightiest man to lay faint and wasted with incurable pain." A simple scratch could result in a gruesome, putrefying wound that turned brave warriors like Philoctetes into pitiful subhumans. Even the superhero Hercules was unmoored by the excruciating pain of the poisoned tunic, uprooting trees and overturning altars, rampaging like a wild beast. "I was the bravest, the mightiest, of all time," he bellowed, tearing at the cloth soaked in Hydra-venom, "but now, a plague is upon me, which no amount of courage can withstand!" Images like these were grim indeed for a culture steeped in a warrior ethic, where bravery and physical might was valued above all and death in battle was expected to be violent, but at least swift and honorable.

In antiquity, as today, a blurry line separated acceptable ruses of war from reprehensible tactics and inhumane weapons. For example, Odysseus's subterfuge of the Trojan Horse seems admirably cunning, until we learn that the trick ushered in Greek atrocities against Trojan women and children. Other myths tell of poisoning rivers and wine to kill enemies, or of giving lethal gifts that concealed poisons or combustible chemicals. But such weapons violated the guidelines of "fair" conflict and corrupted the meaning of courage and skill on the battlefield, for both victor and victim alike. In the face of hidden poisons and biochemical subterfuge, a warrior's valor, physical strength, and prowess were nullified. In the words of Ovid, subversive weapons of poison were feared and detested because they dealt a "double death." They killed a man, and extinguished his honor as well.[15]

The sheer number of great warriors felled by poison arrows and the numerous unintended casualties in the myths illuminate the powerful impact of the idea of warfare with bio-weapons in antiquity. The payoff of such practices in actual conflicts could be substantial. Dipping one's arrowheads into something toxic or infectious would greatly magnify the damage inflicted, and it could be done at a safe distance. Poison projectiles gave confidence to unskilled archers or weak warriors. Even if one's aim was not very accurate (like Paris, who needed Apollo's guiding hand), a contaminated weapon would guarantee a high body count.

The mythic messages about bio-toxic weapons were important to the ancient Greeks and Romans, as shown by the many examples of artwork depicting Hercules killing the Hydra and decimating the Centaurs with poison arrows, the accidental wounding of Hercules' son Telephus by Achilles, and Hercules done in by his own toxic weapons and bequeathing his quiver to Philoctetes. Hercules dying in the poisoned robe was painted by the famous Greek artist Aristeides in about 360 BC. Another painting in the Acropolis of Athens that showed Odysseus trying to steal the bow and arrows from Philoctetes was admired by tourists as late as the second century AD. Hercules' death, Telephus's wounding, and Philoctetes' anguish were also performed on the stage in tragedies still admired today. And as noted earlier, travelers used to point out the boulder that trapped the Hydra's immortal head under the earth, and they honored Philoctetes, the inheritor of the first biological weapons, in at least three different shrines in Italy and the Aegean. Tourists in antiquity could even bathe in the hot stream Thermopylae, where Hercules, driven mad by the shirt of burning venom, was said to have plunged.

The legendary tales of Hercules and Philoctetes and other mythic figures were viewed by the ancient Greeks and Romans as reflections of actual historic episodes in their own very distant past. In popular memories, more recent historical events could also blur into legend, and ancient historians' accounts of real military campaigns sometimes echo mythological ones. The detailed reports written by numerous Greek, Roman, and other historians, however, provide powerful evidence of how biological and chemical weapons were actually used in warfare.

Alexander the Great and the Arrows of Doom

> To make wounds twice as deadly, these men dip
> In viper's venom every arrow-tip.
> —Ovid, on the Scythians

> It was their custom to throw javelins
> steeped in noxious juices,
> thus disgracing the steel with poison.
> —Silius Italicus, on the Nubians

"There is nothing more dangerous than poisons and the bites of noxious animals," wrote Galen, the great Roman physician to gladiators and emperors. We can avoid most dangers by fleeing or defending ourselves, he noted, but the toxins from plants and venomous creatures are treacherous weapons because they strike without warning. The ancients particularly dreaded encounters with poisonous snakes, a problem that plagued Alexander the Great and his army in India. Things only got worse when the Greeks learned that Indian archers tipped their arrows with snake venom, and Alexander's soldiers may well have recalled the scene in the Homer's *Iliad,* when the Trojan archer Paris recoiled from face-to-face battle with the Greeks. Homer compared Paris to "a man who stumbles upon a viper in a mountain glen. He jumps aside, knees trembling, face pallid, he backs and backs away." The scene neatly juxtaposes the ancient terror of snakebites with the fear of envenomed arrows.[1]

Facing battle required great courage, and knowing that one's enemies used deadly poisons on their weapons raised the horrors of war to exponential levels. From numerous Greek, Roman, and Indian texts, one learns exactly how virulent arrow poisons were concocted, who used them in the ancient world, and what sorts of countermeasures were attempted.

*   *   *

Venomous animals enjoy "great confidence" in attacking, commented the natural historian Aelian, in the third century AD, and they are hated by man because they are blessed with such powerful weapons. Based on his own observations of nature, Aelian surmised that Hercules and other Greek heroes got the idea of using venom on their arrows from seeing wasps buzzing around the corpses of vipers. In antiquity, it was widely believed that stinging insects increased the potency of their stings by drawing venom from dead snakes, and in turn, that snakes fortified their venom by devouring poisonous plants. A similar principle was applied to harmful flowers, like aconite or monkshood, which were believed to draw their nutrients from entrances to the Underworld, with its unwholesome vapors. In the same fashion, man could amplify the strength of his weapons by adding natural plant and animal toxins to them. In Aelian's words, "Hercules dipped his arrows in the venom of the Hydra, just as wasps dip and sharpen their sting."[2]

Today, many people think of biological and chemical weapons as inventions that depend on modern technology, toxicology, and epidemiology. Yet, the idea of treating projectiles with noxious substances originated long ago in pre-scientific cultures, who observed that nature endowed certain plants with toxins to defend themselves and certain creatures with venom to hunt prey and kill enemies. Observation and experiment led to some simple—as well as some surprisingly sophisticated—ways of borrowing natural poisons for projectile weapons.

A great variety of toxins—from wolfbane to snake venom—were weaponized as arrow poisons in antiquity. Snake venom may have been one of the first. In antiquity, the old myth of Hercules and the Hydra was thought to be a poetic exaggeration of the historical invention of arrows tipped with snake venom in the very deep past. Several authors, such as the historians Diodorus of Sicily (30 BC) and Pausanias (AD 150), and the poet Quintus of Smyrna (AD 350), assumed that Hercules' arrows were actually "besmeared with deadly venom of the fell water snake" or an adder common in Greece. Pointing out that the ancient Greek word *hydra* meant water snake, Pausanias suggested that perhaps an extra-large *hydra* specimen had inspired the myth of the Hydra monster.

Ancient toxicology treatises from the Mediterranean and India described an impressive array of poisonous plants, minerals, marine creatures, insects, and snakes, along with scores of antidotes and remedies, some useful and others quite dubious. In about 130 BC, for example, the toxicology manual compiled by Nicander, a priest of Apollo at the Temple of Claros in Asia Minor, listed twenty vipers and cobras known in the Greco-Roman world. Descriptions by Nicander and other writers often provide enough details for modern herpetologists to identify the species. Moreover, the medical symptoms of snakebites and arrow wounds contaminated by venom are accurately described in the ancient accounts. First, necrosis appears around the wound, with dark blue or black oozing gore, followed by putrid sores, hemorrhages, swelling limbs, vomiting, wracking pain, and "freezing pain around the heart," culminating in convulsions, shock, and death. Only a very few lucky victims recovered from snake-venom bites or arrows, and sometimes the wounds festered for years, as described in the myth of Philoctetes.[3]

* * *

An effective poison needs an effective delivery system, and the technology of the bow and arrow was perfectly suited for the task of killing with confidence from afar, whether the poisoned arrows were used for hunting or for combat. The first poison arrows were probably used for hunting, and later turned toward enemies in war. This progression, from hunting to war, is clear in the Greek mythology of poison arrows. Hercules' great quiver held "some arrows for hunting and some for smiting foes." And indeed, the first victims of the Hydra arrows were not humans, but a deer with golden horns, the Stymphalean Birds, and the half-man, half-horse Centaurs. Then, after Hercules' death, the arrows were inherited by Philoctctes, who intended to use them in the war against Troy. But their use on the battlefield was delayed until the tenth and final year of the war, while Philoctetes was marooned on the desert island. Philoctetes used the poison arrows to hunt birds for food for a decade before slaughtering any Trojans.

According to the Roman medical writer Celsus, hunters in Gaul (Celtic people of western Europe) used serpent venom to bring down game, because it did not poison the meat (snake venom is safely digestible). Mirko Grmek, a leading scholar of the history of medicine, and the classicist A. J. Reinach have suggested that the Greeks and Romans thought of poison arrows as essentially weapons for hunting, and therefore disapproved of their use against fellow humans. In fact, arrow poisons intended for hunting and those prepared for war differed in crucial ways.

To be effective in hunting, the ideal toxin should be fast-acting and lethal even if the wound was slight, and poisons that ruined meat should be avoided. But war arrows were very different. The most malignant toxins were selected, with the deliberate intention of inflicting a horrible death or an incapacitating, unhealing wound. Pure snake venom might be used on hunting arrows, for example, but for combat the venom was contaminated with the most debilitating or disgusting ingredients for maximum physical and psychological impact. Killing cleanly and swiftly was *not* the point of poisoned military projectiles.

Surprising the enemy with biochemical weapons was one option, but there were significant advantages to be had if your enemies *knew* that archers were shooting arrows coated in virulent substances. The armies that used poisoned arrows in war seem to have calculated the terror impact on potential enemies. They made sure that their recipes for treating war arrows promised a gruesome death, and that these formulas were well publicized. Just as today, deterrence was an important factor in creating biological weapons.[4]

*   *   *

Looking first at the botanical options for arrow poisons, the ancients knew of at least two dozen dangerous plants that were used for medicinal purposes and could also be employed to create toxic weapons. As in modern pharmacology, the dosage drew the line between therapy and death. In very small amounts, many plant toxins are beneficial, while in larger amounts they are lethal—though some poisons, like aconite, can kill even in minute doses.

Some substances mentioned by Greek and Roman historians, such as *helenion* and *ninon,* smeared on arrows by the Dacians and Dalmatians (ancient people of Romania, Hungary, and former Yugoslavia), have not been identified by modern scientists, but most of the arrow poisons used in the ancient world are well-known toxins. One of the most popular was hellebore, the all-purpose medicinal herb and the favorite prescription of doctors, including the father of medicine, Hippocrates. Two kinds of hellebore were identified by the ancients: black hellebore, the Christmas rose of the buttercup family (*Helleborus orientalis*), and white hellebore, a Liliacea (*Veratrum*). Interestingly, the plants are not related, but both are laden with dangerous chemicals so plentiful and diverse that it is surprising that anyone ever survived treatment. It was well known that hellebore killed horses and oxen, and people who collected hellebore sometimes fell ill or died. The plants were "not easy to gather, and very oppressive to the head," noted Pliny the Elder, the natural historian of the first century AD. In tiny doses, the roots caused sneezing or blisters, but in heavier doses they induced severe vomiting and diarrhea, muscle cramps, delirium, convulsions, asphyxia, and heart attack.

It was the immediate purgative effect that made hellebore a pet prescription for all manner of complaints: it's clear that some patients survived merely because the vomiting and diarrhea were so violent. As Pliny remarked, hellebore's reputation evoked such "great terror" that treatment required much courage—on the part of both doctor and patient. Indeed, wrote Pliny, "the various colors of the vomits are terrifying to see, and after that comes the worry of watching the stools!"

Hellebore was obviously an excellent choice for arrow poison. Ancient writers reported that hellebore was one of the "arrow drugs" used by the long-haired Gauls to hunt wild boars and other game. The hunters had to "run hastily" to cut away the flesh around the arrow before the poison sank in and the meat rotted, although the Gauls claimed that a small amount of hellebore tenderized the flesh of hares and deer. Today, traditional hunters in Tanzania, who use the plant poison *panjupe* on their arrows, also rush to pull out the arrow and discard the meat around the wound.

The fact that the Gauls knew of at least two antidotes for hellebore poisoning suggests that they worried about self-inflicted injuries from hellebore arrows. The act of collecting of hellebore and many other baneful plants in antiquity was surrounded by special rituals to avoid accidental poisoning, and the preparations of arrow drugs were time-consuming and delicate. To dig up hellebore, for example, one first prayed facing east, then incised a circle around the plant with a sword, all the while keeping an eye out for an eagle—to spot one spelled death for the herbalist.[5]

Another oft-mentioned arrow drug, aconite or monkshood (sometimes called wolfbane), is one of the most dangerous plant poisons known to mankind and is found in many parts of the world. Its first effect is like that of a stimulant, but then it paralyzes the nervous system, causing drooling and vomiting. Finally, the limbs go numb and death results. The excessive salivation may be the reason the poison was associated in Greek myth with a mad dog foaming at the jaws. Aconite may have been the arrow toxin sought by Odysseus in Ephyra, near the mouth of the Underworld. According to Pliny, a town on the Black Sea, Aconae, was held in "evil repute" because of its abundance of aconite.

Himalayan aconite (called *bish* or *bikh*) was so lethal that sheep had to be muzzled in its vicinity. This "mountain aconite" was used in ancient India for poisoning arrowheads, and aconite is still used in

FIGURE 7. *Black hellebore (Christmas rose), a toxic plant used to poison arrows and water supplies in antiquity.*
(Curtis Botanical Magazine, 1787)

India by poachers who kill elephants for ivory. In the early 1800s, the Gurkhas of Nepal considered the plant "a great protection against enemy attacks," for they could destroy entire armies by poisoning wells with crushed aconite. During the war between the Spanish and the Moors in 1483, the Arab archers wrapped bits of cotton or linen around their arrows and dipped them in distilled aconite juice. Five centuries later, in World War II, Nazi scientists extracted the chemical toxin aconitine from aconite plants, in order to manufacture poisoned bullets.

According to Aelian, *hyoscyamus* or henbane, the sticky, gray-green, and bad-smelling weed (*Hyoscyamus niger*) that contains the powerful narcotic poisons hyoscyamine and scopolamine, had to be collected without touching any part of the plant (all parts of henbane are in fact poisonous). One arcane method was to loosen the soil around the root with a dagger, then attach the stem to the leg of a trained bird. As the bird flew up, it uprooted the henbane. Pliny expounded on the dangers of henbane, which was sometimes used, in tiny doses, as an anaesthetic. "In my opinion," he wrote, "it is a dangerous drug in any form," for it deranges the brain. Henbane poisoning can cause violent seizures, psychosis, and death. It was another of the several arrow poisons said to be collected by the Gauls. Perhaps they used hellebore (with its meat-tenderizing effect) and fast-acting snake venom for game, and reserved deadly henbane for their human foes.[6]

Preparing weapons from poisons evoked a lot of anxiety about self-inflicted wounds and "friendly fire" accidents in antiquity. The risks of handling bio-toxins were (and still are) very real, as shown by complex preparation methods described by the ancient writers. One can gain further insights into ways the ancients may have avoided self-poisoning problems by looking at some special procedures for creating poison weapons among more contemporary people in Asia, Africa, and South America.

In South America, for example, many rainforest tribes use "poison arrow" frogs to treat arrows and blowgun darts. The frogs secrete an extremely deadly chemical through their skin: one frog contains about two hundred micrograms of poison, and just two micrograms are instantly fatal to a human. The toxin of one frog can tip about fifty arrows, and to avoid touching the powerful poison, most archers pin down a living frog with a stick and carefully wipe their arrows on the slimy skin. But a safer method invented by the Choco Indians in Colombia yields an even greater amount of concentrated poison. They roast a skewered frog on a stick over a fire, catching the dripping toxin in a bottle, into which they can safely dip their darts.

The Choco practice sheds some light on a puzzling passage in Pliny's natural history about the Psylli, a mysterious nomadic tribe of North Africa. The Psylli were snake charmers, and as masters of myriad venoms from snakes to scorpions, they were said to be immune to all of them. After describing poisonous frogs and toads known in antiquity, Pliny claims that he once witnessed the Psylli placing toxic toads in heated pans. Scholars have wondered why the Psylli "irritated" the toxic amphibians in this way. Taking into account the Choco methods, however, a more logical explanation might be that the Psylli were roasting the toads to obtain their poison, which was said to bring death more rapidly than the bite of an asp.

The Spanish conquistadors were terrified of the poison darts of the South American Indians, and despite the thick leathern cuirasses they wore to deflect the arrows, many early explorers died from weapons coated with deadly frog slime, or the plant toxins strychnine or curare, an alkaloid that causes fatal paralysis. A mere pinprick from a small curare blowgun dart can bring down a human or a large animal. In the Amazon rainforest, natives carried as many as six hundred tiny curare darts in a quiver, and there were horrifying reports that curare was not only used on projectiles, but in hand-to-hand combat too: it was rumored that the natives painted their fingernails with the toxin.

The art of preparing curare was extremely hazardous, yet a remarkable number of different combinations of curare arrow poison have been invented over the ages. The naturalist-explorer Alexander von Humboldt was the first Westerner to witness the mysteries of curare preparation by shamans, in 1807. The process took many days and was fraught with danger. In view of the secret powers of the Psylli and all the complicated ancient rituals for gathering poisons described around the Mediterranean, it seems likely that in antiquity, too, shamans or mystical herbalists were responsible for creating the dangerous arrow poisons and their antidotes. In Gaul, for example, the Celtic wizard-priests called Druids may have prepared the poisons from henbane, hellebore, and snake venom.

An expert in concocting poisons would have mixed the lethal dose of hemlock for the Athenian philosopher Socrates, who was condemned to die by drinking hemlock in 399 BC. Hemlock juice (*Conium maculatum*) killed by "congealing and chilling the blood," in the words of Aelian, but the effects are debated by modern philosophers and toxicologists. Did it really bring a pleasant death for Socrates, as famously described by his friend Plato? Or is death by hemlock excruciatingly painful, as others claim? Some believe that Socrates' "gentle" death draught was actually hemlock mixed with enough opium and wine to numb the violent effects. At any rate, pure hemlock sap on a projectile point would bring sure death, and some ancient writers stated that hemlock was one of the poisons used by the fearsome Scythian archers of the Black Sea area.[7]

Yew, the very poisonous tree known as *taxus* in Latin, has symbolized danger and death since antiquity, and was long used to poison arrows. The tall, dark, and dense tree, often planted in graveyards, has a "gloomy, terrifying appearance," observed Pliny, and was so lethal that "if creeping things go near it and touch it at all, they die." Indeed, Pliny claimed that people who napped or picnicked beneath a yew tree had been known to perish. Yew berries contain a strong alkaloid poison, which brings sudden death by suppressing the heartbeat. Pliny also reported that in Spain, which had been brutally conquered by the Romans in the second century BC, souvenir canteens were carved from yew wood and sold to Roman tourists, many of whom died after drinking from the flasks. Could this have been a sly biological sabotage by the Spanish against their hated oppressors?

Belladonna, the deadly nightshade, was known as *strychnos* (hence the word strychnine) to the Romans. Proof that strychnine was a very old weapon poison lies in its other name, *dorycnion*. The Latin word means "spear drug" and, as Pliny commented, "before battle, spear points were dipped in *dorycnion*, which grows everywhere." He also noted that strychnine-treated spears retained toxicity for at least thirty years. The poison causes dizziness, raving agitation, then coma and death. According to legend, ancient Gaelic berserkers took belladonna before battle as an "herb of courage."

Yet another candidate for arrow poison was the sap of rhododendron, which flourishes throughout the Mediterranean, around the

Black Sea, and in Asia. The showy pink and white flowers contain neurotoxins, and the nectar yields a poisonous honey, which was used as a biological weapon against the Romans in Asia Minor.[8]

*　　*　　*

Besides plants, poison creatures could provide arrow drugs. An exotic bio-toxin of mysterious origins was said to be collected in the high mountains of India. First described by Ctesias, a Greek physician living in Persia (Iran) in the late fifth century BC, and then by Aelian in the third century AD, the powerful poison was supposedly excreted by a tiny orange "bird" called the *dikairon*. A miniscule amount of the "droppings" was supposed to bring death in a few hours, and this rare substance was one of the most costly gifts exported from the King of India to the King of Persia and kept as a valuable poison in the royal pharmacy—a useful agent for assassination or suicide.

But what was the poison? Scholars have speculated on the true identity of the *dikairon*, which was said to be the size of a tiny partridge egg. Some suggest that it was really a type of winged dung beetle whose droppings were confused with opium, another exotic product of India. The creature's size does match the size of a dung beetle, and "droppings" may have been a Greek translation for insect excretions or insides. Certain types of dung beetles are even found in birds' nests. The notion that the little orange bird was actually a dung beetle seems like a good answer, except for the fact that dung beetles are not toxic.

There are many other species of highly toxic beetles that can be used to make weapons, however. For example, *Diamphidia* beetle larvae are used to poison arrows by the present-day San Bushmen of the Kalahari Desert. Could the ancient Greek tale of the little "droppings" of the mysterious *dikairon* have originated in a garbled report of a similar beetle toxin gathered in India? Some species of poisonous beetles were recognized in antiquity; for example, Aristotle and the toxicologist Nicander described deadly substances obtained from blister and *staphylinus* beetles, whose poisons are strong enough to kill cattle that accidentally eat them.

A recent discovery by entomological pharmacologists may solve the mystery of the fabled *dikairon* of India. In the 1980s, scientists began investigating the toxic properties of the little-studied *Paederus* beetles of the large Staphylinidae family (rove beetles), found in many areas of the world, including northern India. These predatory flying insects can be either orange and black, or entirely orange, and are about an inch long. Some species inhabit birds' nests, a fact that may account for their being confused with tiny birds as the story traveled west. It transpires that the beetle was known to Chinese medicine twelve hundred years ago. A pharmacopia written by Ch'en in AD 739 accurately described the *Paederus* beetle, called *ch'ing yao ch'ung*, and stated that its "strong poison" could be used to remove tattoos, boils, and polyps from the skin.

Indeed, these blister beetles secrete a virulent poison and their insides or hemolymph contains *pederin*, one of the most powerful animal toxins in the world. On the skin, *pederin* raises angry, suppurating sores, and in the eyes it can cause blindness. But if *pederin* is ingested, or if it enters the bloodstream—as would occur with a poison arrow—the toxicity is more potent than cobra venom![9]

In the Mediterranean, encounters with venomous jellyfish, sea urchins, and stingrays may have suggested the use of marine biotoxins as arrow poisons. The intense pain of a jellyfish sting is like a strong electric shock: it can depress the central nervous system and bring cardiac arrest and death. Sea urchins have been mentioned as another possible source of arrow poison, since the spines deliver a sting similar to a jellyfish's, and life-threatening infections ensue if the wound is near tendons, nerves, or bone. Stingrays were also greatly feared for, as Aelian wrote, "nothing could withstand the barb of the Sting-ray (*trygon*). It wounds and kills instantly and fishermen dread its weapon." It seems that people had experimented with the stingray's weapon of self-defense. So deadly was the *trygon*, declared Aelian, that "if you stab the trunk of a large, healthy tree with the stingray spine, it withers as though scorched and all the leaves shrivel up and fall off."

In the poetic justice of Greek myth, in which a poisoner is fated to die of poison, Odysseus succumbed to a wound from a spear tipped with the spine of a stingray, wielded by the son he never knew, Telegonus. The spear was forged for Telegonus by the god of invention and fire, Hephaestus, from a large ray killed by a Triton (merman) friend of Telegonus's mother, Circe. Several species of toxic rays inhabit Mediterranean waters and the most common is the marbled stingray *Dasyatis chrysonata marmorata* (*Trygon pastinaca*). The stiff, viciously serrated spine is filled with extremely painful poison and makes a jagged, deep, and very bloody puncture. A stab in the chest or abdomen brings quick death. Without modern treatment, a wound anywhere would be likely to develop a fatal infection.

Some classical commentators have considered the legend of Odysseus's strange death an example of overwrought creative mythmaking but, as it turns out, the idea of a stingray spear is not so far-fetched. Modern discoveries in Central and South America give credence to the Greek legend of death by a stingray spine affixed to a spear. In the 1920s, archaeologists were mystified by numerous stingray spines that they found among worked obsidian javelin points in ancient burial sites in Mexico and Latin America. The wooden shafts had long since rotted away, but it seems obvious that the sharp ray spines had served as ready-made arrowheads. Confirmation comes from Brazil where, as late as the 1960s, the Suya Indians manufactured arrows from stingray barbs, which they attached to wooden shafts.[10]

*   *   *

By far, the most feared toxic creatures in the ancient world were hidden snakes whose fangs brought sudden, agonizing death. Numerous species of poisonous snakes inhabit the Mediterranean region and Asia. The terror aroused by the idea of serpents was intensified when a soldier was the target of arrows steeped in their venom.

FIGURE 8. *Poisonous snakes were deeply feared in antiquity, but some ancients were adept in handling snakes and using their venom to make arrow poisons and antidotes. Amphora, detail, Perseus 1991.07.0133.*

(University of Pennsylvania Museum)

According to Greek and Roman writers, archers who "sharpened their arrows with serpent's poison" included the Gauls, Dacians, Dalmatians, Soanes of the Caucasus, Sarmatians of Iran, Getae of Thrace, Slavs, Africans, Armenians, Parthians dwelling between the Indus and Euphrates, and Indians. Poisoned arrows of various sorts were also known in China, demonstrated by ancient texts of the second century AD that describe the surgeon Hua T'o treating a general's poison arrow wound (with a game of chess and wine serving as the anaesthetic). In the same era, the king of the Parthians was killed by a poisoned arrow in the arm, shot by the nomadic Tochari of the Chinese steppes.

In Ethiopia of the first century BC, according to the ancient geographer Strabo, a tribe called the Akatharti hunted elephants with arrows dipped "in the gall of serpents." ("Ethiopia" referred to East Africa north of the Equator.) Several African cultures of more recent times still use snake venom on weapons: perhaps the Akatharti were the ancestors of the present-day Akamba people of Kenya in East Africa, elephant hunters renowned for their special arrow poison. According to the historian Silius Italicus, writing in about AD 80, Roman soldiers fighting in North Africa faced "twice harmful missiles, arrows imbued with serpent's poison." The Nasamonians of Libya were "skilled at disarming serpents of their fell poison," and the Nubians of upper Egypt and Sudan steeped their throwing javelins "in noxious juices, thus disgracing the steel with poison."[11]

Of all the groups who wielded envenomed arrows, however, the most inventive—and the most dreaded—were the Scythians of Central Asia. In the fifth century BC, Herodotus thrilled and shocked the Greeks with his reports of these barbarians who drank from the gilded skulls of their enemies and fashioned quivers from human arms with the hands still attached. The nomad women rode to war too, and were nicknamed "man-killers."

Warlike nomads whose vast territory stretched from the Black Sea east across the steppes to Mongolia, the Scythians dominated the region until about AD 300. For four centuries they were invincible. They successfully repelled the Persian army led by King Darius I in the fifth

FIGURE 9. *Battle between Greek hoplites and Scythian archers. The fallen warrior had decorated his shield with the image of a snake, perhaps to frighten enemies or to magically deflect snake venom arrows. Red-figure kylix.*

(University of Pennsylvania Museum)

century BC with their guerrilla raids and ambushes. Their consummate archery skills led the Athenians to hire Scythian bowman to fight along-side hoplite phalanxes in the fifth century. In 331 BC, Scythian horse-archers even defeated the large army of Alexander the Great.

Scythian victories were due partly to their skill with the bow and their hit-and-run tactics, and partly to special weapon technologies. Indeed, they possessed the ultimate delivery system for pernicious bio-logical agents: they had perfected a composite reflex bow whose power far exceeded other bows, allowing impressive velocity and accuracy at great distances. Each Scythian warrior carried more than 200 arrows into battle, and as crack archers and expert bio-warriors, the Scythians were truly the "sons of Hercules."

When Herodotus traveled around the Black Sea interviewing Scythians in about 450 BC, he discovered that the nomads revered the hero Hercules—the mythical inventor of biological weapons—as their founding father. Parts of the story the nomads told were misunderstood and omitted by Herodotus, who relied on a series of translators, but some intriguing details emerge. What survives of the lost mythology of the Scythians hints that it may have had some parallels to the Greek myth of Hercules and the Hydra-snake, and may have explained the origin of the Scythians' poison arrows. According to the Scythians, Hercules encountered a monstrous Viper-woman in Scythia and fathered three sons with her. He left his bow, arrows, and special belt to the youngest son, Scythes, the ancestor of the Scythians.

The Scythians told Herodotus that Hercules' belt had a buckle of unusual design. The tongue of the buckle was in the form of a little gold vial. And "to this day the Scythians wear belts with little gold cups attached," remarked Herodotus. Herodotus, who was apparently unaware of the Scythians' use of poison arrows, did not speculate on the purpose of the belt. Why would the buckle be fitted with a little cup? I think that the cryptic passage in Herodotus can be explained by the nomads' reliance on toxic arrows. It seems logical that the gold container held the infamous *scythicon*—literally, "Scythian toxin"—the substance the Scythians used for poisoning their arrows. Pure gold would be unaffected by contact with poison. Recalling the Choco method of gathering frog poison in a bottle for dipping, one can imagine that it would be efficient before a battle to dip one's arrows into a vial of *scythicon* at one's waist. It is interesting that in several early vase paintings of Hercules killing the Hydra, the goddess Athena is shown holding out a vial with a narrow opening to catch the Hydra's venom.

The Scythians also invented a special combination bow case–quiver, called a *gorytus*. Artistic representations of these cases on vase paintings and gold artifacts—as well as actual bow cases excavated from fifth-century BC Scythian tombs—show the ingenious design of the case. The *gorytus* hung from a belt and had two separate compartments: one held the bow and the other was a pocket for arrows that could be tightly closed with a flap. Each Scythian archer carried two of these cases. This practice and the unique design of the quiver guaranteed that bows and arrows of various sizes and types were at hand for any hunting or battle situation, and the safety flap helped prevent contact with the razor-sharp, poisoned points.

FIGURE 10. *Right, Scythian archer shooting poison arrows at Greek hoplites. Left, running Scythian archer with bow, arrow, and quiver, about 500 BC.*

(© The British Museum)

As recently as the 1970s, the Akamba tribe of Kenya (mentioned earlier) carried their poisoned arrows in a similarly combined bow case–quiver of smoked leather, fitted with a cap to prevent scratches from the points. The Akamba followed further precautions to avoid the perils of handling poison arrows. Not only did the arrows have very small, sharp retractable metal tips to carry the toxin, but the points were wrapped in leather to keep the poison moist and to prevent accidental injury. It is possible that this was also done in antiquity.

Going into battle, the Scythians may have stored pre-coated arrows in the special safety pocket of the *gorytus*. But when hunting or during a sniping ambush, an archer could dunk an arrow in *scythicon* in the cup or vial on his special belt just before shooting it. This practice would help avoid the kind of nightmarish accident that befell Philoctetes when he was carrying Hercules' quiver of arrows.[12]

The most blood-curdling ingredient of the dreaded *scythicon* was viper venom. Scythian territory is home to several poisonous snake species: the steppe viper, *Vipera ursinii renardi*; the Caucasus viper, *Vipera kasnakovi*; the European adder, *Vipera berus;* and the long-nosed or sand viper, *Vipera ammodytes transcaucasiana*. Simply dipping an arrow in one of these venoms would create a death-dealing projectile, since even dried snake venom retains its neurotoxic effect for a long time (herpetologists working with snake skeletons have suffered envenomation by accidentally puncturing themselves with the fangs of dried-out snake skulls). But the Scythians went much further in manufacturing their war arrows.

The complex recipe for *scythicon* can be reconstructed from statements attributed to Aristotle; from fragments of a lost work by the natural philosopher Theophrastus (fourth century BC); and from the formula given by Aelian. Since psychological terror is a chief aspect of bio-war, the method for brewing the poison and its nauseating ingredients were probably gleefully recounted by the Scythian archers serving with the Athenian army in the fifth century BC.

First, the Scythians killed poisonous vipers just after they had given birth, perhaps because the snakes were sluggish then and easily caught.

(Most vipers, also called adders, give birth to live young.) Then, the bodies were set aside to decompose. The next step required very specialized knowledge, and because shamans were important figures in Scythian culture and the keepers of arcane knowledge, they probably oversaw the complicated preparation of the poison, which required several ingredients. One was taken from humans. "The Scythians," Aelian wrote, "even mix serum from the human body with the poison that they smear upon their arrows." According to Aristotle and Aelian, the Scythians knew a means of "agitating" the blood to separate the plasma, the "watery secretion that somehow floats on the surface of the blood." Theophrastus is cited as the source for this remarkable forerunner of modern blood-plasma separating technology, but unfortunately the full description of the technique is lost.[13]

The human blood serum was then mixed with animal dung in leather bags and buried in the ground until the mixture putrefied. Dung or human feces itself would be a simple but very effective biotoxin for poisoning weapons, and even without an understanding of modern germ theories, experience would have taught the dangers of dung-contaminated wounds. As the historian Plutarch remarked in the first century BC, "creeping things and vermin spring out of the corruption and rottenness of excrement." Excrement is loaded with bacteria that can cause morbid infections. The "pungee sticks" deployed by the Vietcong against U.S. soldiers during the Vietnam War are a modern example of the use of feces on sharp weapons intended to inflict deep, septic wounds.

In the third step, the Scythians mixed the dung and serum with the venom and matter from the decomposed vipers. The stench must have been powerful. A comment by Strabo, who was a native of the Black Sea region, confirms this. The Soanes, a Scythian tribe of the Caucasus Mountains near the Black Sea, "used remarkable poisons for the points of their missiles," he wrote. "Even people who are not wounded by the poison projectiles suffer from their terrible odor." The reek of poisoned arrows may have been an intentional feature, an ancient version of modern "stench weapons" designed by military chemists to be "psychologically toxic" to victims.

Scythian arrow poison was obviously *not* intended for hunting animals. The laborious process of contaminating putrid venomous snakes with blood and feces created a bacteriological weapon clearly meant *only* for human enemies, since no one would eat game tainted by such toxins. As Renate Rolle, an expert on the ancient Scythians, has stated, the result was "a pernicious poison" calculated to cause agonizing death or long-term damage, since "even slight wounds were likely to prove fatal."

Likely indeed: putrefied human blood and animal feces contain bacteria that cause tetanus and gangrene, while the rotting vipers would contribute further bacterial contaminants to wreak havoc in a puncture wound. Rolle consulted Steffen Berg, a forensic physician, who theorized that the poison delivered by a Scythian arrow would probably take effect within an hour. As the victim's blood cells disintegrated, shock would ensue. Even if the victim survived shock, gangrene would set in after a day or two. The gangrene would bring severe suppuration and black oozing of the wound, just as described in the ancient myths of envenomed wounds on the battlefield at Troy. A few days later, a tetanus infection would probably be fatal. Even if a victim miraculously survived all these onslaughts, he would be incapacitated for the rest of his life, like Philoctetes and Telephus in the Greek myths, by an ever-festering wound.[14]

And as if the horrific effects of the poison were not enough, archaeological evidence reveals that Scythian arrowsmiths added yet another feature to their airborne weapons: hooks or barbs. Deploring the odious Scythian missiles for their "promise of a double death," the Roman poet Ovid described how victims were "pitifully shot down by hooked arrows" with "poisonous juices clinging to the flying metal." Poison arrows with ingeniously designed breakaway barbs had decimated a Roman army facing mounted archers in Armenia in 68 BC, according to the historian Dio Cassius.

"In order to render the wound even nastier and the removal of the arrow more difficult," writes Rolle, thorns were affixed to the arrowheads, and others were barbed or hinged. Even a superficially lodged barbed arrow would be extremely tricky and painful to pull out. Projectiles "fitted with hooks and soaked in poison were particularly feared," notes Rolle. Such weapons modified to inflict more injury and pain than conventional arms aroused moral disapproval among Greeks and Romans, who conveniently ignored their own legacy of biological weapons. Interestingly, the ancient criticism of weapons specifically designed to intensify suffering foreshadows modern war protocols that prohibit projectiles that cause "superfluous injury or unnecessary suffering."[15]

So, the Scythians not only formulated their own extremely potent toxin and figured out how to increase damage by adding barbs to arrows shot from technologically advanced bows, they also invented ways of safely handling their hazardous ammunition with their quiver and belt designs. But it seems their creativity did not stop there.

In the 1940s, the Soviet archaeologist Sergei Rudenko was the first to excavate several tombs of Scythian warriors, from the permafrost of the Russian steppes. The tombs, dating to the fifth century BC, were filled with equipment, weapons, and artifacts, many of which were accurately described more than two thousand years ago by Herodotus. Gold, wood, leather, wool and silk, metal, and even the mummified bodies of tattooed warriors, were unearthed from the frozen mud, which Rudenko thawed with boiling water. Since Rudenko, other Russian and American archaeologists have excavated more tombs containing male and female warriors and a wealth of artifacts. So far, nothing matching the little gold cup buckles mentioned by Herodotus has been found in the burials, but many bow case–quivers and arrowheads carved from antler, horn, and bone, and cast in bronze have come to light. Wooden artifacts are rare in most archaeological sites, but the Russian permafrost preserved quantities of wooden arrow shafts in excellent condition, with the vivid colors of paint still visible. And, here, an additional aspect of Scythian creativity comes to light.

Many of the shafts (they were about thirty inches long) were painted solid red or black, while others had red and black wavy lines and zigzags. Rudenko illustrated numerous examples of these arrow shafts in his book, *The Frozen Tombs of Siberia,* but no scholars have commented on the curious decorations. Our knowledge that the Scythians treated their arrowheads with snake venom, however, leads to an intriguing idea. Were the striking designs inspired by patterns on the skins of snakes? Most poisonous vipers have zigzag or diamond patterns. The Caucasian viper, for example, has a serrated black stripe along its red body, and *Vipera berus* has bold zigzags.[16]

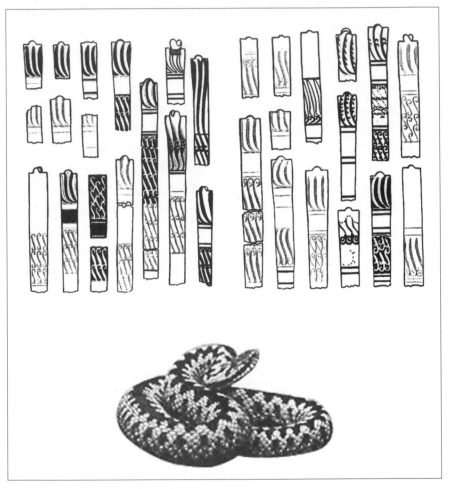

FIGURE 11. *Top, wooden arrow shafts for snake-venom arrows, painted with red and black designs, found in fifth-century* BC *Scythian tombs. After Rudenko,* Frozen Tombs of Siberia. *Bottom, the venom of the poisonous European adder,* Vipera berus, *may have been used by the Scythians to treat their arrows.*

The designs may have been intended to magically empower the envenomed arrows, or they could have been a psychological device aimed at demoralizing the enemy. By painting the shafts to resemble much-feared vipers and affixing arrows with barbs that replicated fangs dripping poison, the Scythians transformed their arrows into the equivalent of flying snakes. "Snake-arrows" zinging through the air certainly would strike fear into the hearts of victims. The effect would be especially harrowing when a warrior impaled by "a bitter-biting arrow" saw that its shaft carried the patterns of a deadly viper.

The painted markings might have also designated different arrow types for the archer. Quintus of Smyrna commented that Philoctetes carried two different sorts of poison arrows in his quiver, some for hunting and others for killing foes, and many cultures around the world use different types of toxic arrows for war and hunting. Perhaps a certain design indicated an arrow coated with pure snake venom to be used for hunting game, while another design indicated arrows tipped with the bacterially enhanced and labor-intensive *scythicon* to be used for battles. Plain shafts may have been used for unpoisoned arrows, to serve for target practice and the many contests the nomads held to show off their skills.

Scythian archers' accuracy and range were phenomenal, even on horseback. Archaeologists have discovered skulls of their victims with arrowheads embedded right between the eyes. Pliny wrote that these nomads were so skilled that they actually used their arrows to dislodge valuable green turquoise gems in the rocks of "inaccessible icy crags" of the Caucasus. From an ancient inscription at Olbia on the Black Sea, we know that a Scythian archer named Anaxagoras won a prize for long-distance shooting. His arrow traveled 1,640 feet (500 meters), far exceeding the average range of an ancient Greek bow, estimated at 900 feet (250–300 meters).

Facing a horde of mounted Scythian warriors was surely a hair-raising experience. The battle would begin with a hail of hideously poisoned arrows blotting out the sun, as each Scythian archer shot about twenty shafts a minute.[17] And the soldiers, crouching behind their shields, had heard all about the dire effects of *scythicon*. In virulence and the ability to inspire terror in the ancient world, only the poison arrows of India could rival the Scythians' flying vipers.

* * *

India, marveled the ancient writers, was fabulously rich in drugs and deadly plants, and infested with noxious reptiles. (For the ancients, "India" meant the lands east of Persia, from Pakistan to Southeast Asia.) Poison weapons could be made from a wealth of nefarious substances, from aconite to bug guts to cobra venom. In the fourth century BC, Alexander the Great's men faced many daunting and marvelous dangers as they marched through India—nearly impassable mountains, strange valleys whose vapors killed birds, weird poisonous plants, scorching heat and thirst, monsoons, deadly serpents of colossal size, and new and bizarre weapons in the form of Indian war elephants—but the worst were the snake-venom arrows.

One of the most feared poisons of India was obtained from the so-called Purple Snake of the "hottest regions" According to Aelian, this snake was short, with a deep purple or maroon body and a head as white as milk or snow. It seemed "almost tame" and did not strike with fangs, but if it "vomited" on a victim, the entire limb putrefied and death was usually quick, although some victims wasted away over several years, "dying little by little."

The Purple Snake has never been identified by modern herpetologists. When I contacted Aaron Bauer, who has studied reptiles in Asia, about Aelian's description, he was struck by two details, the remarkable white head and the habitat in the "hottest part of Asia." If Aelian's account came third- or fourth-hand from Southeast Asia, suggested Bauer, the Purple Snake may refer to the rare, white-headed viper that was unknown to science until the late 1880s, *Azemiops feae*. This viper is the only tropical Asian venomous snake with a distinctive white head. The short and stout body is dark blue-black with red marks and looks

FIGURE 12. *The dreaded Purple Snake of India, as described by Aelian and Ctesias, had a distinctive white head. It may have been the poisonous* Azemiops feae, *discovered by scientists in the late 1800s.*

(Photo © R. W. Murphy)

purplish, especially as the scales reflect light or if a preserved specimen is observed. This primitive viper has relatively short fangs and small venom sacs. Described by herpetologists as "docile but dangerous," the white-headed viper is found in modern Tibet, China, Burma, and Vietnam. The lack of fangs and disastrous result of "vomiting" on a victim described by Aelian probably referred to venom that accidentally dripped into an open sore. The venom of *Azemiops* has not been fully analyzed, but the "long-term effects would be devastating with significant necrosis."

Collecting the toxin of the Purple Snake was difficult and dangerous, Aelian recounted. To extract the venom, the Indians suspended the reptile alive and head down over a bronze pot to catch the dripping poison, which congealed and set into a thick amber-colored gum. When the snake eventually died, the first pot was replaced with another to catch the watery serum flowing from the carcass. After three days, this foul liquid jelled into a deep black substance. The two poisons of the Purple Snake were kept separate, as they killed in different ways, both dreadful. The black poison caused a lingering, wasting death over years, from spreading necrosis and suppurating wounds. The amber poison (the pure venom) caused violent convulsions, and then the victim's "brain dissolves and drips out his nostrils and he dies a most pitiable death."[18]

Feeling queasy? That reaction was exactly the intention of poison arrow makers in Scythia and India. Just dipping arrows in pure venom would be deadly enough. But soaking war arrows in the most grotesque poisons and broadcasting the horrid recipes to potential enemies was an important psychological aspect of biological warfare. The very idea of facing archers supplied with *scythicon* or Purple Snake poison was terrifying.

When Alexander the Great and his army advanced over the Khyber Pass from Afghanistan into Punjab in 327–25 BC, India was still an unknown land of fabled wonders. The Greek veterans brought back more accurate information about the natural history of India, along with some tales that defied belief. In a decisive battle on the Hydapses River in northern India, Alexander's soldiers were astounded by the sight of the giant King Porus atop his huge elephant. This was the first time the Greeks had encountered war elephants in action, but Alexander's army managed to defeat Porus by hemming in the elephants and shooting the mahouts (drivers) who controlled them.

After that victory, many cities and kingdoms acquiesced to Alexander, but others still resisted. It was Alexander's dream to push eastward to the Ganges River and thence to the ocean, but his troops were exhausted by the long campaign so far from home and dispirited by rumors of invincible armies led by King Chandragupta of the Mauryan Empire in northeast India. Demoralized by the drenching monsoons and the strange deadly plants and terrible serpents of India, the Greeks mutinied and refused to advance.

Alexander conceded to his men's wishes. They did not have to fight King Chandragupta's formidable forces (the king would later make alliances with Alexander's successors and supplied them with Indian war elephants for their wars). Alexander followed the Indus River south to the Indian Ocean, where his army divided, half heading home by sea and the others trudging west through the waterless wilderness of Gedrosia (southern Pakistan and Iran) with their leader.

As they pressed south, Alexander's men met with many adventures and battles with exotic peoples. They encountered an herb that instantly killed their pack mules and the soldiers suffered eye injuries from the blinding, squirting juice of prickly cucumbers. Men perished from thirst, tropical diseases, and eating unripe dates. And then there were the deadly cobras and vipers. "In the sand-hills," wrote Strabo, "snakes crept unnoticed and they killed every man they struck." Snake-bites soon became such a menace that Alexander was obliged to hire Hindu physicians to accompany his army. Any soldier who was bitten was to report to the royal tent for emergency treatment by the Hindu healers.[19]

It was after conquering the Kingdom of Sambus that Alexander and his men arrived at the fortified city of Harmatelia, in 326 BC (probably Mansura, Pakistan). Here, the Greeks faced a "new and grave danger," wrote the historian Diodorus of Sicily. The Harmatelians were reported to be oddly confident of victory. When three thousand warriors rushed out of the city to meet Alexander's army, the Greeks discovered the source of their confidence.

The Harmatelians "had smeared their weapons with a drug of mortal effect." The historian Quintus Curtius mentions poisoned swords, and Strabo says they used poisoned arrowheads carved of wood and hardened in fire. Diodorus elaborated further: he says the poison was derived from dead snakes, but by a different technique than that used for the Purple Snake. Like the Scythian adders, the snakes of Harmatelia were killed and left to rot in the sun. As the heat decomposed the flesh, the venom supposedly suffused the liquefying tissue. It is interesting that both the Scythians and the Indians used the entire bodies of vipers to make arrow poisons. A recent herpetological discovery suggests a good reason. Not only would the rotting flesh of whatever prey was in snake's stomach contain harmful bacteria, but researchers have learned that vipers retain surprisingly large amounts of feces in their bodies over many months. In a dead viper, the volume of rotting excrement would provide further foul bacteria to the mixture.

Diodorus's description is vivid. The wounded men went immediately numb, then suffered stabbing pains and wracking convulsions. Their skin became cold and livid, and they vomited up bile. Black froth exuded from the wound and then purple-green gangrene spread rapidly and "brought a horrible death." Even a "mere scratch" brought the same gruesome death.

Because India is so famed for its cobras, modern scholars have simply assumed that the poison was cobra venom. I asked herpetologist Aaron Bauer for his expert opinion. Considering Alexander's route through India and the detailed symptoms recorded by Diodorus, Bauer concluded that the venom probably came from the deadly Russell's viper, *Vipera russelli russelli,* rather than from a cobra species. The symptoms suggest that pure snake venom was used on the arrows; Diodorus apparently conflated other accounts of rotting viper poisons into his description, or perhaps the story was circulated by the Harmatelians to discourage attackers. The Russell's viper venom causes numbness and vomiting, then severe pain and gangrene before death, just as described by Diodorus, whereas death from cobra venom is relatively painless, caused by respiratory paralysis.

Watching so many of his men, even those with only slight wounds, die one after another in agony, deeply distressed Alexander. He was especially aggrieved by the suffering of his beloved general Ptolemy, who had been grazed on the shoulder by an envenomed arrow. According to Diodorus and Curtius, one night Alexander dreamed of a snake carrying a certain plant in its mouth (according to Strabo's version, a man showed him the plant). The next morning, Alexander found the herb and applied a poultice of it to Ptolemy's blackened wound. He also made an infusion of it to drink. With this therapy, Ptolemy recovered, as did a few other wounded men. Seeing that the Greeks had discovered the antidote to their arrows, the Harmatelians surrendered.

Strabo surmises that the fantastic story of Alexander's healing dream was fabricated after someone—probably one of the Hindu doctors accompanying the Greek army—informed him of an antidote for the snake-venom arrows. Indian physicians were very experienced in treating snakebites and wounds made by snake-venom arrows. They would have immediately recognized by the symptoms what kind of venom Harmatelians were using on their weapons.[20]

The use of poisoned arrows for war was common in India and yet, as in many other ancient cultures, the practice aroused mixed reactions. Toxic weapons violated the traditional Hindu laws of conduct for Brahmans and high castes, the *Laws of Manu*. The laws, recited over generations in oral verses, date back to about 500 BC (some say even earlier), and were therefore known at the time of Alexander. The *Laws of Manu* explicitly proscribed the use of arrows that were "barbed, poisoned, or blazing with fire."

The *Laws of Manu* principles of correct and noble warfare for Brahmans were countered, however, by another treatise from the time of Alexander's adventures in India, the *Arthashastra*. An infamous book on ruthless statecraft written by Kautilya, King Chandragupta's Brahman military strategist, the *Arthashastra* has been described as "revolting" and "cynical" by the medical historian Guido Majno, while political scientists and historians see it as a fascinating example of ancient realpolitik. Kautilya advised King Chandragupta to use any means, with no moral constraints, to obtain his military goals, and enumerated an astonishing number of methods to secretly poison enemies, including several complex recipes for creating biochemical weapons based on venomous snakes and other noxious ingredients. The Harmatelians (identified as Brahmans by the ancient Greek historians) probably felt justified in using toxic measures similar to those recommended by Kautilya, to defend themselves against such a formidable foreign invader as Alexander the Great.

How many of Kautilya's biochemical recipes were actually put into practice is unknowable, but the deterrent effect of the weird and loathsome ingredients may have been part of the book's impact. Indeed, Kautilya himself referred to the valuable propaganda effects of exhibiting the frightening effects of his poisons and potions to induce "terror among the enemy."

In a startling revival of ancient bio-warfare in modern India, Kautilya's *Arthashastra,* compiled some twenty-three hundred years ago, became the subject of intense study by Hindu military experts and Pune University scientists in 2002. Funded by the Indian Defence Ministry, the scientists began researching Kautilya's ancient "secrets of effective stealth warfare" and biochemical armaments, to use against India's modern enemies. According to reports by the BBC and other news agencies, the military scientists have begun experimenting with ancient recipes reputed to give armies special biological powers. For example, a potion of fireflies and wild boar's eyes are believed to endow night vision, and special shoes smeared with the fat from roasted pregnant camels or the ashes of cremated children and bird sperm are supposed to allow soldiers to walk for hundreds of miles without fatigue. The scientists are also studying Kautilya's formulas for powders from nefarious substances that were intended to cause madness, blindness, or death in one's adversaries.

The Indian military experiments might be dismissed as useless experiments with magic. Yet the Hindu scientists are not alone in the search for unusual biochemical agents to give armies special biological powers. In 2002, for example, military scientists funded by the Defense Advanced Research Projects Agency (DARPA) of the U.S. Defense Department initiated a search for special stimulants and agents based on "magical genes in mice and fruit-flies" that would eliminate the need for sleep in American soldiers.[21]

* * *

The possibilities for creating arrow poisons from natural toxins were myriad in the ancient world, and the search for antidotes and treatments for poison wounds kept pace. Remedies for envenomed wounds in Greek myths reflected the actual treatments used by battlefield doc-

FIGURE 13. *Achilles treating Telephus's poison wound by scraping rust from his spear. Roman bas relief sculpture, found at Herculaneum.*

(Museo Archeologico Nazionale, Naples)

tors. For example, the festering wound suffered by Hercules' son Telephus, caused by a puncture from Achilles' poisoned spear, was cured with iron rust. Pliny described a famous painting that depicted Achilles using his sword to scrape rust from his spear into Telephus's wound (a relief sculpture of the same scene was found in the ruins of ancient Herculaneum). According to Pliny, scrapings of iron rust and bronze verdigris mixed with myrrh staunched oozing poisoned wounds, and indeed, archaeologists have discovered sets of rusty nails and old metal tools for this very purpose in Roman military surgeons' kits.

The physician Rufus of Ephesus (first century AD) advised military doctors to ask deserters and prisoners of war about their army's use of poisons, so that antidotes could be prepared. Purple spurge and the gum resin from giant fennel were supposed to be effective against envenomed arrows, according to Pliny, who also recommended a plant called "centaury" or "chironion" (*Centaurium*), after the Centaur Chiron. An astringent for drying up septic wounds, its power to close torn flesh was "so strong that pieces of meat coalesce when boiled with it." Supplies of centaury have been discovered by archaeologists in the ruins of ancient Roman military hospitals in Britain.

Pliny claimed there was an antidote for every snake venom, except the asp (cobra). Aelian agreed that the victim of asp venom was "beyond help." Some antidotes, such as rue, myrrh, tannin, and curdled milk, were beneficial or at least harmless; others were dangerous, and still others seem downright silly, such as boiled frogs, dried weasel, and hippopotamus testicle.[22]

There were also notions of trying to develop resistance to snake and other venoms. It was well known that natives of lands with venomous creatures such as scorpions or snakes often had some immunity to the toxins, so that a scorpion sting simply itched or a snakebite merely stung. The resistance of some natives was said to be so powerful that their breath, saliva, or skin repelled vipers or cured their bites. The Psylli of North Africa were considered the outstanding example of this kind of resistance. According to the Romans, the Psylli were so habituated to snakebites that their own saliva was an effective antivenin. Antivenin is derived from antibodies to live snake venom, and the implication is that the Psylli immunity was achieved by the same antiserum principle. Psylli spit was eagerly sought by the Romans to counteract snakebites during their African campaigns.

It was also a common belief in antiquity that ingesting poisons in small amounts, along with the proper antidotes, could offer protection against the poisons, a concept related to the modern techniques of immunization. The idea is evident in the ancient Hindu *Laws of Manu,* which advised kings to mix antidotes to poisons in their food. King Mithridates VI of Pontus on the Black Sea was the most famous practitioner of this systematic poison-resistance program in antiquity. But even today, in Indonesia, jungle military training includes inuring soldiers to snake venom by having them drink snake blood.[23]

Another remedy for snake poison was to try to remove the venom from the victim. Philoctetes' festering wound from the Hydra-venom arrow was cured by sucking out the poison and applying a poultice. This was the standard remedy for snakebite and poison-arrow wounds, both of which were detected by black gore instead of bright red blood. Warriors felled by toxic arrows were immediately tended by army doctors who either sucked the venom themselves or applied leeches, salves, or suction cups to draw out the poison.

Sucking out snake venom by mouth could be hazardous for the doctor. The death of a medicine man in Rome in about 88 BC demonstrated the peril. While exhibiting his snake-handling skills to fellow practitioners, he was bitten by one of his cobras. He managed to successfully suck out the poison himself, but was unable to rinse out his mouth with water soon enough. Aelian tells the horrible result: the venom "reduced his gums and mouth to putrescence" and spread through his body. Two days later he was dead. To avoid such an accident, Trojan doctors used leeches, while Indian doctors stuffed a wad of linen in their mouths as a filter.

The medical writer Celsus, writing about a hundred years after the Roman snake handler's death, recommended a cup to draw out the poison, but if none was available, the alternative was to send for someone adept at drawing venom by mouth. The fabulous reputation of the Psylli, whose saliva was said to neutralize serpent venom, was probably a misunderstanding on the part of inexperienced observers who had watched a Psylli healer sucking out venom. Celsus revealed that their skill actually came from "boldness confirmed by experience." He correctly pointed out that anyone "who follows the example of the Psylli and sucks out a wound will be safe," provided that "he has no sore place on his gums, palate, or mouth."

Snake venom can be digested safely, as long as no internal abrasions allow it to enter the bloodstream. That fact was also understood by Lucan, a Roman historian in the first century AD. Lucan described, in page after page of lurid details, the "unspeakable horrors" of death by various snakebites and scorpion stings during Cato's arduous civil war campaigns in the North African desert in the first century BC. The Psylli came to Cato's rescue. Just as the Hindu doctors skilled in treating snakebites aided Alexander the Great in India, the Psylli joined Cato's army to treat the constant stream of snakebite victims carried into their tents. Whereas the Hindu doctors recognized the species of venom on the Harmetalian arrows by the symptoms of the wound, Lucan claimed the Psylli could identify the species of snake by the taste of the venom. The Psylli apparently encouraged the notion of their special immunity to boost their monopoly on curing envenomed wounds. In fact, soon after the civil war, some Psylli practitioners had set up shop in Rome, plying their arcane toxicology skills. They were criticized by Pliny and Lucan for importing deadly poisons and venomous snakes and scorpions of many exotic lands into Italy for profit—apparently the Psylli had become purveyors of poisons for nefarious plots.[24]

In ancient India, doctors were well versed in dealing with snakebites, but removing arrows, including those coated in venom, was a special skill of the *shalyahara* ("arrow-remover"). These surgeons had to decide whether to pull the shaft out or push it all the way through the body. Sometimes they used magnets to locate and help draw out iron arrowheads, and sometimes tree branches or horses were used to jerk a deeply embedded arrow out speedily, with the hope that it was not barbed. Barbed weapons "have always been the curse of battlefield surgery," remarks the historian of battle-wound treatments, Guido Majno. In the Mediterranean world, however, special instruments were designed to deal with barbed arrowheads, like those of the Scythian nomads. In about 400 BC, Diokles of Karystos invented a tool, called the "spoon of Diokles," to ease a hooked arrow out without further damage to the flesh.

But in spite of all the remedies, antidotes, panaceas, and drastic emergency treatments—and Alexander the Great's legendary dream—the grim sight of black blood trickling from an arrow wound was cause for despair. A terrible toxin was already coursing through the body, which almost always spelled doom. The survival rate of real-life warriors pierced by poisoned projectiles was slim, probably no better than the dismal rate of recovery in Greek myth, where only two victims, Telephus and Philoctetes, recovered, and then only after years of suffering. Even Chiron the Centaur died despite treatment with a special healing plant, and antidotes were futile in the cases of Achilles, Paris, Odysseus, Hercules, and the many other mythic warriors felled by poison weapons. In the event of biologically contaminated wounds on real-life battlefields, the reaction among warriors was undoubtedly "gloom and frustration."[25]

Despite the perils of obtaining and handling the hazardous materials to make toxic weapons—and the moral disapproval that often clouded their use—the guaranteed casualty rate, the vast arsenal of natural toxins and the lack of effective antidotes, plus the advantages of long-distance projectiles, made poisoned arrows the most popular bioweapon in antiquity. But a great many other natural agents were also manipulated to achieve military victories. The next two chapters look at delivery systems for poisons and disease, capable of destroying enemies en masse. With the ancient myths as models, one could not only pick off one's foes arrow by arrow as did Hercules or Odysseus, but one could copy the sorceress Circe and poison entire bodies of water—or even imitate the god Apollo and spread contagion.

3

Poison Waters,
Deadly Vapors

> Aquillius finally brought the Asiatic war
> to a close by the wicked expedient of
> poisoning the springs of certain cities.
> —Florus, 130 BC

Succumbing to thirst is a terrible way to die.

The Greek historian Thucydides described the horrific outcome of the rout of the Athenians after they invaded Sicily in 413 BC, their worst defeat in the Peloponnesian War. In their failed siege of Syracuse, the Athenians had destroyed the pipes conveying drinking water to the city, a common practice in ancient warfare. But the tide shifted and the Syracusans retaliated in kind. They chased the demoralized Athenian forces overland, constantly denying them access to water. When the parched army, already sickened by swamp fevers, finally reached a river, chaos erupted as the mass of delirious soldiers trampled each other trying to reach the water. The Syracusans stood on the cliffs above and slaughtered the Athenians, who kept on drinking the muddy water, now fouled with blood and gore, until the river was dammed up with heaps of bodies.

In the next century, in India, the Greek army of Alexander the Great was so wracked by thirst that the desperate soldiers would leap into wells, armor and all. The historian Strabo wrote that the crazed men drowned trying to drink while submerged. Their bloated corpses floated to the surface, corrupting their only available source of water. In this case, the Greek army polluted their own water, but Indian strategists of that era knew many ways of poisoning water along enemy routes.

Cutting off an enemy's water supply to force surrender was an effective—and common—method of attack, but thirst could be compounded by compelling foes to drink foul waters. Actually poisoning the water was a more subtle strategy, especially effective in siege-craft. A related large-scale biological ploy was to take advantage of unhealthy terrain. The enemy could be maneuvered into malarial marshes or other environments where bad water or air ensured that illness would take a high toll.[1]

*   *   *

The earliest historically documented case of poisoning drinking water occurred in Greece during the First Sacred War. In about 590 BC, several Greek city-states created the Amphictionic League to protect the religious sanctuary of Delphi, the site of the famous Oracle of Apollo. In the First Sacred War, the League (led by Athens and Sicyon) attacked the strongly fortified city of Kirrha, which controlled the road from the Corinthian Gulf to Delphi. Kirrha had appropriated some of Apollo's sacred land and mistreated pilgrims to Delphi. According to the Athenian orator Aeschines (fourth century BC), the Amphictionic League consulted the Oracle of Apollo at Delphi about Kirrha's religious crimes.

The oracle responded that total war against the city was appropriate: Kirrha was to be completely destroyed and its territory laid waste. The League added a curse of their own, in the name of Apollo: the land should not produce crops, all the children should be monstrous, the livestock should also have unnatural offspring, and the entire "race should perish utterly." The biological disaster described in the curse evokes an eerie "nuclear winter" scene. Then, taking into their own hands Apollo's divine powers of sending sickness, the League destroyed the city of Kirrha by means of a biological stratagem. The event received a remarkable degree of attention from ancient historians.

During the siege of Kirrha, someone "thought up a contrivance."

Depending on whose account one reads, four different historical indi-viduals were credited with variants of the plan. According to the military strategist Frontinus (writing in the first century AD), it was Kleisthenes of Sicyon, the commander of the siege, who "cut the water-pipes leading into the town. Then, when the townspeople were suffering from thirst, he turned on the water again, now poisoned with hellebore." The vio-lent effects of the poison plant caused them to be "so weakened by diar-rhea that Kleisthenes overcame them."

In the account of Polyaenus (second century AD), "the besiegers found a hidden pipe carrying a great flow of spring water" into the city. Polyaenus says it was General Eurylochos who advised the allies "to col-lect a great quantity of hellebore from Anticyra and mix it with the water." Anticyra was a port east of Kirrha, where hellebore grew in great profusion. The Kirrhans "became violently sick to their stomachs and all lay unable to move. The Amphictions took the city without opposition."[2]

Pausanias visited the site of Kirrha in about AD 150, more than seven hundred years after its destruction. "The plains around Kirrha are completely barren, and people there will not plant trees," he wrote, "because the land is still under a curse and trees will not grow there." Pausanias attributed the fateful plan to Solon, the great sage of Athens. In this account, Solon diverted the channel from the River Pleistos so that it no longer ran through Kirrha. But the Kirrhans held out, draw-ing water from wells and collecting rainwater. Solon then threw "a great quantity of hellebore roots into the Pleistos." When he deter-mined that "the water was drugged enough, he sent it back through the city." "The parched Kirrhans glutted themselves on the contaminated water, and of course became extremely ill," wrote Pausanias. "The men defending the walls had to abandon their positions out of never-ending diarrhea." Helpless to respond to the attack, the people of Kirrha were annihilated as the League hoplites overran the city.

The use of a treacherous ruse to breach a city's defenses, which then resulted in further atrocities inside the city, echoes what happened in Troy, in the aftermath of the Trojan Horse trick. That subterfuge was followed by the rape of Trojan women and the massacre of children and old people by the Greek warriors. In both myth and history, there is evidence that once an army has resorted to insidious strategies outside the conventions of combat, it is not uncommon for further violations to ensue, such as the mass killing of noncombatants. Unconventional strategies often result from frustration, and when devious or unscrupulous behavior appears to be the only way to victory, the door is then opened to atrocities.

The destruction of Kirrha in 590 BC features some other striking mythological coincidences. The town happens to be located near the place where the Centaur Nessus was said to have died of the Hydra-venom arrow shot by Hercules, just west of Delphi. According to ancient legend, the Centaur's rotting carcass poisoned the area's water, making it unhealthy to drink. In the mid-nineteenth century, H. N. Ulrichs of the Bavarian Academy of Sciences discovered a brackish spring near Kirrha that induces violent diarrhea. Possibly, the besiegers' knowledge of that naturally foul spring was the inspiration for their idea of poisoning the Kirrhans' water with the violent purgative hellebore.[3]

The fourth man credited with the plan to poison Kirrha was a doctor named Nebros, an *asclepiad,* or follower of the legendary healer Asclepius, son of Apollo. According to ancient medical sources, Nebros was an ancestor of the great physician Hippocrates, author of the Hippocratic Oath in the fifth century BC. The account that implicates Nebros is the earliest known source, written only a century after Kirrha's destruction and during Hippocrates' lifetime. It comes from the medical writer Thessalos, reportedly a son of Hippocrates. Thessalos visited Athens in the late fifth century BC as an ambassador from Cos, the seat of Hippocratic medicine. He wrote that after a horse's hoof had broken open the secret pipe carrying Kirrha's water supply during the siege, Nebros helped the besiegers "by introducing into the aqueduct a drug that brought intestinal illness to the Kirrhans, allowing the allies to take the town."

The involvement of a doctor in the destruction of the populace of Kirrha is startling. By sending sickness to Kirrha, did Nebros see him-self as carrying out Apollo's wrath on the town? That seems possible, given the sacred oracle and the curse used to justify total war. Perhaps in an attempt to rationalize Nebros's participation in the town's destruction, Thessalos avoided naming the drug, although it was identified by all the other sources as hellebore. And he implied that its debilitating effects were only temporary.

But the implication that the drug's effects were only temporary was duplicitous in this case. Everyone—especially doctors—knew that hellebore was extremely dangerous and that the dosage in medical treatments was notoriously difficult to calibrate. Hellebore was known to kill large animals, and it was used as a deadly arrow poison. Doctors never prescribed hellebore for the old or weak, or for women or children. Clandestinely contaminating a city's drinking water with "a great quantity of hellebore" would sicken not just the guards and soldiers of Kirrha, but all the people inside the city walls, young and old. Taken by surprise and already suffering from thirst, they would have had no time to try to prepare antidotes. To deliberately harm noncombatants was proscribed by the ancient Greek notions of fair war, but during sieges of cities the entire population was considered the enemy.

The ancient attempt to justify use of a "temporary" toxin to soften resistance was echoed in a modern biochemical attack on noncombatants in Iraq, in 1920. After the fall of the Ottoman Empire in 1917, the British occupation of Iraq was resisted by the Kurds. According to Geoff Simons in his 1994 book, *Iraq: from Sumer to Saddam*, in 1920 the colonial secretary Winston Churchill proposed a "scientific expedient" to quell the "turbulent tribes" of Kurdistan. He suggested using poison gas as a preliminary measure in bombing operations against the villages. Some British authorities protested that the villagers were defenseless and had no medical knowledge of antidotes. Discounting the protestors' "squeamishness about the use of gas . . . against uncivilised tribes," Churchill claimed that the chemical gas—which had only recently caused such devastation and moral revulsion in the First World War—would inflict "only discomfort or illness, but not death," and would be a good way to demoralize the enemy.

In reality, however, the gas caused blindness, and killed children, the infirm, and the old. Like Kirrha, the Kurdish villages were easily wiped out after the poison was administered. And in keeping with the timeless tendency to further violate codes of war once a rule of fair war has been transgressed, several newly developed inhumane weapons were first tested in Kurdistan with devastating effects.[4]

Mirko Grmek, the Croatian historian of science who devoted his career to medical ethics, has given some thought to the story of Kirrha. He points out that it was in the interest of Thessalos, a practitioner of the healing arts and a son of Hippocrates, to try to exonerate Nebros, a fellow physician and an ancestor of Hippocrates, for devising a plan that so obviously violated the Hippocratic ideal that a doctor should do no harm. The famous Hippocratic Oath was not formally written down until the time of Thessalos in the fifth century, but earlier doctors in the tradition of Asclepius, like Nebros, were still supposed to heal, not injure. The poisoning of Kirrha is a classic example of using specialized natural knowledge to harm humanity rather than to do good. The incident makes one wonder: Was the unscrupulous role of his ancestor Nebros at Kirrha what moved Hippocrates to write the oath?

We can't know that, of course, but it is fascinating to find a doctor implicated in the oldest version of the first recorded incident of poisoning a civilian population in war. This is the earliest report of a medical professional helping to wage biological warfare, but it is certainly not the last. Nebros's actions have been repeated down through history, and around the globe. For example, an Italian physician was responsible for deploying contagion against French forces in 1495, and French doctors carried out similar acts during the Franco-Prussian War. An American surgeon was court-martialed for deliberately spreading yellow fever during the Civil War and medical horrors on a vast scale were perpetrated by Nazi and Japanese doctors during World War II. In South Africa, revelations during the 1999 trial of Dr. Wouter Basson, the eminent cardiologist who founded the government biochemical program in the 1980s to create an arsenal of poisons to be used against anti-apartheid activists, led to his sobriquet "Dr. Death."[5]

* * *

The oracle and the curse against Kirrha were used to justify the unusual ferocity of the First Sacred War in 590 BC. A few scholars have suggested that the destruction of Kirrha may have been a legendary event, but the fact that it is mentioned in a recorded speech by the Athenian orator Isocrates and so many other credible writers has convinced most historians that it really took place. As Grmek concluded, whether the defeat of Kirrha by hellebore was legend or fact, the story of the poisoned water—and the attention it received from historians of the age—reveals the deep ambivalence over using biological measures in antiquity. Even the fact that four different men were implicated implies that people were uneasy about assigning blame or taking credit for the act.

Was there a debate outside the walls of Kirrha among the League allies about the morality of using hellebore, just as some British authorities protested Churchill's plan to gas the Kurds in 1920? That, we'll never know, but we do know that remorse about the method of the destruction of Kirrha was acted upon in the aftermath of the destruction. In an ancient forerunner to the 1924 Geneva Convention (in response to the bio-terror of gassing in World War I), after the battle of Kirrha the defenders of the sacred site of Delphi agreed that poisoning water was unacceptable in a religious war, or among the allies of Delphi should they ever find themselves at war with one another. According to the Amphictionic League's new rule of war, articulated by the Athenian orator Aeschines, contaminating drinking water was to be forbidden in conflicts of a special, sacred nature.

As military historians note, rules against using biological weapons are nearly "as old as the weapons themselves," but their effect has always been fleeting and inconsistent. For example, the *Laws of Manu*, the code of conduct for high-caste Hindus dating to about 500 BC, is considered the earliest attempt to prohibit biological and chemical strategies in a culture where poisons and subterfuges were pervasive and widely accepted. As described in chapter 2, however, the Harmatelians of India attacked Alexander the Great's army with deadly snake-venom arrows, even though the *Laws* prohibited them. When one "fights foes in battle," stated the *Laws,* "let him not strike with concealed [or treacherous] weapons, nor with weapons that are barbed or poisoned or blazing with fire." Yet the *Laws* also advised "spoiling the enemy's water," and the military treatise of the same era, the *Arthashastra,* urged rulers to use a vast arsenal of biochemical weapons.[6]

Despite the good intention of the rule against tampering with water, drawn up after the First Sacred War, many incidents and rumors of poisoning besieged towns and enemy troops were recorded after Kirrha. Not all instances evoked criticism, however. Purely *defensive* biological tactics seemed justified. For example, in 478 BC the Athenians deliberately fouled their own cisterns as they abandoned their city to the Persian invaders led by Xerxes. They were following an accepted, age-old defensive practice—known as the "scorched earth" policy—of burning one's own crops and spoiling foodstuffs and water and other resources in order to leave nothing of use to conquering armies.

The defensive principle legitimated biological strategies against aggressors. But the idea of an *aggressor* surreptitiously poisoning the water supplies of unsuspecting people trapped inside a city, as happened to Kirrha, was more troubling. Evidence that such practices were suspected in antiquity appeared in *The History of the Peloponnesian War,* by the Athenian historian Thucydides. While the Athenians were trapped in their city by the Spartans in 430 BC, a devastating plague broke out suddenly in the harbor of Athens, and—perhaps recalling the famous story of Kirrha—the Athenians' first reaction was to accuse the Spartans of poisoning their wells.

After the Peloponnesian War, the general known as Aeneas the Tactician drew on his own and others' wartime experiences to write (in about 350 BC) a siege-craft manual for military commanders. Aeneas recommended several biological tactics. One was to "make water

FIGURE 14. *Women drawing water at a fountain house. During a siege, a city's water supply could be poisoned. Hydria, 520–510 BC.*

(Toledo Museum of Art, Libbey Endowment, Gift of Edward Drummond Libbey)

undrinkable" by polluting rivers, lakes, springs, wells, and cisterns. In 1927, the British commentators on Aeneas were shocked, and declared that "this horrible practice was against the spirit of Greek warfare." But as the Kirrha episode showed, the expedient has appealed to ruthless war leaders from early antiquity onward. Examples can be found around the world, from ancient India and China to the New World. In North America, for example, more than one thousand French soldiers were decimated by illness after Iroquois Indians deliberately polluted their drinking water with flayed animal skins in 1710. Tossing animal carcasses into wells was a standard practice during the American Civil War, and in countless conflicts before and since.[7]

*   *   *

Interfering with water by diverting rivers was another age-old environmental ploy in war. Frontinus, the Roman commander and author of *Stratagems,* had campaigned against the savage Silures of Wales, the

Chatti of Germany, and "other troublesome people" at the fringes of the Roman Empire. His book, written in a popular style accessible to military leaders, presents numerous examples of clever and successful war strategies from Greek and Roman history, including the poisoning incident at Kirrha. Frontinus's interests in quelling bellicose tribes, and later his office as Manager of Aqueducts at Rome, were combined in a section of his book titled "On Diverting Streams and Contaminating Waters."

On diverting rivers, he wrote of Semiramis, the legendary queen of Assyria (seventh century BC), who boasted in an inscription that she had extended her borders with courageous and cunning conquests: "I compelled rivers to run where I wanted, and I wanted them to run where it was advantageous." According to Frontinus, Semiramis conquered Babylon with a brilliant water trick. The Euphrates River flowed through the city, dividing it in two. Semiramis, who undertook many waterworks projects in her reign, had her engineers divert the river, so that her army could march right into the city in the dry riverbed. The very same feat was attributed by other authors to the mythical witch Medea and to two historical conquerors of Babylon, the Persian king Cyrus and Alexander the Great.

A stream was diverted to literally flush out an enemy by the Roman commander Lucius Metellus, fighting in Spain in 143 BC. The Spaniards had foolishly camped in an easily flooded plain alongside a stream. The Roman legionaries damned the stream and waited in ambush to slaughter the panicked men as they ran for high ground. Some years later, in 78–74 BC, Rome began a difficult campaign in a rugged region of Asia Minor called Isaura (in eastern Turkey). The Isaurians were fiercely independent mountaineers, labeled as "brigands and bandits" by the Romans. Publius Servilius, leader of the campaign, finally reduced the fortified towns of Isauria by diverting the mountain streams where the Isaurians drew their water, "and he thus forced them to surrender in consequence of thirst." A couple of decades later, Julius Caesar, on his campaign in Gaul (now France), diverted the water of the city of

Cadurci. Because the town was surrounded by a river and many springs, this took a lot of labor, digging extensive networks of underground channels. Then Caesar stationed his archers to cut down any Gauls who attempted to reach the river. The stratagem was successful: Cadurci surrendered in 51 BC.

Polyaenus, a Macedonian lawyer from Bithynia, wrote a military treatise for the Roman emperors Lucius Verus and Marcus Aurelius in AD 161. In it he claimed that the mythic hero Hercules had changed the course of a river in Greece to destroy the Minyans because he was afraid to face such skilled cavalrymen in open battle. The story was intended to justify reliance on devious tricks, instead of risky face-to-face battles, for the co-emperors who were facing a daunting war against the invincible Parthians of Central Asia. The Parthians, renowned for their armored cavalry and formidable horse archers, had just invaded the eastern empire and, in fact, were never defeated by the Romans.

Cunning tricks like diverting rivers to gain access to a city or to cause floods are examples of creative unconventional warfare, not true biological strategies based on special natural knowledge. Unless such ploys killed entire populations by drowning (as occurred in some Islamic attacks by flooding in the early Middle Ages) diverting rivers aroused little moral tension, because a well-prepared city or army should be able to anticipate or counter such tactics. But secretly poisoning the water or food supplies that the enemy must depend on was another matter—and such insidious practices often raised ethical questions in ancient societies. In the Punic Wars against Carthage in North Africa (264–146 BC), for example, the Romans were accused of polluting wells with carcasses of animals. But many Romans bristled at the idea of resorting to poisons of any sort in warfare, as not in keeping with traditional ideals of Roman courage and battle skills.[8]

After a revolt was quelled in Asia in 129 BC, for example, disturbing reports circulated in Rome claiming that the consul Manius Aquillius had defeated the rebelling cities by pouring poison in their cisterns. Aquillius was a cold-blooded general notorious for his harsh military discipline—whenever his lines were broken by the enemy, it was his habit to behead three men from each century (a unit of one hundred) whose position was breached. The historian Florus, who compiled his grandiose *History of All the Wars over 1,200 Years* in about AD 140, described what happened in Asia.

The insurrection, led by Aristonicus of Pergamum, challenged Roman rule in the newly declared Province of Asia Minor. The rebellion was especially threatening to the Romans because Aristonicus was mobilizing slaves and lower classes, and he was succeeding: Several important cities in Asia Minor had joined the revolt before the Romans arrived in 131 BC. Aristonicus was captured at last and executed in Rome, and Aquillius, wrote Florus, "finally brought the Asian war to a close." But his victory was a clouded one, because Aquillius had used "the wicked expedient of poisoning the springs to procure the surrender" of the rebel cities. Florus was clear about the immorality of such measures. "This, though it hastened his victory, brought shame upon it, for he had disgraced the Roman arms, which had hitherto been unsullied by the use of foul drugs." Aquillius's measures, thundered Florus, "violated the laws of heaven and the practice of our forefathers."

Florus's ringing condemnation of "un-Roman warfare" would have appealed to many Romans. His patriotic nostalgia obscured earlier incidents of well- and crop-poisonings in the Romans' ruthless wars against Carthage, however, not to mention countless political assassinations by poison during the republic and empire. Tacitus, the moralistic historian of the reigns of Rome's first two emperors, Augustus and Tiberius, referred to similar nostalgic ideals of honor in his *Annals of Imperial Rome*. In AD 9, a rebellion in Germany led by the brilliant chieftain Arminius had resulted in the treacherous destruction of three Roman legions. The Germans had cleverly lured the legionaries into the marshy Teutoburg Forest (near Osnabruck) and slaughtered them as the men and horses foundered in the difficult terrain. A war-chief of the neighboring Chatti tribe wrote to the emperor Tiberius offering to poison Arminius.

Professing to be deeply offended by the offer, the emperor replied to the Chatti chief: "Romans take vengeance on their enemies, not by underhanded tricks, but by open force of arms." By this "elevated sentiment," commented Tacitus, Tiberius compared himself to noble "generals of old" who had rejected plans to poison the invader Pyrrhus when he was ravaging Italy in the third century BC. "We Romans have no desire to make war by trickery," had been their reply to the would-be assassins.

Historians like Tacitus and Florus and their audiences greatly admired Virgil, the poet-propagandist commissioned by the emperor Augustus to write the epic saga of the glorious origins of Rome and the story of how the legendary forefathers of Rome, the Trojans, had colonized Italy after the Trojan War. The imperial historians chose to overlook a salient passage in Virgil's *Aeneid,* in which stated that among Rome's founders there was an expert at poisoning arrows and spears.[9]

*　　*　　*

Besides poisoning a city's wells, one could take advantage of naturally unhealthy environments—or even create a contaminated environment to sicken and disable foes. Contaminating water and vegetation along the route of an enemy's march was a well-known stratagem in ancient India and Kautilya's *Arthashastra* suggested several poison mixtures for polluting the foodstuffs and drink of the enemy. In Book 14, chapter 1, "Ways to Injure an Enemy," he described powders and ointments made from various plants, animals, insects, and minerals that caused blindness, disease, insanity, lingering death, or instantaneous death. Some of the ingredients were thought to have magical properties (crabs, goat hoof, snake skin, cow urine, ivory, peacock feathers), but many others were truly poisonous. There was special smoke to destroy "all animal life as far as it is carried off by the wind," and certain compounds that would poison grass and water to kill livestock. One powerful mixture of toxic plants and minerals could contaminate a large reservoir "one hundred bows long": it killed all the fish and any creature who drank or even touched the water. One could even poison "merchandise," such as spices or cloth, and send it to the foe.

Notably, Kautilya also provided remedies for these biological weapons, in case of backfire that threatened one's own troops, or retaliation in kind by enemies. Other Indian writers explained how to counter military poisons, too. According to an ancient medical treatise by Susruta, the *Susruta Samhita,* composed between the sixth century and first century BC, deliberately polluted water could be detected and purified with mineral and plant antidotes, and special rituals. Water that has been poisoned, wrote Sushruta, "becomes slimy, strong-smelling, frothy, and marked with dark lines on the surface. Frogs and fish die without apparent cause [and] birds and beasts on its shores roam about wildly in confusion from the effects of the poison." Countermeasures against biological contaminants combined practical agents such as charcoal or clay and alcohol, each of which have natural filtering and purifying capabilities against toxins and bacteria, along with magical incantations. For example, Sushruta recommended purification of contaminated water with ashes, an effective form of charcoal filtering. For earth, stone slabs, and animal fodders that had been poisoned, Sushruta listed antidotes such as sprinkling with perfumes, wine, black clay, and the bile of brown cows, and beating drums smeared with "anti-poisonous compounds." Again, alcohol in wine and the absorptive clay would have had disinfectant and filtering effects.[10]

*   *   *

Avoidance of diseases and unwholesome environments that endangered their men was a key concern for military leaders. Xenophon, the Greek mercenary commander who recorded his memoirs in the fourth century BC, advised leaders to vigilantly guard the health of their soldiers. "First of all, always camp in a healthy place." By this he meant camping where the air and waters were pure, avoiding swamps and other places where the water and atmosphere were insalubrious and caused illness.

Some lakes, streams, and valleys were infected by "miasma," an exhalation or atmosphere known to be harmful to living things (*miasma* is the ancient Greek word for "pollution"). These vapors and waters were said to be so deadly that animals died on the spot and birds flying overhead dropped out of the sky. A number of these locales were places like Ephyra in western Greece, identified as entrances to the Underworld, where noxious plants thrived. Modern sciences shows that some of these locales were in fact geologically active thermal sites, where fumeroles and hot springs emitted bad-smelling sulphurous and other poisonous gases from the earth. In antiquity there was a strong association between foul odors and disease, based on experience and observation, and geologists have shown that methane and other fumes released from the earth can adversely affect humans and wildlife.[11]

A mythic explanation was also offered to explain the origin of a stinking marsh in the Peloponnese so baneful that the fish in it were toxic. It was rumored to be the place where a group of Centaurs, wounded by Hercules' poison arrows, had attempted to wash away the Hydra venom. A similar place of toxic exhalations, caused by the poison arrows that killed the Centaur Nessus, was known to exist near Kirrha, the town destroyed by poison. The ancient idea that the water, land, and atmosphere had been contaminated by poison weapons from the past finds a modern counterpart in the deadly environmental pollution caused by testing or dumping biochemical and nuclear weapons.

Swamps and marshes in general were considered dangerous to the health, and with good reason: wetlands with stagnant water were breeding places of mosquitoes carrying malaria, which was endemic in certain areas in antiquity. The exact causes of fevers that emanated from swamps were not understood, but the health benefits of draining marshes was already recognized as early as the fifth century BC, when the natural philosopher–doctor Empedocles alleviated the raging fevers (now known to be malaria) that beset the Sicilian town of Selinus, by devising a sophisticated hydraulic engineering plan to drain the swamps there. (Malaria was not fully eradicated from Italian marshlands until the 1950s.)

Varro (116–27 BC), Rome's most erudite scholar, anticipated modern epidemiology when he stated, "Precautions must be taken in the neighborhood of swamps," because they "breed certain minute creatures which cannot be seen by the eyes, but which float in the air and enter the body through the mouth and nose and cause serious diseases." Lucretius, a natural philosopher writing in about 50 BC, also offered a perceptive theory of invisible microbes. "In the earth there are atoms of every kind," and although "certain atoms are vital to us, there are countless others flying about that are capable of instilling disease and hasten death." When these harmful atoms accumulate in mists or in earth rotted by too much water, the "air grows pestiferous." These "hurtful particles enter the body [and] many noxious ones slip in through the nostrils" when we breathe; some enter through the skin; and many are ingested through the mouth. By inhaling polluted atmospheric particles from places like swamps, wrote Lucretius, "we can't help absorbing these foreign elements into our system."

According to the historian Livy (first century BC) the pernicious effects of making camp in stagnant swamps brought disease to the Gauls who had sacked Rome in about 390 BC. Livy and the historian Diodorus of Sicily both described the contagion that assailed the Greeks and the Carthaginians fighting around Syracuse (Sicily) in 397 BC. The Carthaginians were harder hit, being unused to the unhealthy climate and water. "They perished to a man, together with their generals."

Looking back to the Plague of Athens during the Peloponnesian War, Diodorus of Sicily surmised that the disease had been a result of floods the previous wet winter, which created marshes filled with "putrid, foul vapors which corrupted the air" and spoiled the crops. The Athenians, trapped in their crowded city by the Spartans that hot summer, he noted, were especially susceptible to disease. By the fourth century AD, it was a commonplace among generals that "an army must not use bad or marshy water." "Foul water is like poison and causes plagues," cautioned the Roman military strategist Vegetius. Moreover, if an army camps too long in one place, the air and water "become corrupt [and] unhealthy." Without frequent changes of camp, he wrote, "malignant disease arises."[12]

Xenophon's advice to always camp in a healthy place was based in part on his knowledge of what befell the Athenians on their ill-fated expedition against Sicily in 415–413 BC. The swamp fevers that decimated the Greeks during the Sicilian disaster were described by Thucydides, Diodorus of Sicily, and Plutarch (first century AD). These historians all agreed that the Athenians' crushing defeat in Sicily was attributable in part to fevers (probably malaria) contracted in the marshes where they made their summer bivouacs. Diodorus of Sicily pointed out that the Carthaginians who were annihilated by pestilence in 397 BC camped in the same place where the Athenians had camped.

It is not clear whether the Athenians made the fatal mistake of camping in malarial swamps on their own, or whether the Sicilians "took particular measures to lead the Athenians into such noxious conditions." But, as Thucydides repeatedly demonstrated, the Sicilians were hyperaware of denying advantageous terrain to the Greeks, constantly depriving them of water and opportunities for foraging. It's very likely that the Athenian invaders succumbed to a biological subterfuge by the Sicilians.

Some modern military writers exclude "maneuvering of armies into 'unsanitary' areas" from their discussions of biological warfare, but as Grmek notes, in antiquity this was an effective strategy based on sound biological knowledge. Knowing the ill effects of local marshes and rank water, an astute commander would ask, "How can I manipulate these naturally malignant miasmas against my enemies?" Luring or driving an enemy into these virtual minefields of microbes could be decisive.[13]

The German tribes were masterful at maneuvering enemies into lethal landscapes. When the Romans were fighting the Teutons in 106 BC, the military writer Frontinus assumed that the Roman engineers "had heedlessly chosen a campsite" near the Germans' stronghold without realizing that the only water supply was the river flowing along the enemy palisades. Teuton archers would pick off anyone who attempted to drink. In this case, though, the site may have been selected by the commander, Marius, on purpose. The historian Plutarch says that Marius intended to goad his men into attacking fiercely by the biological expedient of thirst. When his desperate soldiers complained, he pointed to the river between the camp and the Teuton fort. "There is your water," replied Marius, "but it must be bought with blood." The Romans begged to be given the order to storm the fort "before our blood dries up!"

Recalling Germanicus Caesar's arduous campaigns in Germany in the first century AD, Pliny the Elder noted that noxious plants and beasts were not the only treacherous things in the countryside. Certain geographical areas and their waters were also "guilty of harm." The Germans consistently forced the Romans to fight and camp in unhealthy marshes and boggy woods (especially around modern Osnabruck), where the legionaries were easily ambushed and suffered extremely heavy losses. Tacitus described the emotions of Germanicus and his men when they came upon the jumbled masses of skeletons of horses and mutilated men, all that remained of the three Roman divisions that had been massacred six years earlier in the "sodden marshland and ditches" of the Teutoburg Forest by Arminius and his men. When the Romans finally managed to maneuver the Germans into fighting on level, dry ground, reported Tacitus, a spontaneous war cry rang out: "It's a fair fight! On fair ground!"

Pliny was intrigued by the experience of the veterans of Germanicus's campaign who had been forced to camp in the coastal wetlands of northern Germany, where there was only one place to draw drinking water. Drinking it caused disease, and even the survivors lost all their teeth and suffered severe degeneration of the joints. Ever optimistic about nature's balance, Pliny pointed out that a remedy for these maladies grew in the swampy area, a kind of aquatic weed called *britannica,* known to the locals. The German manipulation of the Roman legions into a place where they would be forced to drink the infected water without knowledge of the antidote was most likely a biological stratagem.[14]

A particularly villainous strategic use of insalubrious terrain occurred a century or so after the Greek defeat in Sicily. What makes this event especially reprehensible is that it was the commander *himself* who plotted the destruction of his own men. The story comes from Polyaenus, the strategist who compiled a history of how to protect armies and overcome barbarians for the emperors at the beginning of the Parthian War.

Drawing on several historical accounts, Polyaenus told how Clearchus, a cruel tyrant (one of several evil tyrants who had studied with the philosopher Plato), took power in Heraclea, on the Black Sea, in 363 BC. He surrounded himself with mercenaries, and ordered them to sneak out at night and rob, rape, and assault the citizens of Heraclea. When the citizens complained, the tyrant shrugged: the only way to restrain the bodyguards was for the citizens to build him a walled acropolis. After ensconcing himself in his new citadel, however, Clearchus "did not check the mercenaries, but granted himself the power to wrong everyone." Using trickery, the tyrant arrested Heraclea's democratic Council of 300, and then he devised a vicious scheme to get rid of the rest of the dissident citizens.

All local men between the ages sixteen and sixty-five were drafted for a bogus campaign against the Thracian city of Astachus. It was the hottest part of the summer of 360 BC, and Astachus, in western Turkey, lies in an area surrounded by marshes. Pretending that he and his mercenaries "were going to bear the brunt of the siege," Clearchus occupied the high ground with shade trees, running water, and refreshing breezes. He commanded all the citizens to camp below in a hot, breathless swamp filled with stagnant water. To exhaust them, he ordered continual guard duty. Then he "stretched out the 'siege' all summer until the unhealthy marshiness of the camp killed his citizen troops." When all of the men had died, Clearchus returned to Heraclea with his mercenaries, claiming that a plague had wiped out the citizens.[15]

This story is shocking but certainly plausible. Any general of Clearchus's day knew that troops forced to endure such conditions would succumb to the diseases we now know to be malaria and dysentery. (Perhaps there is grim satisfaction in knowing that a few years later, Clearchus himself was murdered.) The story of a tyrant who turned biological agents against his own people almost sounds too evil to be true, but there are too many modern examples to dismiss the tale as pure invention.

In a widely publicized attack in March 1988, for instance, Saddam Hussein responded to Iraqi Kurds' resistance by bombing villagers with poison gas. An estimated five thousand men, women, and children were killed. After the fall of apartheid in South Africa, trial testimonies before the Truth and Reconciliation Commission in the late 1990s revealed that the South African government planned to systematically poison citizens who protested apartheid in the 1980s and early '90s. The tale of Clearchus's premeditated elimination of his own citizens and soldiers by forcing them to endure a deadly environment also stirs disquieting memories of well-documented, clandestine U.S. government experiments with nuclear, bacterial, and chemical agents on its own citizens and soldiers during the Cold War of the twentieth century.

As Grmek has pointed out—and as demonstrated by the numerous ancient examples of manipulating poisons and disease-ridden atmospheres to sicken foes on a large scale—it would be a mistake to assume that the ancient preoccupation with "miasmas" or "vapors" as the source of illness presented any conceptual "obstacle to utilizing contagion for military ends." In antiquity, long before the modern terminology of epidemiology was developed, experience and observation led to insights into how disease could be used as a blunt instrument of war. Could that instrument somehow be refined into a capacity to spread epidemics among entire populations?[16]

4

A Casket of Plague in the Temple of Babylon

The plague arose in Babylonia,
when a pestilential vapor escaped from
a golden casket in the temple of Apollo.
—Julius Capitolinus

ONE OF THE MOST oft-cited incidents in the early annals of biological warfare occurred in AD 1346. That year, the Mongols catapulted bubonic plague-ridden corpses of their own soldiers over the walls of Kaffa, a Genoese fortress on the Black Sea, thereby introducing the dread disease in Europe. This macabre incident occurred centuries before epidemiology was formally understood, but modern science shows that even if the cadavers themselves were not the main vector of the flea-borne Black Plague, inhalation of airborne *Yersinia pestis* microbes remaining on the corpses or their clothing could cause the highly fatal respiratory form of the plague. To carry out an act of germ warfare like this, the Mongols only needed to know that proximity to corpses of people who had died of an epidemic would almost certainly lead to more deaths.

Apart from the biological outcome of the Mongols' act, the psychological impact was horrendous, and horror has always been one of the goals of biological warfare. Terrifying the enemy was the sole object of a catapulting incident in 207 BC, when the Romans hurled the head of the Carthaginian general Hasdrubal into the camp of his brother,

Hannibal. Hasdrubal's head probably carried nothing more contagious than lice (although lice can in fact carry typhus), but the act served to demoralize Hannibal, dashing his hopes of getting the reinforcements he needed to conquer Italy. Interestingly, Hannibal himself would later use catapults to fling venomous vipers at a different enemy in Asia Minor.[1]

So far no clear reports of *catapulting* disease-bearing cadavers or clothing have come to light before the fourteenth century, but the purposeful spread of contagion among enemies by other means could have occurred much earlier than Kaffa. Although the exact mechanisms of infection remained mysterious, people of many ancient cultures recognized that "foul and deadly miasmas arose" from plague-stricken cadavers and that cloth or other items that had touched a plague victim could be deadly. That knowledge made possible the use of disease-ridden animals, and people and their clothing, as weapons of war.

An incident reported by the historian Appian described how a besieging army was defeated by contagion from dead bodies. In 74 BC, King Mithridates of Pontus began a long siege of the city of Cyzicus on the Black Sea. The defenders of Cyzicus resisted with every strategy they could come up with, from breaking the invaders' siege machines with rope nooses to hurling burning pitch. As the siege wore on, Mithridates' troops began to suffer from hunger and sickness. Then, when "corpses that were thrown out unburied in the neighborhood brought on a plague," Mithridates gave up the siege and fled. Although it is not clear if the defenders deliberately spread pestilence by throwing out their dead, or whether the corpses belonged to the besiegers themselves, the account shows that the link between the corpses and the plague was well understood.[2]

Greek and Latin historians demonstrated perceptive insights about epidemics, noting that those who tended the sick fell ill and that unburied or unburned corpses spread disease. As the Roman historian Livy remarked in the first century BC, during epidemics "the dead proved fatal to the sick and the sick equally fatal to the healthy." Thucydides, in his history of the Peloponnesian War, described the great Plague of Athens, which originated in Egypt, spread to Persia and

FIGURE 15. *It was realized early in human history that contact with corpses of victims of epidemics, or their possessions, could spread disease. Roman skeleton mosaic, Via Appia, Italy.*

Libya, and arrived in Athens in the summer 430 BC. The virulent epidemic (probably smallpox, but possibly typhus, measles, or bubonic plague, according to competing theories offered by modern medical historians) killed more than a quarter of the population. Thucydides, one of those who survived the plague, recognized the role of contact with the sick in transmitting the disease.

Some scholars have noted that the symptoms suffered by Hercules' dying in the Hydra-poisoned cloak share some similarities to death from smallpox. In Sophocles' version of the myth, written in about 430 BC when the epidemic was raging in Athens, the playwright used medical terminology for pustules and plague to describe the burning torment of the tunic. His play reflects the knowledge that not only poison but disease could be transferred by clothing. That idea was also expressed by Cedrenus, a historian who described the Plague of Cyprian (a pandemic that spread from Egypt to Scotland in about AD 250), when he remarked that the disease was transmitted not just by direct contact but also by clothing.[3]

Actually, the recognition that diseases could be transmitted by contact with the ill and their personal belongings goes back much earlier in recorded history, to ancient Sumer (in Syria). The evidence comes from several royal letters inscribed on cuneiform tablets in about 1770 BC, from the archives of Mari, a Sumerian outpost on the Euphrates in Mesopotamia. One of the letters forbade people from an infected town from traveling to a healthy town, to avoid "infecting the whole country." Another letter described a woman whose cup, chair, bed, and physical presence were to be avoided because of the danger of contracting her disease, which was very contagious (*mustahhizu*, literally "keeps on catching or kindling").

The modern epidemiological term for articles like cups or clothing that harbor infectious pathogens is *fomites*. The principles of fomite contagion and quarantine were evidently understood 3,800 years ago, but the accounts of epidemics were often expressed in symbolic language or metaphors such as "angels of death smiting armies" or gods shooting "arrows of plague." Because of the metaphorical imagery, descriptions of epidemics in Near Eastern and biblical texts, and in Greek mythology have often been viewed by scholars as superstitious explanations, even though they may have been based on sound empirical knowledge, as shown in the Mari letters.[4]

The Kaffa event of 1346 is considered by historians to be the first documented case of a deliberate attempt to spread contagion to achieve military victory, but much earlier incidents of transmitting disease for strategic purposes can be found in the ancient sources. Some of the evidence is legendary or inconclusive, like the Cyzicus event, but many other historical accounts record clear intentions to transmit disease to enemies in chillingly feasible ways.

The earliest clear examples of deliberate attempts to spread contagion appear in cuneiform tablets of the ancient Hittite civilization of Anatolia (1500–1200 BC). The tablets tell of driving animals and at least one woman infected with epidemics out of the city and into enemy territory, accompanied by a prayer: "The country that accepts them shall take this evil plague." The intention is unmistakable and the means would have been quite effective.[5]

*　　*　　*

The ancient Hittites and Babylonians worshipped the archer-god Irra, who was said to shoot arrows of plague at enemies in military contexts. In Greek mythology, it was the god Apollo who destroyed armies with his invisible plague-arrows—and by sending infestations of rodents, which were widely recognized in antiquity as harbingers of pestilence. These mythic images reflect the fact that epidemics did frequently coincide with military invasions, due to overcrowding and unsanitary conditions, stress, lack of food and pure water, infestations of rodents and other disease vectors, and exposure to new germ pools. When people of antiquity implored the gods to inflict pestilence on invaders, diseases that broke out among the enemy forces were seen as answered prayers. In an example from the fourth century BC, the people of Pachynus, Sicily, prayed to Apollo to strike the approaching Carthaginian fleet with pestilence. And, in fact, in 396 BC, a devastating epidemic did break out among the Carthaginians, causing them to abandon their plan to attack Sicily.[6]

It must not have been long before humans began to wonder if, instead of relying on requests to the gods, they could also take matters into their own hands and sow contagion and biological calamities among their adversaries by practical means, as the Hittites did by sending infectious animals into enemy lands. Some commentators have speculated on whether the ten plagues that Moses called down on the Egyptians (in about 1300 BC), might represent the earliest incidents of "using nature to gain strategic goals."

Thinking along these lines, one might wonder if the first plague, the red waters of the Nile that killed fish and fouled the water for drinking, could have been due to deliberate contamination by the Israelites. According to Exodus, the Pharaoh's "magicians" were able to produce a similar phenomenon, which would place them among the world's first biochemists. Indeed, techniques for poisoning fish, by dumping powdered roots of deadly plants mixed with toxic chemicals such as lime, were also practiced in early Roman times in the Mediterranean, according to Pliny the Elder. The blood-red, polluted water of the Nile, however, could have been a natural phenomenon such as an algae bloom or an influx of red sediment.

Seasonal occurrences account for the frogs and insects of the second, third, and fourth plagues, as well as for the hailstorm, locusts, and hot dust storm (*khamsin*) of the seventh, eighth, and ninth plagues. But what about the diseases of the fifth and sixth plagues? In the fifth plague sent by Yahweh, the Egyptians' herds and flocks were killed, followed by the sixth plague, a rain of "ashes" that caused black boils on beasts as well as humans. The progression here from infected animals to infected humans strongly suggests that what is being described is the spread of pulmonary anthrax, and the boils caused by powdery black "ashes" could describe the black sores of the cutaneous form of anthrax (the word comes from the Greek for "coal").

A similar plague appeared in Homer's *Iliad*, when the Greeks laying siege to Troy in about 1200 BC were assailed by a plague sent by Apollo. Homer's details are realistic: first to sicken from Apollo's "black arrows" were the pack animals and dogs; then the men began to die. Outbreaks of anthrax are devastating to both livestock and humans. The "Black Bane" anthrax epidemic that swept Europe in the 1600s, for example, killed millions of animals and at least sixty thousand people. Like smallpox and other infectious material, anthrax spores can remain viable for a very long time and they can conceivably be manipulated by humans. But natural cycles of anthrax have attacked periodically throughout history, and the fact that the Israelites' cattle were spared while the Egyptian herds were struck has been attributed to the separate pastures of the Israelites.

Although neither the *Iliad* nor Exodus implicates humans in the anthrax-like plagues, the priests of Apollo and Yahweh took credit for summoning the epidemics, and that definitely reveals both the human *desire* and *intention* to wage what we now call germ warfare. The ten plagues of Exodus were most likely a series of natural calamities that were advantageous for the Israelites, but inherent in the story is the strong suggestion that plagues and biological disasters could be powerful weapons against enemies.[7]

The tenth plague, the sudden death of the Egyptians' firstborn children, has been called the ultimate biological weapon. Although the Israelites' children were spared the final plague, again there is no hint of human agency in Exodus. It is true, however, that if one could systematically destroy the genetic material of an enemy people that would indeed constitute biological strategy with a devastating effect on the population. Blocking an enemy's genetic reproduction by killing entire populations or, alternatively, by slaying all males and/or systematically raping the women was an effective way of wiping out an enemy "root and branch" in antiquity.

The most notorious modern examples of such biological strategies are the Nazis' attempt to eliminate all Jews and Gypsies in World War II, and the ethnic cleansing and systematic rapes by soldiers that occurred in former Yugoslavia and Burma and in Rwanda in the late twentieth century. After the fall of apartheid in South Africa, the Truth and Reconciliation investigations (1998) revealed that government-sponsored doctors had researched "a race specific bacterial weapon" and "ways to sterilize . . . the black population." In 2003, a U.S. military report described a proposal for creating "non-lethal" weapons based on "genetic alteration." With the very real ability to manipulate genetic material in the laboratory, the specter of an "ultimate biological weapon" that affects enemy DNA looms in the near future.[8]

Ancient examples of attempts to interfere with genetic reproduction are numerous. Before the onset of the ten plagues in Egypt, for instance, the Pharaoh had ordered midwives to kill all male offspring born to Hebrew women. Later, in the first century BC, King Herod's preemptive biological strike—his order to kill all Jewish boys under age two—was another example of the strategy. In Greek myth, during the sack of Troy, the Greek warriors killed the infant son of Hector to make sure that none of the Trojan champion's stock would survive (the tragic scene was featured in many Greek vase paintings). Greek and Roman historians report wars in which the victors killed all the males of an enemy population and raped and abducted the women en masse (the legendary Rape of the Sabine women by the founders of Rome is a famous example). Polyaenus referred to this legend when he noted that the Roman founders invited the Italian natives, the Sabini, to a festival and then abducted all the virgins. The Indian manual on devious ways of war, the *Arthashastra,* insinuated that there were secret ways of interfering with opponents' reproduction: "When an archer shoots an arrow he may miss his target, but intrigue can kill even the unborn."[9]

*   *   *

The Latin expression *pestilentia manu facta,* "man-made pestilence," shows that intentionally transmitted contagion was a suspected biological weapon in Roman times. The term was coined by the philosopher Seneca, Nero's advisor in the first century AD, to refer to epidemics attributed to deliberate human activity. Livy and other Latin historians referred to the malicious transmission of plagues without giving specifics, but Dio Cassius, a Greek historian born about AD 164, reported on two man-made epidemics in detail.

According to Dio Cassius, the plagues were begun by saboteurs acting in Rome and in the provinces, apparently to spread chaos and undermine unpopular emperors' authority. The first occurred before his time, in AD 90–91, during the reign of Domitian (himself suspected of poisoning his brother and predecessor Titus). Conspirators dipped needles in deleterious substances and secretly pricked many victims, who perished of a deadly illness. Dio Cassius says that the plague-spreaders were caught and punished after informers spoke out.

A similar plot occurred in Dio Cassius's lifetime, during the reign of Commodus. Commodus had succeeded his father, the emperor Marcus Aurelius, who died in AD 180 of a plague that was brought back to Italy and Europe by Roman troops fighting in Babylonia. While Commodus was emperor, in about AD 189, another plague wracked the empire, killing 2,000 people a day in Rome. This pestilence was said to have been spread by saboteurs who "smeared deadly drugs on tiny needles [and] infected many people by means of these instruments."

These accusations may or may not have been true, but they do reflect the idea circulating in antiquity that humans—not just the gods—could propagate disease at will. The method, sticking victims with infected needles, was certainly plausible, and rumors of bio-sabotage aroused panic in Rome. Indeed, the rumors were in themselves a form of bio-terror that has proven effective through history. During the ravages of Black Plague in the Middle Ages, rumors that enemies were deliberately spreading the disease caused widespread hysteria. Similarly, fears fueled by rumors rose in the United States in the aftermath of the anthrax attacks of 2001 and amid continuing alarms over bio-terrorist activities.[10]

In India, during the fourth century BC, the ruthless strategist Kautilya demonstrated a clear intention to transmit infectious diseases to enemies. In the *Arthashastra*, he claimed that burning frog entrails and plant toxins would produce a smoke that would infect adversaries with gonorrhea; the addition of human blood to the recipe was supposed to bring a wasting lung disease. Powdered leeches, bird and mongoose tongues, donkey milk, plus jimsonweed (a toxic plant related to deadly nightshade) and other poisons were intended to cause fevers, deafness, and various diseases. Four different recipes were said to spread leprosy: one called for special seeds kept for a week in the mouth of a white cobra or lizard, then mixed with cow dung and parrot and cuckoo eggs. The ingredients of the concoctions may seem silly to modern readers but, once again, one of Kautilya's stated purposes was to terrify his enemies with biological threats.

The idea of "manufactured pestilence" has taken on a new, sinister meaning in view of some recent scientific discoveries. One finding, reported by Richard Preston, whose popular books chronicle what he terms "Dark Biology," showed that scientists could easily create a virulent version of mousepox by adding a mammalian gene to the smallpox-like virus. Much more ominous, however, are the experiments with diseases that attack humans, which were sponsored by the Pentagon in 2002. Scientists at the State University of New York proved that synthetic replicas of epidemic viruses could be created chemically in the laboratory from scratch, without live cells, simply by replicating the published DNA sequence of a natural virus. The laboratory used a blueprint for polio virus downloaded from the Internet and chemical material available by mail order. As one scientist remarked, the findings suggest that terrorists might soon be able to replicate viruses for "evil intent." Some two thousand years after Seneca coined the phrase *pestilentia manu facta* to refer to pestilence manipulated by man, actual man-made pestilence has become a scientific reality.[11]

*   *   *

The Greek myth of Pandora, who unwittingly opened the jar or box that held plagues and pestilence, is one of the earliest expressions of the ancient notion of confining disease in a sealed container. The related idea of sealing a virulent contagion in a container with the specific intention of inflicting plague on enemies who break open the seal is a widespread folk motif—and one that has scientific and historical plausibility. Some of the traditional stories about such bioattacks may reflect wishful thinking or imaginative worst-case scenarios, but the potential for deliberately spreading epidemics like smallpox or bubonic plague was real, since infectious matter on fomites and aerosols (tiny airborne particles) can retain virulence over long periods of time.

The story of the Philistines' problems with the Ark of the Covenant, recounted in 1 Samuel, is a provocative, early example. In the twelfth century BC, when the Philistines were at war with the Israelites, they feared that Yahweh would smite them with plagues as he had done to the Egyptians. Sure enough, when the Philistines captured the Ark of the Covenant from the Israelites and took the sacred wooden chest to their capital, an epidemic marked by swollen buboes in the groin (a

FIGURE 16. *The Greek myth of Pandora's box is one of the earliest expressions of the idea that contagion could be "trapped" in a sealed container. Red-figure amphora by the Niobid Painter, 460–450 BC.* (The Walters Art Museum, Baltimore)

classic sign of bubonic plague) decimated the population. The survivors sent the Ark away to a series of Philistine towns, and each was struck with the same epidemic. The Philistines attributed the plague to Yahweh and also related it to an infestation of rodents in their land (bubonic plague is carried by fleas on rodents).

The coincidence of a plague breaking out upon the arrival of a special casket in each town raises interesting questions. It may simply have been that the Philistine escorts of the Ark brought the disease with them. But, given the worldwide occurrence of tales of plague begun by opening sealed containers from enemies and the modern knowledge that such a scenario is plausible, one wonders: Does the story of the Ark suggest that the chest might have contained some object, such as cloth, that harbored aerosolized plague germs, or an insect vector that infected the rodents in Philistine territory? The Ark of the Covenant was recovered and placed in Solomon's great temple in Jerusalem. Notably, the Ark itself was never to be touched by the

FIGURE 17. *The Ark of the Covenant, a wooden chest that the Israelites were forbidden to touch, brought plague to each Philistine town that it visited in the twelfth century* BC. *James Tissot,* The Ark Passes over the Jordan. (© De Brunoff 1904)

Israelites themselves, but was always carried suspended by poles through rings. One Israelite, named Uzzah, accidentally touched the Ark and died instantly.[12]

Two other narratives about the temple in Jerusalem suggest that material carrying plague could very well have been hidden away, stored in a safe place against the possibility of a military invasion. Consider, for example, the ancient legend about sealing up "plague demons" and placing them in the temple at Jerusalem. This story appears in the *Testament of Solomon* and other ancient texts of Hebrew, Gnostic, and Greek origins, dating from the first to fourth century AD, but based on earlier traditions. Solomon was a historical king who built the first temple in Jerusalem in the tenth century BC. According to legend, King Solomon summoned a crew of evil spirits of disease and disaster and forced them to help build the magnificent temple of Jerusalem. Then he imprisoned the demons inside copper vessels and sealed them with silver. These vessels were placed inside large jars or casks and buried in the foundations of the temple.

The legend can be seen as evidence of the belief that evil spirits could be magically imprisoned in containers, like genies or djinns in bottles. But, as the Mari tablets from Sumer showed, people of the ancient Near East also understood that things such as cloth and cups could actually transmit fatal disease. That knowledge, and the Old Testament tale of the Ark accompanied by outbreaks of plague among the enemy, gives the legend about Solomon deeper significance.

Indeed, the biblical stories of the plagues sent by Yahweh against the Egyptians in the time of Moses, and against the Philistines who stole the Ark, had already planted the idea of contagion as a weapon, and Solomon's reserves of plague seem to be intended as a weapon. The *Testament of Solomon* predicted that when the temple of Jerusalem would be destroyed by the king of the Chaldeans, the plague spirits would be released. And in fact, in 586 BC, Nebuchadnezzar (the cruel king of the Chaldeans, or Neo-Babylonians) sacked and burned Solomon's temple in Jerusalem. "In their plundering," the invaders found the copper vessels and assumed that they contained treasure. The Babylonians broke open the seals and the pestilential demons flew out and "plagued men again."

The ancient legend of Solomon imprisoning the evil spirits in the temple at Jerusalem is well known in Islamic lore. Today, among Muslim fundamentalists who practice "Islamic science"—a hybrid of modern scientific terminology and Islamic mysticism—invisible djinns are identified as the sources of nuclear energy and epidemics. These scientists point to Solomon's ability to "harness energy from djinns" as evidence that special "spirits" of atomic power and contagion such as anthrax could be manipulated by secret knowledge. In 1988 and 1991, the leading Pakistani nuclear scientist, Bashiruddin Mehmood, spoke of the possibility of "communicating" with the invisible but powerful djinns or spirits that were long ago "harnessed by King Solomon." In

2001, Mehmood was detained for questioning in Pakistan after plans and diagrams for creating anthrax-spreading devices were found in his offices in Afghanistan.

Solomon's temple was rebuilt in the fifth century BC. In 1945, a trove of early Christian writings buried in about AD 400 were discovered at Nag Hammadi in Egypt. One of the scrolls contains a different version of the Solomon legend that dates to the first or second century AD. During the siege of Jerusalem by the future Roman emperor Titus in AD 70, the second temple was destroyed and, according to the scrolls, Roman soldiers discovered the ancient jars and broke them open looking for plunder. The plague demons, imprisoned in the foundations since the time of Solomon, escaped. Suetonius, the Latin biographer of Titus, records that "Titus's reign was marked by a series of dreadful catastrophes," including "one of the worst outbreaks of plague ever known."[13]

*   *   *

Almost a century later, in the same geographical region, a remarkably similar scenario was played out again, when looting soldiers destroyed a Greek temple in Babylon.

The terrible Plague of AD 165–180 swept out of Babylonia and raged across the Mideast and Mediterranean, reaching Rome and even Gaul and Germany. The great doctor Galen described the symptoms in enough detail for medical historians to suggest that the disease may have been smallpox. The epidemic is the second most famous in antiquity after the Plague of Athens during the Peloponnesian War.

Accusations detailed in two fourth-century Latin accounts of the Parthian War in Babylonia—one in the *Lives of the Later Caesars* and the other in a history by Ammianus Marcellinus—strongly suggest that this plague belongs in the annals of biological sabotage. The epidemic began during the Roman campaign against the Parthians in Mesopotamia, led by the co-emperors Lucius Verus and Marcus Aurelius. The Parthians dominated Central Asia from the Indus River to the

FIGURE 18. *The Great Plague of* AD *165–80 began when a Roman soldier broke open a golden chest in the Temple of Apollo in Babylon, allowing the "spirits of plague" to escape. The "spirits" in this drawing are taken from a Greek vase painting of "spirits" in 460* BC.

Euphrates, and constantly threatened Roman power. "The pestilence is reported to have arisen in Babylonia, when a *spiritus pestilens*, a pestilential vapor, escaped from a golden casket in the temple of Apollo," wrote Verus's biographer, "Julius Capitolinus" (one of the pseudonyms used by the anonymous authors of the *Lives of the Later Caesars*). A Roman soldier had "cut open the casket and from thence [the plague] filled the Parthians' land and then the world," extending all the way from Persia to the Rhine.

Lucius Verus was accused, by the Syrians and others, of deliberately spreading the plague. But the plague was not really Verus's fault, claimed Capitolinus, who said that the blame really lay with Verus's ambitious general, Avidius Cassius. In AD 164, the bloodthirsty Cassius had stormed Seleuceia, a Greek city on the Tigris River in the district of Babylonia (the Parthians had used the city as their summer quarters).

Cassius's army committed atrocities and laid waste to Seleuceia, one of the last bastions of Hellenic culture, despite the fact that the Seleuceians had welcomed the Romans. Cassius thereby violated a generally accepted convention of war not to attack a friendly city or break a truce. It was Cassius's soldiers who plundered the Greek temple and released the contagion, according to Capitolinus and Ammianus Marcellinus.[14]

The idea that plundering a temple or sacred site would be punished by plague was a very old one. The capture of the Ark of the Covenant by the Philistines followed by outbreaks of plague is one of the earliest examples. Another example comes from Diodorus of Sicily, who, as we have seen, noted that the Carthaginian army was struck by plague in 396 BC—and that plague began after the Carthaginians had pillaged a Greek temple in Syracuse. Appian told how plague ravaged the Gauls during their attempt to loot Apollo's Oracle at Delphi in 105 BC. Capitolinus's account also conveyed the strong implication that Cassius and his men had offended Apollo, who scourged invading armies with plagues. According to inscriptions discovered by archaeologists, the oracle at the Temple of Apollo at Claros (on the coast of Turkey) issued many dire warnings during the pandemic, attributing the plague to the anger of the god and advising cities to erect statues of Long-Haired Apollo wielding his bow to ward off the contagion released by the Roman looters.

Stories implying that biological weapons were stored in temples raise a flurry of questions. Why would biologically dangerous materials be stored in temples? And were the releases of the plagues accidental or intentional?

In the Greco-Roman world, temples often served as museums of revered relics, and all sorts of weapons with mythic and historical significance were treasures commonly displayed in temples. Indeed, Hercules' original bio-weapons—the Hydra-poisoned arrows—were famously stored in a temple in Italy by the archer Philoctetes who dedicated them to Apollo, the god whose arrows carried pestilence.

But surely items of deadly biological potential were not merely retained for posterity. Evidence from antiquity relates that priests of the temples of Apollo were very knowledgeable about poisons and studied their effects. For example, the celebrated toxicologist Nicander was a priest of Apollo at the Temple of Claros, the same temple that issued oracles about the plague of AD 165, and Nicander compiled an encyclopedia on venomous snakes, plants, and insects. Apollo was also the patron of doctors, and we know that the doctor Nebros used his knowledge of poison to help destroy the town of Kirrha, which had offended Apollo. With these clues in mind, one is tempted to ask whether some temples may have functioned as ancient laboratories for experiments with poisons and antidotes, with diseases and even primitive vaccines.

In fact, some Greek temples were repositories of real disease vectors. Apollo was the guardian of rodents (in antiquity, no distinction was drawn between mice, rats, and voles). Rodent swarms were a presage of epidemics—and all sorts of rodents can be vectors of bubonic plague, typhus, and other diseases. At least one temple of Apollo—at Hamaxitus near ancient Troy—actually housed a horde of sacred white mice or rats around the altar, which were fed at public expense.

Another intriguing example of disease vectors associated with temples involves Athena, the Greek goddess of war. Her temple at Rhocca, Crete, was notorious for its rabid dogs, and Athena of Rhocca was invoked to cure human victims of rabies. Aelian described a complicated experiment by an old shaman-like character that took place in the vicinity of Rhocca, in which marine bio-toxins (the stomach acid of seahorses) were administered to counteract rabies in a group of boys bitten by mad dogs. But, as Aelian acknowledged elsewhere, the bite of a mad dog was always fatal. Notably, in his section on various venoms and arrow poisons, Aelian included a reference to rabid dogs. The saliva of a mad dog could even imbue a piece of cloth bitten by the dog, noted Aelian, causing secondhand, fatal rabies to anyone who came in intimate contact with it. This ominous remark insinuates that mad dog "venom" could have weapon potential, although no evidence survives that the idea of using rabid dog "venom" on arrows was pursued in ancient Greece or Rome. There are two bio-weapon recipes in the *Arthashastra* of the fourth-century BC, however, that appear to be evidence of such an attempt in India. One describes how to make a poison arrow with a mixture of toxins and "the blood of a musk rat." Anyone pierced with this arrow will be compelled to bite ten companions, who will in turn bite others, wrote Kautilya. The other weapon, concocted from red alum, plant toxins, and the blood of a goat and a man, induces "biting madness." These symptoms of biting mania sound suspiciously like rabies. Two thousand years later, in 1650, the possibility of weaponizing rabies in projectiles occurred to an artillery general in Poland. He referred to catapulting "hollow spheres with the slobber from rabid dogs [to] cause epidemics."

Going back to the original line of thinking, involving temples as places where toxins or pathogens and antidotes were sometimes stored, and taking the idea a step further, the question arises: Were some priests in temples of Apollo or Athena the keepers of lethal biological material that could be weaponized in times of crisis? One can imagine that a garment or other item contaminated with, say, dried smallpox matter, could have been sealed away from heat, light, and air in a golden casket in the temple of Apollo in Babylon, until a time of need. The items could maintain "weapons-grade" virulence for many years.[15]

Besides the literary evidence that temples might serve as emergency arsenals of disease vectors and fomites, there is archaeological evidence that very special weapons were actually stored in temples. For example, in the 370s BC a cache of catapult bolts was kept in the Parthenon, the great temple of Athena on the Acropolis in Athens. That was just a generation after the invention in Syracuse of the crossbow-style catapult, a terrifying weapon that took warfare to a higher level of destruction. Sacred sites and weapons have been linked in later times, too. During the Crusades, for example, when Greek Fire, the new chemical incendiary weapon based on naphtha inspired terror, Arabic sources reported

FIGURE 19. *A woman placing a cloth in a chest. If the material had belonged to a victim of an epidemic such as smallpox, it could retain virulence for many years. Terracotta pinax from Lokri.* (Museo Archeologico Nazionale, Calabria)

that great stocks of naphtha were stored in Byzantine churches. Earlier, in the fourth century AD, it was rumored that the "Devil" was responsible for smuggling naphtha into the church of Saint Nicholas in Myra (on the coast of Turkey)." In 2003, there were allegations by the United States that Saddam Hussein had hidden biological and chemical "weapons of mass destruction" in mosques in Iraq.[16]

In classical antiquity, the storage of catapult bolts in Athena's temple suggests that the most deadly, technologically advanced ballistic armaments were watched over by the goddess of war. Likewise, it seems that the most virulent biological ammunition was guarded by the god of plagues, Apollo.

*   *   *

It is notable how often plague gods like Apollo were "invoked in defensive military contexts [to] bring plague against an invading or besieging army," remarked Christopher Faraone, a scholar of ancient religion. Like other commentators, he saw the story of the casket of plague in Apollo's temple in Babylonia as simply another "curious historical anecdote," further proof that Apollo was worshipped as the source of epidemics, which often coincided with invasions by armies.

But the story is much more complex, with significant implications for the history of attitudes toward justifiable biological warfare. There are many ancient accounts of people calling on gods who control plague to help them *resist* an invading enemy or oppressor, which seems to suggest a sense that using biological weapons was acceptable in situations of defense but less permissible as a "first strike." In Exodus, the Israelites called on Yahweh to send plagues against their Egyptian captors. In Homer's *Iliad,* the priest of Apollo called down the god's plague arrows on the invading Greek army after they destroyed the priest's city, Chryse, and captured his daughter. Even the bio-warrior–hero Hercules, who was regularly invoked for help by Greek armies, could only offer aid in defensive situations. For example, when the Syracusans sacrificed to Hercules to ask for assistance during the Athenians' invasion of Sicily, Hercules could only promise to help "provided they did not seek battle, but remained on the defensive."[17]

The principle of summoning plague for self-defense may be related to the reality that invaders are "immunologically naive" and therefore more vulnerable to endemic diseases in foreign lands than the local population. Simply put, epidemics often strike invading forces more severely than indigenous populations. But, another factor appears to be a strong intuition from earliest times that poisoning and spreading contagion could be justified when it was reserved for desperate emergencies. This principle allowed the practice of polluting water in advance of an invading army or booby-trapping an abandoned outpost. The same defensive principle appears in the modern Biological Weapons Convention (ratified in 1972 by 143 nations), which prohibits offensive weapons but allows "defensive" research to continue.

Various military leaders in modern history have hesitated to approve biochemical weapons for aggressive purposes. Louis XIV, for example, rewarded an Italian chemist for inventing a bacteriological weapon, but on the condition that the man never reveal the formula, and, in a similar account, Louis V declined an offer of the "lost" formula for Greek Fire. In 1969, President Richard Nixon supposedly terminated the offensive biological weapons initiative that the United States had begun in World War II. Even Hitler, a fan of Greco-Roman culture, reportedly forbade offensive biological weapons research in 1939, although his scientists continued to develop nerve gases and other bio-chemical agents. Of course, there have been, and still are, countless systematic violations of bans against offensive uses of weaponized contagion. For example, many modern nations simply label bio-weapons research and production as "defensive security," even though nothing precludes the weapons from being used in a first strike. The salient point in these ancient accounts, though, is the surprising antiquity of the attitude that there is something heinous about *attacking* with contagion, but as a weapon of resistance, self-defense, or retaliation, it is acceptable as a last resort.[18]

In AD 165, the Syrians and others accused the Romans of intentionally spreading the plague and taking it back to Rome. But the Romans themselves were the main victims of the epidemic. Even Emperor Marcus Aurelius succumbed to the plague—despite his daily dose of a special antidote to protect himself from biological attack. It seems more likely that the Romans were the victims of a biological timebomb, a kind of booby-trapped Pandora's box, set against the invader, activated despite the dangers of friendly fire (the Parthians were also affected). If so, the chest in the temple may have been a very early precursor of the booby-trapped treasure chests in the late Middle Ages that were rigged with primitive explosives. In this case, trying to direct contagion only at the Roman enemy, without incurring collateral damage, must have been seen as a drastic last resort.

Imagine the scene at the Temple of Long-Haired Apollo, god of plague, in Babylon. Lucius Verus's generals are laying waste to Babylonia, and Cassius has utterly destroyed the friendly Greek city of Seleuceia. Roman soldiers burst into the temple, looking for loot before setting it afire. They spy the golden casket, and the priests of Apollo allow the biologically devastating "accident" to happen, knowing that at least the Roman army will contract the plague and spread it across their provinces all the way back to Italy. As Faraone points out, soldiers far from home and living in crowded conditions were "excellent targets for a variety of new viruses and bacteria for which they had no immunity."

The plague of AD 165–180 has been identified as smallpox, based on Galen's description. Some of the local populace may have been immune to the pestilence stored in their temple, but the dangers of keeping plague as a secret weapon inside one's own city would be considerable. Just as those who handled poison arrows and toxic substances suffered friendly-fire accidents, handling contagion always involves the chance of self-contamination.

Indeed, the backlash problems associated with handling contagion as a weapon persist in modern times. A prime example of the "poisoners poisoned" effect occurred in 1941, during Japanese attacks with infectious agents against eleven cities in China. The Japanese troops themselves are reported to have suffered 10,000 biological casualties and 1,700 fatalities trying to spread contagion in the city of Changteh alone. In grim irony, Dr. Shiro Ishii, the director of attacks, became a casualty of his obsession with germ warfare: he suffered from chronic dysentery. During the offensive bioweapons research program in the United States in 1943–69, there were reports of more than four hundred inadvertent "occupational infections," and since the 1950s, military experiments with germ warfare agents have been linked to several outbreaks of disease in civilian populations. After smallpox was eradicated in the 1970s, routine vaccinations were halted and laboratories around the world supposedly destroyed their stores of the virus (except for two authorized sites in the United States and the Soviet Union). But in 2002, evidence emerged that Russia may have continued to create staggering amounts of the virus and that vials of smallpox strains (rumored to be resistant to vaccines) lurk in lab freezers across the globe. The perilous situation is chronicled in Richard Preston's 2002 book, *The Demon in the Freezer,* a striking title that calls to mind the ancient plague demons trapped in stoppered vials in temples.

Ancient recognition of the danger of trying to weaponize plague is evident in traditional Greek prayers urging Apollo to set aside his bow and quiver of plague-arrows during peacetime. And an ancient Hittite prayer bluntly requested their own plague-bringing god to "Shoot the enemy, but when you come home, unstring your bow and cover your quiver."[19]

*　　*　　*

The biological sabotage that I have suggested may have been planned by the priests at the temples at Babylon, and perhaps Jerusalem, took advantage of the invading enemies' greed and lust for loot. The contagion was delivered in the form of something attractive. Indeed, the next chapter shows how military commanders could take advantage of adversaries' desires, vices, or overindulgence, but before we turn to toxic sweets and tainted wine as weapons, let's consider another unique subterfuge that concealed doom in an alluring gift.

In India, where all manner of toxic substances could be had, poisoning was a favored method of political assassination in myth and history. One of the most ingenious methods described in Sanskrit literature was to send an irresistible gift in the form of a so-called Poison Maiden. In the *Katha Sarit Sagara,* a collection of Indian lore compiled by the poet Somadeva (about AD 1050), King Brahmadatta "sent poison-damsels as dancing-girls among the enemy's host." In an ancient twist on the modern idea of "sleepers," the term for undetected, lurking assassins or terrorists who await orders to kill, Poison Maidens were carefully "prepared" and dispatched as secret weapons. A touch, a kiss, or sexual intercourse with one of these ravishing but deadly damsels brought sure death.

The idea that certain individuals were personally poisonous, capable of killing with their mere touch or breath, is a folk motif of great antiquity. According to popular belief, one way that the toxicity could be achieved was by a lifelong regimen of ingesting poisons and venoms. (Nathaniel Hawthorne's short story "Rappaccini's Daughter," about a Poison Maiden, and the Poison Sultan Mahmud Shah are two famous examples of the theme in Western and Indian-Persian folklore). The tales reflect folk knowledge of gaining immunity to venoms (exemplified by the Psylli, the snake charmers of North Africa), but they also were early attempts to explain how contagion is mysteriously passed from person to person.

According to ancient Indian and Arabic legends, both King Chandragupta and his Greek rival Alexander the Great were the intended victims of Poison Maidens. King Chandragupta's Mauryan Empire was the most powerful dominion in India when Alexander invaded in 327 BC and defeated the king's ally, Porus. In the seventh century AD, the historian Visakhadatta described how a plot to send a Poison Maiden to the king's bedchamber was thwarted by Kautilya, Chandragupta's minister and the author of the *Arthashastra*, the book of Machiavellian statecraft. Kautilya cleverly rerouted the girl to one of the king's enemies instead.

A similar intrigue was said to have been hatched to kill Alexander the Great, according to a body of ancient and medieval legends. The earliest description of the conspiracy to send a Poison Maiden to the Macedonian conqueror appeared in about AD 1050 in a Latin book, based on an earlier Arabic translation of a lost Greek manuscript. In that story, the King of India sent Alexander many precious gifts, among them a "beautiful maiden whom they had fed on poison until she had the nature of a venomous snake." Smitten by her beauty, Alexander "could scarcely contain himself and rushed to embrace her." Her touch or bite, even her perspiration, it was said, would have killed Alexander—had not *his* trusted advisor, the philosopher Aristotle, foiled the plot and prevented him from contact with the "messenger of death."

The story of Alexander is clearly legendary (for one thing, Aristotle never visited India). But the concept of a Poison Maiden may contain a germ of truth. Comparing the beautiful girls to snakes plays on the idea that snake charmers gained immunity by ingesting small doses of venom, and as folklorist Norman Penzer points out, there was a popular notion in antiquity that the bite of a snake charmer might be as venomous as the snakes they handled. Penzer also investigated the possibility that the "poison" transmitted by intimate contact with deadly maidens was really venereal disease or other fatal infectious illnesses, such as small-pox, transmitted by personal contact.

The strategy of sending disease-ridden but alluring women to foes appeared again in later military history, too. During the Naples Campaign of 1494, for example, the Spanish not only poisoned French wine with contaminated blood, but according to the medical writer Gabriele Falloppia, they also "intentionally chased beautiful, infectious prostitutes into the French army camp."[20] Although the biological strategies are nearly three thousand years apart, this Spanish "poison prostitute" plot also has parallels to the ancient Hittite ritual of driving a plague-infected woman into enemy territory. Offering something tempting but lethal to a foe is an age-old path to victory via biological agents.

5

Sweet Sabotage

> Men by their unbridled appetites
> are the victims of plots against
> their food and drink.
> —Aelian, *On Animals*

> He'll come with a deadly poison,
> pour it in our wine, and kill us all.
> —Homer, *Odyssey*

Xenophon was pleased with the campsite he had selected in the territory of Colchis in Pontus, along the southeastern shore of the Black Sea. The land was fertile and well-watered. It was 401 BC, and the great general was leading ten thousand Greek mercenaries on the long march home from Babylon, north through Mesopotamia, Armenia, and Asia Minor. The hoplites had fought with distinction in the attempted coup d'état by the Persian rebel Cyrus the Younger against the grand army of his brother, Artaxerxes II, king of Persia. But when Cyrus was killed by Artaxerxes' men in the battle of Cunaxa (near modern Baghdad), the cause was lost. The Persians had invited the Greek generals to negotiate. At the supposedly friendly banquet, however, all the generals were assassinated and the Greek army was left stranded in a precarious situation with no leaders, thousands of miles from home.

Xenophon emerged from the ranks as their new leader. The murder of the Greek generals and his knowledge of Persian history made Xenophon exquisitely aware of treachery, but even he was unprepared for what happened in Colchis, the homeland of the legendary sorceress Medea and her magic potions and poisons.

Xenophon always followed his own advice to military leaders, "Above all, camp in a healthy place." His men had battled natives and plundered towns for supplies all along the march from Babylon. Here, in Colchis, it seemed safe for the ten thousand homesick soldiers to rest and dream of soon reaching Greece. "There was nothing remarkable about the place," wrote Xenophon in his memoir of the expedition, "except for extraordinary numbers of swarming bees." The Colchian villages were well-stocked with food and there was even the special treat of wild honey for the taking. The men soon discovered the beehives and raided them for the sweet.

After feasting on the honey, however, the soldiers "succumbed to a strange affliction," and began to act like intoxicated madmen. Soon they were staggering about and collapsing by the thousands. Xenophon reported that his troops were sprawled over the ground like victims of a terrible rout. As though under a spell, the men were totally incapacitated. Some even died. A "great despondency prevailed," wrote Xenophon. The next day, the survivors began to recover their senses but were unable to stand until three or four days later. Still feeling weak, the army broke camp and continued west. The vulnerability of his men to an ambush in enemy territory while they were unconscious greatly troubled Xenophon.

Unknown to Xenophon, the culprit in this situation was naturally toxic honey, produced by bees that collected nectar from poisonous rhododendron blossoms. The powerful neurotoxins of the flowers have no effect on the bees, but the inhabitants of the Black Sea region knew all about the beautiful but baneful rhododendron plant. Its sap could be used as an arrow poison, and in very tiny doses the honey was a *pharmakon,* taken as a tonic or mild intoxicant. Today in northern Turkey and the Caucasus, the honey is called *deli bal* ("mad honey") and known to Westerners as *miel fou.* A small spoonful in a glass of milk is a traditional pick-me-up, and a dollop in alcoholic beverages gives an extra kick. In the eighteenth century, *deli bal* was a major export from the Crimea, and tons of toxic honey were shipped to Europe to be added to drinks sold in taverns.

Strangers unfamiliar with the delicious honey made from poison flowers are liable to overdose, like Xenophon's soldiers who eagerly devoured the honeycombs. I interviewed an American anthropology student who barely survived a bout with toxic honey in the 1970s, in Nepal, where great rhododendron forests thrive. His hosts, nomadic yak herders, had warned him about the dangers of wild honey, and told him how to distinguish toxic from safe honey—one method is to hold a handful: a tingling sensation indicates toxicity. But the student also knew that the herders purposely gathered the toxic honey. Assuming that it was a hallucinogenic drug, he sought out a hive in the rhododendron forest, identified the toxic honey, and ate an ounce or so. The high began pleasantly enough, he recalled, but soon turned ferocious. Tingling and numbness progressed to vertigo, severe vomiting, and diarrhea. His speech became garbled and the psychedelic visual effects were frightening, with whirling colored lights and tunnel vision. Delirious, he was able to reach the village just before muscle paralysis caused complete collapse. The villagers nursed him back from near death. A few days later, following the same course of recovery experienced by Xenophon's men, the student was still weak, but able to stand. Later, he learned that the herders fed tiny doses to their livestock as a spring tonic. They told him the amount he had ingested was enough to kill a huge Tibetan mastiff.

By Roman times, the "mad" honey of the Black Sea area was well-known to natural historians. Pliny the Elder mused on the paradox that the "sweetest, finest, most health-promoting food" could be so randomly lethal. Noting that nature had already armed bees with venomous stings, Pliny surmised that the bees borrowed the toxins from poisonous plants to create an additional weapon, one intended to protect their honeycombs from human greed.

Xenophon's close call was due to accidental poisoning, but it was only a matter of time before someone figured out how to use the honey as a biological weapon. As John Ambrose, a historian of insects in warfare, commented, the ancients "were clever enough to realize that the honey . . . could have a military usage not unlike that of poison gas today." Honey was just one of many attractive lures that could serve as a secret biological weapon to disable or kill enemies in antiquity. Fears of biotoxins inspired the search for antidotes and immunities, which were themselves sometimes based on poisons.[1]

*   *   *

Four centuries after Xenophon's experience with toxic honey, a Roman army marched through the same region, in about 65 BC. They too feasted on the delicious honey of the Pontus, this time with fatal consequences. The commander of the army was Pompey the Great, attempting to complete the long campaign to conquer Rome's most dangerous enemy in the first century BC, the brilliant King Mithridates VI of Pontus. Mithridates' colossal army—much feared for its hellish war-chariots with rotating scythes attached to the wheels—had swept across Asia, slaughtering tens of thousands of Romans. He had captured Greece, and was poised to attack Italy (89–85 BC). Pompey's predecessor, Licinius Lucullus, had failed to finish the war against the elusive Mithridates in an arduous campaign of 74–66 BC, despite victories from Pontus to Mesopotamia. Pompey's legions finally defeated Mithridates' grand army in 65 BC, but the wily king slipped away over the Caucasus to Crimea, and began to plan an audacious land invasion of Italy.

Mithridates was a ruler obsessed with a phobia of assassination by poison, and with good reason: he had murdered his own mother, his brother, his four sons, and many others, and poison was a favorite weapon in his milieu. A team of Scythian shaman-doctors, called the Agari, accompanied Mithridates at all times. Famed for their healing potions made from various snake venoms, the Scythian shamans had cured several grave arrow wounds suffered by the king. (The paranoid monarch's sleep was guarded by a bull, a horse, and a stag, who alerted him with a three-alarm cacophony—bellowing, whinnying, and bleating—whenever someone approached the royal bed.)

FIGURE 20. *King Mithridates VI of Pontus, arch-enemy of Rome, was a toxicologist searching for the most effective poisons and their antidotes. Here, he tests a poison on a prisoner, while his royal pharmacists display aconite and other toxic plants. Painting by Robert Thom.* (Courtesy of Pfizer Inc)

Early in his life, Mithridates had devised a remarkable personal poison-survival plan. His program was based on the concept of ingesting a minute amount of a toxin or contagion, just enough to confer immunity when the body encounters the toxin again (the same principle of modern vaccines). The king dined on smidgens of poisons and antidotes every day. Extremely erudite, Mithridates studied texts in many languages. Indian medicine was much admired, and disseminated as far as Rome by his day. The king may have known that in ancient India fears of assassination by poisoning were addressed in the *Laws of Manu*, the Hindu sacred code of conduct dating to about 500 BC. Perhaps the idea for his special regimen was influenced by the verse that instructed: "Let the king mix all his food with medicines that are antidotes against poisons."[2]

Searching for the fabled *theriac*, a so-called universal antidote to all poisons, Mithridates also tested various *pharmaka* on prisoners whom he caused to be poisoned or bitten by venomous snakes and scorpions. Eventually he created an elaborate compound of the fifty-four best antidotes mixed with honey—possibly the toxic honey of his native land—into a single drug for his own protection. His special *theriac* became known as *mithridatium*. Over the years after his death, the formula was improved on by various Roman toxicologists, including the personal physician to the emperor Nero (in about AD 60), who added ten more ingredients, including chopped viper flesh and opium. The imperial physician Galen prepared daily doses of this new, improved *mithridatium* for three emperors who feared biological attack, including Marcus Aurelius.

Complex concoctions thought to have panantidotal powers were also created in ancient India and China. The Indian medical writers Charaka and Sushruta (about 400 BC) mention two universal antidotes to poisons, one called *Mahagandhahasti*, with sixty ingredients, and another with eighty-five. Vials of *theriac* continued to be very popular in Europe in the Middle Ages and Renaissance—and they were still dispensed by French and German apothecaries up to the late nineteenth century.[3]

Commanders who used poison weapons were especially sensitive to the need for antidotes or immunities. In his Indian military manual, the *Arthashastra*, Kautilya included a chapter on preparations to be administered to an army (and its animals) "before the commencement of battles and the assailing of forts," to protect them against the enemies' biological weapons and the potential backfire of their own biochemicals. The ingredients included known poisons, such as aconite, along with numerous plant, animal, and mineral substances of varying medicinal effects, such as jackal blood, mongoose and crocodile bile, gold, turmeric, and charcoal (these last three are effective agents in modern medicine). In a modern echo of Kautilya's plans, in 2002, as the United States threatened invasion of Iraq (ancient Babylonia) to destroy its stores of bio-weapons, Saddam Hussein attempted to obtain antidotes for nerve gases in vast quantities, in an effort to protect his army from their own weapons.

Mithridates' and Kautilya's efforts to ensure immunity to poison weapons are mirrored in other crude—and sophisticated—methods carried out today. For example, in 2002 it was reported in the *New York Times* and other news media that Indonesian military training included drinking the blood of venomous snakes and undergoing snakebites to boost soldiers' immunity to venom and poison arrows. In the United States, the ancient dream of a *mithridatium* that would protect civilians against modern germ warfare is promoted by a New Age organization called Tetrahedron. In 2001, the company began selling "Essential Oils for Biological Warfare Preparedness" via the Internet. One oil is said to have been originally compounded by Moses to protect the Israelites from the plagues called down on the Egyptians. Other oils are claimed to protect against bio-terrorist attacks with anthrax and bubonic plague.

But in a variation on the perils of accidental self-contamination with poison arrows or bottled plague, ancient and modern methods of seeking immunity to poison weapons can also have boomerang effects. In World War II, a complex example of the unanticipated results of attempting to protect against one's own biological weapons occurred after the Germans had polluted a large reservoir with sewage, which caused outbreaks of highly contagious typhus. The Nazis themselves relied on taking blood tests of local people to avoid going into areas with typhus. In Poland, however, their defense was turned against them when local doctors secretly injected the Poles with a vaccine that gave false-positive readings for typhus in the Nazis' blood tests, leading the Germans to stay away from the region.

More deleterious problems with attempts to protect an army from biochemical attack occurred in the Gulf War of 1991. The U.S. military vaccinated American soldiers against biochemical weapons expected to be unleashed in Iraq. In the years after the war, however, the vaccinated veterans have been afflicted by serious health problems, referred to as Gulf War Syndrome, attributed in part to the vaccinations that were intended to protect them. Since the terrorist attacks with anthrax in the United States in 2001 and the decision to vaccinate the U.S. armed forces and American citizens against smallpox in 2003, the public health hazards of mass vaccinations against anthrax and smallpox have been widely discussed in medical journals and the popular media.

In antiquity, Emperor Marcus Aurelius, fearing assassination by poison and plague, ingested a dose of Galen's opium-fortified *mithridatium* every day. (The emperor himself was not immune to accusations of poisoning—it was rumored that he had murdered his co-emperor Lucius Verus with poison.) In a prime example of the backfiring of an antidote, not only did Marcus Aurelius become an opium addict, but he died of the great plague that was brought back to Rome from Babylon by his own army, commanded by Verus.[4]

Even King Mithridates fell victim to his search for immunity to poisons. Having escaped from Pompey, he was hiding out in his Crimean kingdom planning his invasion of Italy, when his fifth son led a revolt against him. Cornered in his castle tower, Mithridates was forced to commit suicide in 63 BC. He took poison, which he always kept at hand. But his attempt to die peacefully was ironically thwarted by his life-long regimen of toxins and antidotes. In desperation, Mithridates tried to stab himself. In the end, he had to order his bodyguard from Gaul to run him through with a sword.

Mithridates' traitorous son sent his father's corpse to Pompey, who interred his formidable foe with honors in the Mithridatic family sepulcher at Sinope on the Black Sea. Meanwhile, Pompey had seized the king's headquarters and royal possessions, including an extensive library of toxicology treatises in various languages (the king spoke twenty-two tongues). There was also a treasure trove of Mithridates' handwritten notes on his experiments with poisons and antidotes. Recognizing their value, Pompey sent the books and notes to Rome with orders that they be translated into Latin.

Pliny, writing a century later, consulted Mithridates' personal toxicology library and cited several antidotes written out in Greek in the king's own hand. Antidotes discovered by Mithridates in his bio-toxins research laboratory included the blood of Pontic ducks, who lived on

poisonous plants; a pink flower he called *mithridatia*; and *polemonia,*
"the plant of a thousand powers." Pliny was deeply impressed by the
"untiring research into every possible experiment in compelling poisons
to be useful remedies."[5]

As king of Pontus and a scholar of toxicology, Mithridates was well
aware of the deadly properties of the rhododendron honey of his kingdom. He would have kept some in his royal laboratory of *pharmaka*
and, as noted earlier, he may have included it in his *mithridatium*. He
would also have been familiar with the arrow poisons concocted by the
Soanes and Scythians of his territory. As a philhellene and scholar of
Greek literature, Mithridates knew all about Medea, the legendary
witch of Colchis who was the archetype of the scheming barbarian in
Greek mythology. Medea, niece of the sorceress Circe, had poisoned the
dragon that guarded the Golden Fleece and devised potions to protect
Jason and the Argonauts from pursuing enemies. Mithridates would
also have known of Xenophon's misadventure with the poisonous
honey. With Medea as his model and with his historical knowledge of
the effects of local rhododendron honey, Mithridates had a great advantage over Pompey and his Roman army, who were unaware of the dangerous honey as they pursued Mithridates north.

Mithridates, like Medea, had eluded his pursuing enemies by a
series of ingenious tricks, and what subsequently happened to Pompey
has the hallmark of Mithridates' schemes. In about 65 BC, Pompey's
army was approaching Colchis. Mithridates' allies there, the
Heptakometes, were described by Strabo as "utterly savage" mountain
barbarians, dwelling in tree forts and living on "the flesh of wild animals
and nuts." The tribe was feared for attacking wayfarers—suddenly leap-
ing down on them like leopards from their tree houses. The Heptakometes may have received specific orders from Mithridates on how to
ambush the Roman army. What we do know for a fact is that they gathered up great numbers of wild honeycombs dripping with toxic honey
and placed them all along Pompey's route. The Roman soldiers stopped
to enjoy the sweets and immediately lost their senses. Reeling and

babbling, the men collapsed with vomiting and diarrhea, and lay on the ground unable to move. The Heptakometes easily wiped out about one thousand of Pompey's men.

Raw honey and its fermented product, mead, were the only natural sweets in antiquity, as irresistible as candy. The Heptakometes simply used a natural resource of their landscape, the delicious honey that also happened to be a deadly intoxicant, as a biological agent to incapacitate the Romans so they could be easily slaughtered. The same effect could be gained with mead, set out as alluring bait to entrap enemies. Later in the same region, for example, the Russian foes of Olga of Kiev fell for a ruse in AD 946, when they accepted several tons of mead from Olga's allies. Was the mead fortified with *deli bal*? That is not known, but all five thousand Russians were massacred as they lay in a stupor. Several centuries later in 1489, in the same area, the Russian army slaughtered some ten thousand Tatar soldiers after they had gulped down great casks of mead purposely left by the Russians in their abandoned camp.[6]

*   *   *

Aelian noted that soldiers on campaign were especially vulnerable to plots involving food and drink. The simplest biological ploy, other than denying an enemy drinking water, was to take advantage of their hunger or their overindulgence in eating and drinking. As Pliny lamented, "Most of man's trouble is caused by the belly . . . it is chiefly through his food that a man dies." Aeneas the Tactician advised commanders in the fourth century BC to wait until the enemy grows reckless and begins "looting to satisfy their greed." They will "fill themselves with food and drink and, once drunk [will] become careless . . . and impaired in performance." Writing in the same era in India, Kautilya told how to administer poisons "in the diet and other physical enjoyments" of the enemy.

Hannibal the Carthaginian relied on this tactic during his invasion of Italy in the third century BC. Noticing the lack of firewood in the district and aware of the dietary habits of the Roman army—they were used to eating cereals rather than meat—he devised a cunning plan.

Hannibal abandoned his camp, leaving herds of cattle behind, and waited until the Romans eagerly took possession of the cows as booty. Then, when they could find no wood for cooking fires, they stuffed themselves with the "raw and indigestible" beef. Unused to such heavy, uncooked fare, the soldiers became severely bilious and lethargic from their steak tartare feast. Returning in the night when the indisposed Romans were "off their guard and gorged with raw meat," wrote the military tactician Frontinus, the Carthaginians "inflicted great losses upon them."

In his first victory, in northern Italy in December 218 BC, Hannibal had used another simple ploy based on biological vulnerability. Drawing up his forces at first light, he tricked the Romans into fighting in the freezing snow before they had eaten breakfast. Hungry and numb with cold, they were easily annihilated by the well-fed Carthaginian troops. Some decades later, Tiberius Gracchus, the Roman commander fighting the Celtiberians in Spain in 178 BC, also used hunger as a weapon. He learned through spies that the enemy was suffering from a lack of provisions. Like Hannibal, he abandoned his camp, leaving behind "an elaborate supply of all kinds of foods." After the Celtiberians "had gorged themselves to repletion with the food they found," says Frontinus, "Gracchus brought back his army and suddenly crushed them."[7]

If setting out tempting food worked to trick enemies, plying them with inebriating liquor was even more effective. Barrels of alcohol could be left for them to find, or they could be sent gifts of wine. Many Greek myths tell how semi-human creatures—Centaurs, Satyrs, and Tritons—were captured or killed after being lured with wine, and this simple bio-subterfuge also figured in many ancient military engagements, especially those fought against "barbarians," who were thought to be especially susceptible to liquor.

A historical example occurred when the ruthless emperor Domitian (AD 81–96), vexed by the revolt by the Nasamonian nomads of Numidia (North Africa), declared "I forbid the Nasamonians to exist!" When Flaccus, Domitian's governor in Numidia, learned that the tribe had

FIGURE 21. *Jugs of wine could be sent to enemies or left in an abandoned camp. Foes who fell into a drunken stupor were easily wiped out. Apulian red-figure amphora, about 400 BC, detail Perseus 1991.07.1066.*

(University of Pennsylvania Museum)

discovered barrels of wine and were lying helplessly unconscious, he sent troops to "attack and annihilate them, even destroying all the non-combatants."[8]

Polyaenus, who compiled the "Stratagems of War" for the emperors Marcus Aurelius and Lucius Verus, offered advice on how to defeat barbarians in Asia in the second century AD. He began his book with an "archaeology" of mythical examples of successful trickery, assuring the emperors that courage and strength in battle were all very fine and well, but the wisest generals should know how to achieve victory *without* risk, by cunning arts and subterfuges. When the god Dionysus marched against India, declared Polyaenus, he concealed his spears in ivy and distracted the enemies with wine, then attacked while they partied under the influence.

Polyaenus also shrewdly twisted the ancient myth of Hercules and the Centaurs. Although the myth says Hercules was forced to fight the Centaurs when an unruly mob of them crashed a party to get wine, Polyaenus claimed that Hercules had planned to wipe out the entire Centaur race all along, and lured them to their death by poison arrows by setting out jugs of wine.

Turning to real-life battles, Polyaenus cited the Celts as an example. Like all barbarians, he wrote, the Celtic race was "by nature immoderately fond of wine." He reminded his readers that during treaty negotiations with them, the Romans sent many gifts, including "a large amount of wine as if to friends." After the Celts "consumed a great deal of the wine and lay drunk," wrote Polyaenus, "the Romans attacked and cut them all to pieces."

It is notable that in the historical accounts of using wine in warfare, the victims were identified as barbarians, considered inferior to the civilized cultures of the Greeks, the Romans, and the Carthaginians. (Similar justifications were expressed in British decisions to use chemical poisons against ignorant and uncivilized tribespeople in Asia and Africa in the early twentieth century.) The Greek and Roman tacticians who recounted the stories consistently stressed the barbarians' inordinate passion for alcohol, as though to justify a biological treachery that would not be employed against more cultured, noble enemies. For example, Polyaenus advised the emperors on how to defeat Asian barbarians by turning their "propensity" for trickery and terrorism and love of intoxicants against them.[9]

Polyaenus, it seems, was rather enamored of the method of defeating enemies with intoxicants. He also described how Tomyris, queen of the Massagetae (a tribe of Scythians), was said to have lured the Persian king, Cyrus the Great, to an ignominious death in 530 BC. But Polyaenus, writing nearly seven hundred years after the event, garbled the story. In his version, Tomyris pretended to flee in fear from the Persians, leaving casks of wine in her camp. The Persians consumed the wine all night long, celebrating as if they had won a victory. When they lay sleeping off their wine and wantonness, Tomyris attacked the Persians, who were scarcely able to move, and killed them all, including the king.

In fact, Cyrus did die an ignoble death during the conflict with Tomyris, but according to the Greek historian Herodotus, it was Cyrus who had tricked the milk-drinking nomads with strong wine. Herodotus's version was based on information he gained from personal interviews with Scythians about one hundred years after the event, so his story is considered more credible.

According to Herodotus, the Massagetae were a tribe of nomadic Scythians living east of the Caspian Sea. These formidable warriors were unfamiliar with wine—their favored intoxicants were hashish and fermented mare's milk. When Cyrus began a war to annex their territory to his empire, his advisors recommended a clever stratagem. Since the Massagetae "have no experience with luxuries [and] know nothing of the pleasures of life," they could be easily liquidated by setting out a tempting banquet for them, complete with "strong wine in liberal quantities."

The Greek historian Strabo, who also discussed the event, made the important point that Cyrus was in retreat after losing a battle with the nomads and therefore had to resort to underhanded trickery. Herodotus also stressed the moral aspect of the story, that Cyrus used biological treachery because his men lacked the skill and bravery necessary for a fair fight.

Cyrus ordered a fancy banquet to be set out under the Persian tents and withdrew, leaving behind a contingent of his most feeble, expendable soldiers. Tomyris's army arrived and in quick order killed the weak men that were sacrificed to the ruse by Cyrus. Congratulating themselves, the nomads then took their seats at the splendid feast laid out for them and drank so much wine that they fell into a stupor. Cyrus returned and slew the drunken Massagetae. He also captured Tomyris's son, but the youth killed himself as soon as he sobered up the next morning.

Enraged by the bloodshed achieved through such base bio-sabotage, Tomyris sent a message to Cyrus equating wine with poison. "Glutton that you are for blood, you have no cause to be proud of this day's work, which has no hint of soldierly courage. Your weapon was red wine, with which you Persians are wont to drink until you are so mad that shameful words float on the fumes. This is the poison you treacherously used to destroy my men and my son." Leave my country now, she demanded, "or I swear by the Sun to give you more blood than you can drink." Cyrus ignored the message.

The battle that ensued was one of the most violent ever recorded, wrote Herodotus. According to his informants, the two sides exchanged volleys of arrows until there were no more, and then there was a long period of vicious hand-to-hand fighting with spears and daggers. By the end of the day, the greater part of the Persian army lay destroyed where it had stood. Tomyris sent her men to search the heaps of dead Persians for Cyrus's body. Hacking off his head, she plunged it into a kettle of blood drawn from the king's fallen men, crying, "I fulfill my threat! Here is your fill of blood!"[10]

Queen Tomyris's milk-drinking warriors from the steppes were unfamiliar with the effects of wine, which made Cyrus's strategy seem especially odious. In other instances, however, taking advantage of an enemy's careless overindulgence in food or liquor did not seem unfair, since it was assumed that a commander should be able to restrain his men's behavior, and also because of the element of free choice in the decision to indulge or not. Contaminating wine with poisonous substances was particularly treacherous, however, because it eliminated free choice, and offering poisoned wine as a gift was even more devious because it violated the ancient principles of trust and fair gift exchange. And yet, ever since the Trojan Horse trick took down Troy, vigilant generals and their armies should have been on guard against accepting "gifts" from enemies.

*   *   *

Two different Carthaginian commanders, Himlico and Maharbal, were credited with defeating barbarian tribes with poisoned wine. According to Polyaenus, Himilco, a "pertinacious soldier" who owed most of his

FIGURE 22. *Queen Tomyris of the Massagetae took revenge on King Cyrus of Persia for poisoning her army with wine.* Head of Cyrus Brought to Queen Tomyris, *oil painting by Peter Paul Rubens, about 1622–23.*

(Juliana Cheney Edwards Collection © Museum of Fine Arts, Boston)

victories to his enemies' errors (in the judgment of modern historians), had lost several battles when plague swept through his armies in 406 and 400 BC. With his forces severely reduced by this apparently natural disaster, he devised a biological strategy to conquer a rebellious North African tribe in 396 BC. Himilco defeated the Libyans by taking advantage of their fondness for wine. He tainted jugs of wine in his own camp with *mandragora* or mandrake, and pretended to retreat.

Mandrake, a heavily narcotic root of the deadly nightshade family (which contains strychnine), originated in North Africa and so was a well-known *pharmakon* in Carthage. Mandrake was a drug surrounded by ancient lore and danger. Like hellebore, there were two kinds of mandrake, white (male) and black (female), and the plant had to be gathered by shamans who knew the proper rituals. With their backs turned to the wind, the diggers first traced three circles around the plant with a sword and then dug it up while facing west. Some believed the root emitted screams as it was pulled from the ground and to hear that terrible sound spelled instant death. To avoid hearing the screams, an herbalist tied the mandrake stem to the leg of a dog, which uprooted the plant when it was later called from a distance. The strong-smelling roots were sliced and sun-dried, and then crushed or boiled and preserved in wine (this practice may have suggested the idea of tainting barrels of wine to Himilco).

According to Pliny, the mere fumes of mandrake made one drowsy and those who inhaled too deeply were struck dumb. The tactician Frontinus described mandrake as a drug whose "potency lies somewhere between a poison and a soporific." A minute dose, either inhaled or drunk, could be used as a sleeping draught or anesthetic before surgery, but "those who in ignorance took too copious a draught"

FIGURE 23. *The collection of mandrake, the deadly root used by the Carthaginians and by Julius Caesar to poison wine, required special precautions. This medieval manuscript illustrates one ancient method, tying the root to a dog.*

fell into a fatal coma. And indeed, the Libyans "greedily drank of the wine" while Himilco feigned his retreat. In what has become a timeworn tactic, the Carthaginians returned and killed the unconscious tribe.

Hannibal's hot-headed cavalry officer, Maharbal, also used mandrake against some unnamed "barbarians." He mixed up a large batch of wine with pulverized mandrake root and left it in his camp. As Frontinus tells it, the barbarians "captured the camp and in a frenzy of delight greedily drank the drugged wine." Maharbal came back and "slaughtered them as they lay stretched out as if dead."

Julius Caesar may have been inspired by these old Carthaginian ruses with mandrake during his tangle with pirates in Asia Minor in about 75 BC. By Caesar's time, Cilician pirates (from what is now the coast of Turkey and Syria) had become a serious threat in the eastern Mediterranean and the Romans undertook several campaigns to wipe out these "barbarians." On a sea voyage from Rome to Bithynia (in northwest Turkey), the young Caesar was captured near Cape Malea by the Cilician pirates prowling the treacherous waters around southern Greece. The pirates sailed on to Miletus, a wealthy Roman city on the coast of Turkey, and demanded a large ransom for Caesar's release.

Caesar managed to send a secret message to the Milesians requesting that they bring double the ransom money, along with provisions for a "great feast"—actually amphoras or jars of wine well-spiked with mandrake and another huge pot with swords hidden inside. "Overjoyed at the large amount of money," the unsuspecting pirates celebrated with the wine and collapsed en masse on the deck of the ship. The Milesians returned and stabbed them all to death, and Caesar returned the ransom money. He then coolly proceeded to catch another ship to Bithynia.

Sometimes the people that the Greeks and Romans called barbarians used this biological tactic against other barbarians. When the Celts and Autariatae were locked in a long war, for instance, the historian Theopompus (fourth century BC) reported that the Celts "drugged their own food and wine with debilitating herbs and left them behind in their tents," then abandoned camp by night. The Autariatae, thinking the Celts had fled in fear, "seized the tents and freely enjoyed the wine and food." The effect was immediate: they "lay about powerless, undone by violent diarrhea. The Celts returned and murdered them as they lay helpless." We can make a good guess at the identity of the toxic herb. The symptoms recall those of hellebore, which we know was employed by the Celtic archers to poison their arrows, and which was used to similar effect by the Greeks when they poisoned the water supply of Kirrha.[11]

The ancient practice of poisoning wine or other tempting goodies—turning what the Indian strategist Kautilya had termed the "enemy's physical enjoyments" into a weapon—turns up regularly in later history, too. The modern examples are vicious enough to make the ancient incidents seem almost quaint. The humanist physician Andrea Cesalpino reported that during the Naples Campaign of 1494–95, the Spanish abandoned a village to the French, leaving behind caskets of wine that had been mixed with tainted blood drawn from leprosy and syphilis patients at Saint-Lazare Hospital and, during World War II, Dr. Shiro

FIGURE 24. *One could secretly mix poisons, such as mandrake, hellebore, or aconite, into wine and leave it for the enemy to find. Detail of an Attic red-figure kylix, about 520 BC.*

(Smith College Museum of Art, Northampton, Mass.)

Ishii, the Japanese master of biological weapons, reportedly handed out anthrax-laced candies to Chinese children in Nanking. A CIA plot to create exploding cigars for Fidel Castro in the 1960s is another example, and as recently as the 1980s, South African government agents poisoned beer, whiskey, cigarettes, chocolates, sugar, and peppermints to murder anti-apartheid dissidents.[12]

*   *   *

In our reconstruction of the murky world of ancient biochemical warfare, many of the insidious weapons and stratagems were developed by experts in natural toxins who remained anonymous, with the credit going to the commanders they worked for, such as Himilco. The arrow poisons concocted from plants and vipers, and the hellebore and mandrake used to contaminate water and wine, for example, were gathered and prepared by shamans, witches, Druids, magicians, and other skilled practitioners of clandestine arts. "Those who possessed knowledge guarded it with jealous care" and encouraged ordinary people to believe "that it was obtained by supernatural means," remarks Vaman Kokatnur, in his article on chemical warfare in ancient India.[13] They usually worked covertly, behind the scenes, and their successes could be described as "revenge of the gods" or magic, to maximize the psychological terror of biochemical warfare. These specialists in early botany, zoology, pharmacology, toxicology—and magic—were actually the first bio-war scientists, but their role has remained obscure to historians because of the secrecy that surrounded their arcane professions. As a result, the identities of only a few of the ancient bio-war professionals can be pinpointed—such as the Psylli of Africa and the Agari snake-venom specialists of Scythia, hired by the military leaders Cato and Mithridates, respectively. Mithridates stands out as a unique example of a famous military commander who was himself learned in toxicology, and Kautilya, the advisor to King Chandragupta, is another military toxicology expert whose name has been passed down.

One extremely early example of rare notoriety for a bio-weapons

maker was Chrysame, a witch of Thessaly who devised a brilliant stratagem based on trickery and drugging the enemy with tainted comestibles.
The legendary account, told by Polyaenus, is very old, dating to about
1000 BC. It was the time of the Greek colonization of Ionia (now western
Turkey) and Cnopus, son of Codrus, the king of Athens in the eleventh
century BC, was waging war with the Ionians who held Erythrae, a
wealthy city on the Aegean coast. Cnopus consulted an oracle about how
to achieve victory. The oracle advised him to send for Chrysame, a priestess of the goddess Hecate in Thessaly, to be his "general."

Thessaly, in northern Greece, was the center of ancient witchcraft,
and Thessalian witches like Chrysame were renowned for their black
magic spells, poison potions, and drugs. Their dark powers were
believed to come from Hecate, the sorceress-goddess of the Underworld, mistress of crossroads and the Hounds of Hell whose worship
involved little cakes illuminated with burning candles and the sacrifice
of puppies. Cnopus sent an ambassador to Thessaly and Chrysame
agreed to sail to Ionia to direct his battle strategies against Erythrae.

As a priestess of Hecate, Chrysame was an expert in poisonous
herbs and deadly *pharmaka,* and once in Erythrae, she surveyed the situation and devised a complex plot based on her special knowledge. She
selected the largest and finest bull from Cnopus's herds, decked it out
in a purple robe embroidered with golden thread, gilded its horns with
beaten gold, and hung garlands of flowers around its neck. Then she
mixed madness-inducing drugs into its food. Meanwhile, in full view of
the enemy encamped in the fields, Chrysame set up a great altar and all
the regalia for an important sacrifice. Her plan was to stage a fake
botched sacrifice.

Chrysame led the magnificently decorated bull toward the altar.
"Crazy from the drug's influence and in a frenzy," wrote Polyaenus,
"the bull leaped away and escaped," bellowing and bucking like rodeo
rough stock. Pretending dismay, Chrysame watched with hidden satisfaction as the bull barreled into the enemy camp. Polyaenus described
with glee the success of her ruse: "When the enemy saw the garlanded

FIGURE 25. *The witch-priestess Chrysame of Thessaly devised a successful military strategy to defeat the Ionians. She drugged a sacrificial bull to deliver incapacitating intoxicants to the enemy. Priestess leading a cow to sacrifice, Athenian lekythos, 520–510 BC.*

(Francis Bartlett Donation of 1912 © Museum of Fine Arts, Boston)

bull with golden horns charging from Cnopus's camp into their own camp, they welcomed it as a lucky sign and an auspicious omen."

Thinking that the gods had rejected Cnopus's sacrifice, the Erythraeans captured the bull and sacrificed it to their own gods. Then, they feasted on the meat as though partaking of a "divine and miraculous omen" of their own victory. But as soon as they devoured the drugged flesh, they too were seized by madness. "Everyone began to jump up and down, to run in different directions, to skip with joy." In this case, we can rule out the strong purgative hellebore. Rather, Chrysame's drug apparently had hallucinogenic properties; perhaps it was strychnine from deadly nightshade, known in antiquity for causing "playful insanity" in certain doses. Whatever the *pharmakon* that Chrysame administered to the bull, it evidently retained enough potency after slaughter and cooking to affect the men who ate the meat.

As soon as Chrysame saw that the giddy guards had abandoned their posts and the whole camp was disordered and deranged, she ordered Cnopus and his army to take up their weapons and "speedily attack the defenseless enemy. Thus Cnopus destroyed them all and became master of the great and prosperous city of Erythrae."[14]

*   *   *

"We need something . . . like calmatives, anaesthetic agents, that would put people to sleep or in a good mood." "I would like a magic dust that would put everyone in a building to sleep, combatants and noncombatants." "In an age of terrorism, it would surely be desirable to develop a mist that could put people to sleep quickly." These recent quotes from U.S. military personnel and a major newspaper editorial echo the ancient desire to disable adversaries with pacifying, sedating, or disorienting agents. The "magic dust" and calmative mists they describe would be the modern versions of the barrels of drugged wine and Chrysame's bull, as well as the scores of chemical projectiles that were developed in ancient India with the express purpose of producing "stupor, enchantment, or hypnosis" and even "prolonged yawning" in the enemy.[15]

Modern efforts to find "nonlethal" ways of pacifying or disorienting a foe began during World War II, with a bizarre initiative by the OSS (the forerunner of the CIA), whose agents attempted to find a way of chemically pacifying Adolf Hitler. One plan—apparently never carried out—was to surreptitiously inject his vegetables with female hormones. In 1965–67, during experiments with LSD-like agents, the Pentagon secretly tested a hallucinogen that was being developed as a chemical weapon, on U.S. citizens in Hawaii. And in 2002, it was reported that the Pentagon's Joint Non-Lethal Weapons Directorate and the U.S. Department of Justice were developing what they call "calmatives or chemical peacemakers." These "counter-personnel" weapons in the form of sedatives or mind-altering agents could be placed in water supplies, sprayed as aerosol mists, or packed into rubber bullets. The idea is to use the weapons indiscriminately on large populations, such as dissidents, refugees, or "hostile mobs." U.S. troops would then sort through the mass of incapacitated people to identify enemies.

It's worth noting that in all of the ancient incidents of narcotizing or incapacitating enemies with intoxicants like wine or other drugs, wholesale slaughter of the unconscious victims, often including non-combatants, was invariably carried out. The Joint Non-Lethal Weapons Directorate has acknowledged the need for "training soldiers to refrain from killing persons unable to defend themselves." It's also worth recalling that in Greek myth, even the master of devious ruses, Odysseus, rejected the morally ambiguous option of drugging the enemies who had taken his family hostage, preferring to trick them into meeting him face-to-face.[16]

The potential for lethal collateral damage with such agents in modern situations was vividly demonstrated in October 2002, when Russian troops pumped a powerful narcotic mist into a Moscow theater where more than seven hundred hostages were held by forty Chechen rebels. The plan was to neutralize everyone in the building with the gas, so that special forces could enter and shoot the unconscious rebels at close range, and then save the hostages. As with the drug hellebore in the water supply of Kirrha in the sixth century BC, however, the effect of the gas proved impossible to control. In the Moscow theater, the gas was responsible for the deaths of 127 innocent hostages and impaired the health of hundreds more.

In defending the Pyrrhic victory over the Chechen rebels, the Russian health minister, Dr. Shevchenko, sounded like the apologists for the Greek doctor Nebros who indiscriminately poisoned all the citizens of Kirrha, and Winston Churchill's defense of the use of allegedly "non-lethal" gas on Kurdish villagers. Despite the high death toll, Dr. Shevchenko argued that the gas "cannot in itself be called lethal."

"There is no such thing as nonlethal weapons," countered Mark Wheelis, an expert on biochemical arms, in the aftermath of the Moscow crisis. The military's attraction to such armaments may be understandable, he said, but one must consider the "grave risks and

costs." Besides generating "unrealistic expectations of bloodless battles" and the problems of overkill and friendly fire, Wheelis pointed out
another drawback: the possibility of enemies obtaining and using the
same technologies. That issue echoes a statement attributed to King
Eumenes of Pergamum, defeated in a naval battle (second century BC)
by Hannibal, who catapulted live snakes onto Eumenes' ships. Eumenes
remarked that he "did not think that any general would want to obtain
a victory by the use of means which might in turn be directed against
himself."[17]

6

ANIMAL ALLIES AND SCORPION BOMBS

The elephant dreads a squealing pig.
—AELIAN, *On Animals*

THE PHARAOH OF EGYPT, deluded by visions of grandeur, had treated his warrior class with contempt, thinking he would never need their services. Now, he was in deep trouble. The invincible Assyrian army, led by King Sennacherib, had just invaded Egypt's borders (in 700 BC). And now the Pharaoh's warriors refused to fight for him. "The situation was grave," wrote the historian Herodotus.

The great Assyrian army camped at Pelusium, in the salt flats and flax fields along the northeastern border of Egypt, poised to overtake the kingdom. The Pharaoh, who was also a priest of the god Ptah, was desperate. Regretting his pride, "not knowing what else to do," he entered the god's temple and bemoaned "bitterly the peril that threatened him." The Pharaoh fell asleep in the midst of his lamentations and the god appeared in a dream. Ptah instructed the Pharaoh to forget his warriors. Instead, he said, call up all the shopkeepers, craftsmen, and market folk into an army, and boldly go out to meet Sennacherib's troops. The god promised to send "helpers" to ensure victory. Confident now, the Pharaoh marched with his ragtag legions to Pelusium and took up a position facing the enemy host.

Night fell, and not a creature was stirring. . . . except for thousands of mice. Into the Assyrian camp crept multitudes of rodents, gnawing through all the leather quivers, shield straps, and bowstrings. The next morning the Assyrians were horrified to find they had no weapons to fight with. In antiquity, mice eating leather military gear was perceived as an omen of imminent disaster and, as already noted, hordes of rodents presaged epidemics. The terrible omen threw the men into chaos; the Assyrians abandoned camp and fled. The Egyptian ad hoc army pursued them, inflicting severe losses on Sennacherib's men.

Herodotus heard this tale personally from the priests at the temple of Ptah, who showed him a memorial statue of the Pharaoh holding a mouse, and historians believe that a core of historical truth lies behind Herodotus's story. Archaeologists at Nineveh have found a series of inscriptions from Sennacherib's reign recording his invasions of Egypt and Palestine. In these, the narrative of the war breaks off abruptly, implying that some sort of unexpected calamity took place during the campaign. Putting together the various literary and archaeological clues about the incident helps clarify what probably happened.

Hebrew sources in the Old Testament also recount the sudden and ignominious defeat of Sennacherib's army in about 700 BC, but they set the event at the gates of Jerusalem. According to 2 Kings, "an angel of the Lord smote 175,000 Assyrian soldiers"—traditional scriptural wording for plagues that destroyed the Israelites' enemies. King Hezekiah, inside the walls of Jerusalem, was also struck by the pestilence.

Josephus, a Jewish historian writing in AD 93, added to Herodotus's account, saying that the omen of the gnawing mice was only one reason for the hasty retreat. According to Josephus's sources, Sennacherib had also heard that a large Ethiopian army was coming to aid the Egyptians. Then, citing Berossus, a Babylonian historian (300 BC), Josephus plainly states that "a pestilential plague killed 185,000 Assyrians" as they retreated from Egypt through Palestine.

Clearly, the Greek, Hebrew, Babylonian, and Assyrian evidence refers to a military campaign that was aborted after Sennacherib's army was beset by disease-carrying rodents who, incidentally, ate the leather parts of their weapons at Pelusium. The bad omen and the rumor of the approaching Ethiopian army caused the Assyrians to abandon their invasion of Egypt and retreat through Palestine while the rodent-borne disease (perhaps bubonic plague or typhus) incubated in the men. As they arrived at Jerusalem, the epidemic swept through the troops, killing tens of thousands.[1]

*   *   *

In the ancient world, mice and rats were believed to be controlled by plague-bringing divinities, such as Apollo, Ptah, and Yahweh. Apollo, the god who controlled pestilence, was worshipped as "Smintheus," killer and master of rodents. Statues of mice were set up in Apollo's temples at Chryse and Hamaxitus near Troy, and (as noted in the discussion of plague in chapter 4), the latter temple actually maintained a horde of live white mice. Three ancient Greek sources—the natural historian Aelian and the geographers Polemon and Strabo—tell the origin of the cult of Apollo's pestilential mice. That ancient myth has intriguing parallels to the bio-disaster that befell the Assyrian army.

Long ago, mice arrived by the tens of thousands and ruined the crops in the region around Troy. The rodents also overran the camp of an invading army from Crete, and ate all of *their* leather shield straps and bowstrings. With no weapons to wage war, the Cretans settled at Hamaxitus. They built the temple to Apollo, to honor the god of mice—lowly creatures who possess the power to take down entire armies.

In ancient times, writers did not differentiate among types of rodents, all of which can harbor plague, typhus, and other diseases, so when mice were mentioned in the texts, rats may have been meant. The modern chronicler of rodent-borne epidemics, William Zinsser, remarked in 1934 that long before any scientific knowledge "concerning the dangerous character of rodents as carriers of disease, mankind dreaded and pursued these animals." The ancient Jews considered all

FIGURE 26. *Rodents carry flea-borne bubonic plague and other epidemic diseases.*

(Dover Pictorial Archives)

varieties of rodents unclean, and Persian Zoroastrians so loathed rats that killing them was "a service to God."

As Zinsser pointed out, "What rats can do, mice may also accomplish." Yet, some modern scholars still take the ancient association of mice and epidemics as evidence of superstition rather than an understanding of a real source of pestilence based on observation. Apparently unaware that no distinction was made among rodents in ancient writings, and assuming that only mice were associated with disease in antiquity, some commentators assert that mice never carry bubonic plague. For example, the scholar of religion, Christopher Faraone, in his discussion of these ancient narratives in 1992, suggested that "faulty reasoning" about the "curious coincidence of swarming mice and man-killing plague" must have led the ancients to believe that vermin "cause epidemic disease." Faraone labels this "a misunderstanding that arises from the frequency with which plague strikes close on the heels" of mouse infestations. In fact, however, science shows that pathogens are carried by the parasites (usually fleas) of rodents, which transmit the diseases to humans, and many ancient texts make it clear that periodic hordes of rodents of any sort were correctly recognized as harbingers of pestilence. The geographer Strabo remarked about infestations of vermin, "From mice pestilential diseases often ensue," and during a rodent-borne plague that attacked the Roman army on campaign in Cantabria, Spain (first century BC), the commanders offered bounties on dead mice.

Further proof that the ancients understood the connection between rodents and epidemics can be found in the Old Testament story of the Philistines who were smote by disease after they captured the Ark of the Covenant during the war with the Israelites in the twelfth century BC. In what may be the earliest account of rodent-borne bubonic plague, the Philistine lands were afflicted by an onslaught of mice that coincided with an epidemic marked by "swellings in the Philistines' private places." Assuming that mice were innocent of plague, some commentators cited by Faraone identified the "swellings" as hemorrhoids and they dismiss any connection with the concurrent mouse infestation. But, as pointed out earlier, a classic sign of the Black Death is grotesquely swollen lymph glands in the groin and thighs. And 1 Samuel 5–6 clearly indicates that the Philistines *themselves* recognized the connection between rodents and the disease.[2]

The rodent hordes that afflicted the Philistines and averted the Assyrians' invasion were natural disasters, since directing multitudes of infected rodents against the enemy would be nearly impossible. But the priests who prayed to their gods of pestilence for deliverance from foes by means of mice certainly *intended* to wage biological war, and when an enemy was routed by plague they credited the gods with the biological victory. The small creatures were considered zoological allies in war. In a striking continuity of the ancient cult of rodent allies, laboratory scientists rely on the very same "helpers" that were kept in Apollo's temple—white mice and rats—to develop today's germ warfare agents.

Tales like Sennacherib's military disaster are included in this chronicle of early bio-warfare because the long observed relationship between infestations of vermin and thwarted invasions suggested the idea of praying to gods to send swarms of rodents, and probably gave people the idea of deliberately trying to turn other noxious creatures against enemies. And, in fact, as the following episodes show, a remarkable variety of creatures from the animal and insect world were recruited to achieve victory in the ancient world.

*　*　*

Mice were not the smallest animal allies in waging biological war. One of the biblical Ten Plagues of Egypt was an infestation of lice that "bugged" both animals and humans (lice can carry typhus). That fortuitous infestation was attributed to Yahweh, but there is plenty of evidence from ancient texts that other insects, such as stinging bees, hornets, wasps, and scorpions (venomous arthropods), were purposefully used in wartime as agents for both offense and defense. Simply by doing what came naturally, these tiny creatures could inflict damage and chaos far beyond their bodily dimensions.

Insects, with their sharp stingers, chemical poisons, and a propensity to defend and attack, have long "served as models for man to emulate in . . . the art of warfare," commented the military historian and entomologist John Ambrose. Bees were admired in antiquity as producers of honey, but they were also respected as aggressive creatures "of exceedingly vicious disposition." In one of the earlier examples of borrowing weapons from nature's armory, we saw how a relatively primitive tribe in Asia Minor decimated Pompey's Roman army by setting out toxic honeycombs. As Pliny noted, the baneful honey was the bees' defensive weapon against human greed. But the honeybees themselves—and wasps and hornets (the largest species of wasps)—were armed with stingers. Swarms had been known to invade cities, forcing entire populations to relocate. Such a disaster had befallen the residents of Phaselis (central Turkey), and the people of Rhaucus, in Crete, had to abandon their city when copper-colored killer bees from Mount Ida arrived in great swarms.

Why not hurl entire hives filled with enraged, venomous insects at an enemy? The painful stings would send any army into wild confusion and retreat, and massive numbers of stings could be fatal. According to folk belief cited by Pliny, it took only twenty-seven hornet stings to kill a man (in fact, even one sting can cause death in individuals who are sensitive to the venom).

Beehive bombs were probably among the first projectile weapons and Edward Neufeld, a scholar of Mesopotamian history, surmises that hornets' nests were lobbed at enemies hiding in caves as early as Neolithic times. Bees have figured in warfare in different cultures of many eras. The sacred text of the Maya in Central America, the *Popol Vuh,* for example, describes an ingenious bee boobytrap used to repel besiegers: dummy warriors outfitted in cloaks, spears, and shields were posted along the walls of the citadel. War bonnets were placed on the heads, which were actually large gourds filled with bees, wasps, and flies. As the assailants scaled the walls, the gourds were smashed. The furious insects honed in on the warriors, who were soon "dazed by the yellow jackets and wasps [and were sent] stumbling and falling down the mountainside."[3]

FIGURE 27. *Wasp nests and beehives were hurled at enemies from Neolithic times onward.* (Dover Pictorial Archives)

Were hornets and other venomous insects marshaled to scourge the Israelites' foes? Neufeld has written that in biblical times insects were "important military agents in tactics of ambush," guerrilla raids, and flushing out primitive strongholds. He also noted that ancient Hebrew and Arab sources refer to hordes of unidentified flying insects that were summoned to attack the enemies' eyes with "acrid poison fluids," blinding or killing them. As Neufeld pointed out, these could belong to any of the dozens of species of noxious insects in the Near East. He suggested that the gadfly, or "eye fly," may have been the unknown insect that ejected blinding poison. But thinking back to poisonous insect "droppings" of India described by Aelian (chapter 2), is it possible that these Near Eastern stories were about infestations of *Paederus* beetles? The beetles excrete the virulent poison *pederin,* a fluid that causes suppurating sores and blindness, and in the bloodstream the effect is as deadly as cobra venom. Plagues of *Paederus* beetles period-

FIGURE 28. *A swarm of bees or hornets attacking men. Amphora from Vulci, about 550 BC.* (© The British Museum)

ically afflict populations in Africa and in the Mideast, but it is difficult to see how the swarms could ever have been directed effectively in a military campaign.

Some biblical passages cited by Neufeld do seem to suggest a *planned* military use of stinging insects. Exodus states that hornets were "sent ahead" of the Israelites to drive out the Canaanites, Hittites, and other enemies, and in Deuteronomy, hornets supplemented ordinary weapons against the Canaanites. In Joshua, hornets, in conjunction with swords or bows, drove out the Amorites. Proposing that these biblical narratives describe "massive assaults" with hornets' nests, "plotted and contrived deliberately," rather than spontaneous swarming insect behavior, Neufeld argued that the "texts clearly reflect an early form of biological warfare." Even the "crudest forms" of such warfare, simply throwing beehive bombs by hand, could rout an enemy hiding in caves with stings and panic.

Deploying stinging insects involved hazards for those who used them in war. The traditional practice of the Tiv people of Nigeria shows one clever method of directing bees at the enemy. The Tiv kept their bees in special large horns, which also contained a toxic powder. The poison dust was said to strengthen the bees' venom, but it is possible that it was a drug to calm the bees in the horn. In the heat of battle, the bees were released from the horns toward the enemy. It was not recorded how the Tiv avoided stings themselves, but it seems that the shape and length of the horns effectively propelled the swarm toward the enemy ranks.

Tossing beehive bombs at enemies also involved the potential for "blow-back." Stinging insects had to be "kept peacefully in their nests before the ammunition was used against the foe; the danger of premature explosion must have been considerable." To reduce "the chances of backfire," noted Neufeld, buzzing bombs had to be "hurled carefully at the enemy, wherein the bursting nest would release hundreds of very nervous hornets on the target." He suggests that hornets' nests may have been plugged with mud and transported in sacks, baskets, and pots, or perhaps bees were persuaded to colonize special containers.

One precaution against misdirected stings was smoke, which was recognized as a tranquilizer of bees very early in antiquity. Another method was to set up hives with trip wires along the enemy's route, a method used by both sides in Europe in World War I. Obviously, a great deal of skill and a variety of releasing devices were required for the entire operation, and it is possible that beekeeping shamans were involved in stunning the hornets with smoke or toxic dust, and in planning the attacks.[4]

There is historical evidence that the old strategy of hurling hives of stinging missiles at enemies continued to flourish even as more sophisticated methods of siege-craft were developed. Catapults, for example, were a very effective delivery system for launching biological weapons of all sorts—including hornets' nests—while avoiding collateral damage. In fact, catapulting beehives at enemy troops became a favorite Roman tactic. In his survey of the use of bugs in battle from biblical times to the Vietnam War, John Ambrose even suggested that the Romans' extensive use of bees in warfare may partly account for the recorded decline in number of hives in the late Roman Empire. Ambrose also pointed out that heaving hives continued in popularity in later times: for example, Henry I's catapults lobbed beehives at the Duke of Lorraine's army in the eleventh century, a tactic used again in 1289 by the Hungarians against the Turks. More recently, in the 1960s, the Vietcong set boobytraps with giant, ferocious Asian honeybees (*Apis dorsata*) against American soldiers. In retaliation, says Ambrose, the Pentagon began developing its own top-secret bee weapon to use against the Vietcong, based on the bees' alarm chemical, a pheromone that marks victims for a swarming attack. Such weapons are, in 2003, still in the development stage.[5]

As the ancient Maya and many others have recognized, bees could provide a very effective *defense,* too. Defenders of the medieval castle on the Aegean island of Astipalaia, for example, fended off pirate attacks by dropping their beehives from the parapets. In Germany in 1642, during the Thirty Years' War, attacking Swedish knights were repulsed with beehive bombs. Armor protected the knights, but the clouds of stinging bees drove their horses crazy. In the same era, the village of Beyenburg (Bee-town) was named in honor of some quick-thinking nuns who overturned the convent hives to repel marauding soldiers. When Mussolini invaded Ethiopia in 1935–36, Italian planes sprayed a fog of mustard gas that devastated civilians and the landscape. The Ethiopians' only recourse was to drop beehives from ridges down onto the Italian tanks, terrorizing the drivers and causing crashes.

Stinging insects certainly helped defend forts in antiquity. In the fourth century BC, Aeneas the Tactician, in his book "How to Survive under Siege," advised "besieged people to release wasps and bees into tunnels being dug under their walls, in order to plague the attackers." This same tactic was employed against the Romans in 72 BC by King Mithridates in Pontus, according to Appian of Alexandria (a historian of the second century AD). Appian relates that Licinius Lucullus (one of several Roman commanders who failed to capture the wily king) laid siege to Mithridates' strongholds at Amisus on the Black Sea, and at Eupatoria and Themiscrya. Lucullus's sappers excavated tunnels under the citadels, passageways so capacious that several subterranean battles were fought in them. But Mithridates' allies routed the Romans by drilling holes that intersected the tunnels and releasing not only swarms of angry bees, but also bears and other rampaging wild beasts.[6]

*   *   *

In AD 198–99, the emperor Septimius Severus began the Second Parthian War, in one of several Roman bids to control Mesopotamia. He failed in two separate attempts to capture the remote desert stronghold of Hatra, a city that derived great riches from its control of the caravan routes. Hatra's impressive remains, south of Mosul, Iraq, reveal the ruins of an enormous double-walled fortress with ninety large towers,

163 small towers, and a moat. The city was located at the top of a precipitous ridge, and surrounded by barren desert.

Holed up inside their fortified city, King Barsamia and the citizens of Hatra prepared strong defense plans as the Roman legions advanced over the desert. One of their defenses was biological. Anticipating by seventeen hundred years the bombs of fragile porcelain filled with noxious insects that the Japanese dropped on China in World War II, the Hatreni filled clay-pot bombs with "poisonous insects" and sealed them up, ready to hurl down at the attackers.[7]

Herodian, a historian from Antioch (Syria), who recounted the story, did not specifically identify the venomous creatures, but simply referred to them as "poisonous flying insects." What sort of insects would have been collected by the Hatreni? In the "wretched," waterless wilderness stretching for miles in every direction around Hatra, nothing grew but dragonwort and wormwood; there were no bees, except for an occasional solitary ground bee. Scorpions, on the other hand, were extremely abundant. The stinging creatures were sacred to the local goddess Ishhara and scorpion motifs abound in Mesopotamian mythology.

In the deserts surrounding Hatra, deadly scorpions lurked "beneath every stone and clod of dirt," wrote the natural historian Aelian. They were so numerous that to make the land between Susa to Media safe for travel, Persian kings routinely ordered scorpion hunts, bestowing bounties for the most killed. Scorpions, declared Pliny, "are a horrible plague, poisonous like snakes, except that they inflict a worse torture by dispatching their victim with a lingering death lasting three days." The sting is intensely painful, followed by great agitation, sweating, thirst, muscle spasms, convulsions, swollen genitals, slow pulse, irregular breathing, and death.

Everyone "detests scorpions," agreed Aelian. The fear factor was put to symbolic military use among the ancient Greeks, who painted scorpion (and snake) emblems on their shields to frighten foes, and by the early first century AD, the scorpion had been taken up as the official

FIGURE 29. *Scorpions abound in the desert around Hatra, and they were used as live ammunition against Roman besiegers.* (Dover Pictorial Archives)

emblem of the dreaded Roman Praetorian Guard, the personal troops of the emperors. It's no coincidence that modern U.S. military weapons carry names like "scorpion" and "stinger," "hornet," and "cobra" to instill confidence among the troops that man them and to inspire fear among the enemy.

According to Aelian, the sting of some scorpion species killed instantly, and in the Sinai peninsula, gigantic scorpions preyed on lizards and cobras. Anyone who even "treads on scorpion droppings develops ulcers of the foot." Eleven types of scorpion were known in antiquity: white, red, smoky, black, green, pot-bellied, crab-like, fiery red-orange, those with a double sting, those with seven segments, and those with wings. Most of these species have been identified by entomologists, but others may have been venomous insects mistaken for scorpions.

True scorpions lack wings, and Herodian referred to *flying*, stinging insects in his account. But ancient authors consistently referred to winged varieties of scorpions and winged scorpions are also depicted in ancient artifacts. The natural historian Pliny explained the error. Scorpions are given the power of flight by very strong desert winds, he said, and when they are airborne, the scorpions extend their legs, which makes them appear to have membraned wings.

The modern commentator on Herodian, C. Whittaker, dismissed Herodian's account of clay pots filled with scorpions as a tall tale based on a special double-firing ballistic catapult that was called the *Scorpion*. But the abundance of scorpions in the desert, and the many other historical reports of hurling hornets' nests and earthenware pots filled with noxious creatures in ancient military engagements make Herodian's account quite plausible. In fact, heaving scorpions by the basketful at attackers was specifically recommended by Leo VI (AD 862–912), in his famous military *Tactics* handbook.

The Hatreni would have gathered the venomous insects in advance and, to avoid getting stung while preparing their live bio-ammunition, they would have followed several safety procedures. Aelian told of the "innumerable devices contrived for self-protection" against the giant Egyptian scorpions (seven inches long) and the multitudes of them in North Africa, where people "devise endless schemes to counter scorpions." Wearing high boots and sleeping in raised beds with each bedpost in a basin of water were just two common defenses.

Scorpion stings were most deadly in the morning, declared Pliny, "before the insects have wasted any of their poison through accidental strikes." The Hatreni may have teased the irascible arthropods into wasting stings before they placed them in the pots. Aelian pointed out that the stinger was a very slender hollow core, so one could temporarily block the tiny opening by very carefully spitting on the tip of the stinger. Or, one could sprinkle scorpions with deadly aconite (monkshood) powder, which was said to cause the creatures to shrivel up temporarily. They could be revived with poisonous white hellebore, once they were inside the earthenware containers.

It's possible that other venomous flying insects, such as assassin bugs, were called scorpions in antiquity. Assassin bugs (cone-nose bugs, *Reduviidae* family) were notoriously used by rulers in Central Asia for torturing prisoners. These predatory, bloodsucking insects cling tenaciously to a victim and push their sharp beaks into the flesh, injecting a lethal nerve poison that liquefies tissues. The bite can be extremely painful. Assassin bugs do have wings, and Herodian's description of the effects of the "poisonous flying creatures" fits these insects' clinging, piercing attack: As Severus's men attempted to ascend the walls, the clay pots were rained down on them. "The insects fell into the Romans' eyes and the exposed parts of their bodies," wrote Herodian, "Digging in before they were noticed, they bit and stung the soldiers, causing severe injuries."

Probably the best conclusion is that the earthenware bombs contained a potpourri of scorpions, assassin bugs, wasps, *pederin* beetles, and other venomous insects from the desert around Hatra.

Military historians are perplexed over what caused Severus to give up his siege of Hatra after only twenty days, just as he had successfully breached the city walls and victory was within reach. Roman sieges were usually grueling ordeals, and they were expected to last several months or even years but they were ultimately successful. So, what could have caused Severus to back off? Citing the "insalubrious desert," mutinous troops, poor planning and disputes over plunder, a possible secret treaty, or other unknown factors, modern scholars seem to be unable to accept the ancient historians' clear indications that it was the brute effectiveness of Hatra's defensive biological and chemical weapons that overcame Roman morale, manpower, and siege machines.

Herodian gives a vivid account of the violent battle, in which nearly every siege technique was tried. He makes it clear that the scorpion bombs were just one of many types of ammunition fired at the Romans. In the scorching desert sun, a great many legionaries had succumbed to the heat and unhealthy climate even before the battle, but the Romans sent their full forces and manned every kind of siege machine. The

Hatreni "vigorously defended themselves" with their double-shot catapults, "firing down missiles and stones." Dio Cassius adds that the
Hatreni also poured burning naphtha on Severus's army, which completely destroyed his siege engines and enveloped his men with
unquenchable petroleum-fed flames.

The last straw must have come when the defenders began firing the
jars full of hideous bugs down on Severus's soldiers as they assaulted
the walls. The terror effect would be quite impressive, no matter how
many men were actually stung. Herodian states that these combined
defense tactics caused Severus to withdraw "for fear his entire army
would be destroyed." And the desert fortress of Hatra remained independent in "splendid isolation" until AD 241, when it was reduced to
ruins by Iranian Sasanids.[8]

*   *   *

Harking back to ancient deployments of stinging insects, Pentagon
experts not only investigated ways of using bees to attack the enemy in
Vietnam, but also tested the ability of assassin bugs (there are thousands of species around the world) to hone in on prey at long distances.
During the Vietnam War, the Army carried out tests using assassin bugs
in special capsules to track down the Vietcong in the jungle. The predatory bugs reportedly detected humans from a distance equivalent to two
city blocks and emitted a "yowling" sound that was amplified to audi-
ble range. It is not known whether the assassin bug tracking device was
ever actually used in the jungle.

The ancient practice of enlisting insects as weapons has been taken
to new levels in the U.S. government's most advanced research. Since
1998, the Pentagon has sponsored experiments in "Controlled
Biological Systems" to create sophisticated war technologies based on
entomology and zoology. The research is overseen by the Defense
Advanced Research Projects Agency (DARPA), the central research and
development unit of the Defense Department. The mission is to exploit
the natural traits of what they call "Vivisystems," living creatures from

insects to intelligent animals, in order to "turn them into war-fighting technologies." Just as the ancients learned to use the natural instincts of bees in waging war, scientists are studying insects whose attributes might be valuable for military purposes. For example, DARPA-funded laboratories are training honeybees to detect minute amounts of substances that indicate the presence of biochemical or explosive agents. The hope is to deploy the hypersensitive insects as spies and sentinels in biochemical warfare.

We have come a long way from praying to plague gods to send mice and lobbing hornets' nests at foes—and yet the Defense Department's sophisticated insect research still relies on the timeless principle of exploiting bees' instincts. But living insects have disadvantages: for example, bees sting indiscriminately and they won't work when cold, at night, or in storms. Accordingly, DARPA scientists are improving on mere Vivisystems by designing "Hybrid Biosystems" and "Biomimetics." With brain-computer interface technology, they can integrate living and nonliving components, for example, by reengineering bee neurology or attaching real bee antennae to a cyborg bee.

In antiquity, biological strategies were often justified in self-defense and, as noted earlier, often modern treaties allow biochemical weapon research for defense, which can serve as a cover for covertly developing biochemical agents with first-strike capabilities. The tendency to justify biological armaments "for defense only" is evident in the public explanations of DARPA's Vivisystems mission. One ambiguous sentence in the DARPA "Objectives" statement of 2003, for example, remarks that "other applications [of insect agents] might involve controlling the distribution of pest organisms to improve operational environments for troops," while the next sentence asserts that "all aspects of the program are for defensive purposes only."

Scientists stress the peaceful applications of their DARPA-funded research, but the military applications are obvious. The most recent Hybrid Biosystem creations, remote-controlled rats, are promoted in the media as "search and rescue" agents, but the project scientists admit that the cyber-rat would also be "an ideal delivery system for biological weapons." What nature (and the god Ptah) brought to Sennacherib's Assyrian army in Egypt back in 700 BC—a rodent-borne plague—could now be delivered by remote-control. The DARPA scientists have also successfully wired monkey's brains to control machines. Transforming animals into living war machines represents a giant step in the militarization of nature. And the use of intelligent animals in war has a very ancient history.[9]

* * *

In antiquity, mice were inadvertent allies in repulsing attackers, and even smaller allies were the stinging insects whose natural aggressive instincts could be directed against foes. But larger creatures, such as the ferocious bears sent against the Roman besiegers in Pontus in 72 BC, could also be drafted for war duty.

Hannibal's masterful use of animals during his invasion of Italy in 218 BC is an excellent example of how creatures could be used for war. The well-known feat of Hannibal's war elephants crossing the snowy Alps was only the beginning, for the Carthaginian general had many ad hoc animal tricks. For example, when he seemed to be trapped in a narrow valley guarded by the Romans, Hannibal terrified the enemy into wild flight by assembling herds of cattle and affixing burning torches to their horns. He made a safe getaway that night, by driving the herd before his army toward the Romans.

Four different historians related another creative zoological ploy thought up by Hannibal during a decisive naval battle against King Eumenes of Pergamum (Asia Minor) sometime between 190 and 184 BC. Hannibal and his allies were far outnumbered in ships. Therefore, explains the Roman historian Cornelius Nepos, "it was necessary for him to resort to a ruse, since he was unequal to his opponent in arms." Hannibal sent his men ashore to "capture the greatest possible number of venomous snakes" and stuff them into earthenware jars. When they had amassed a great many of these, he prepared his marines for the battle. The biological secret weapon boosted the confidence of the out-numbered men, reports Nepos. When the clash came and Eumenes' ships bore down on Hannibal's fleet, the marines let fly the jars, cata-pulting them onto the enemy decks.

The enemy's first reaction to the smashing pottery was derisive laughter. But as soon as they realized their decks were seething with poisonous snakes, it was Hannibal's turn for mirth, as the horrified sailors leaped about trying to avoid the vipers. Eumenes' navy was overcome and it may have been this incident that led Eumenes to make his famous remark that an honorable general should eschew victory by underhanded means that he would not like to have turned against himself.

Hannibal's idea was to terrorize Eumenes' crew so that they were unable to fight and similar ideas have occurred to commanders in other times and places. For example, in Afghanistan in about AD 1000, during the siege of Sistan, Mahmud of Ahazna ordered his men to catapult sacks of serpents into the stronghold to terrify the defenders of the fort.[10]

Animals could also be used to give the enemy an illusion of vast numbers of attackers, a ploy that was advised by Polyaenus and other ancient strategists. Alexander the Great, for one, resorted to such a trick in Persia, tying branches to the tails of sheep to raise clouds of dust, which the Persians took as the sign of a massive army. He also tied torches to the sheep at night, so that the whole plain looked to be on fire. Alexander's successor, Ptolemy, did the same thing in Egypt in 321 BC, when he attacked Perdiccas, binding loads of brush to herds of pigs, cattle, and other domestic animals to raise dust as he approached with his cavalry. Perdiccas, imagining a very great cavalry was galloping toward him, fled and took heavy losses.

Much earlier, in the sixth century BC, the Persian king Cambyses lay siege to Pelusium, which had remained the same entry point for invaders of Egypt since Sennacherib's mouse-borne disaster there in the eighth century BC. This time, the Egyptian defense was very well-organized, holding off the Persians with batteries of artillery that shot stones, bolts, and fire. Cambyses responded by placing a unique zoological shield before his ranks: a phalanx of yowling cats, bleating sheep, barking dogs, and silent ibexes. All these animals were worshipped by the Egyptians, and just as Cambyses hoped, the warriors halted their fire to avoid harming any sacred creatures. Pelusium fell and the Persians conquered Egypt. [11]

All the creatures dispatched against the enemy discussed so far have been involuntary zoological allies: from Chrysame's poisoned bull (in the previous chapter), swarms of mice, and innocent sheep dragging branches, to venomous creatures whose aggressive nature leads them to attack human targets. But, unlike hordes of wasps or rodents whose instincts might work to the advantage of one side in military contexts, large, intelligent animals could be specially prepared for battle. Almost every army in antiquity maintained baggage animals (mules, oxen, donkeys, camels) and used dogs for sentry duty, and some large animals were trained to actively participate in war: horses and camels were cavalry mounts, while dogs and war elephants could be used to attack the enemy.

*   *   *

Ever since dogs became man's best friends they have served as sentinels to warn of intruders. Their acute senses and their loyalty, vigilance, speed, and intelligence make them valuable for military purposes. To guard the citadel of Acrocorinth against Philip of Macedon in 243 BC, for instance, the great guerrilla general Aratos set out fifty dogs, while an inscription from the small Greek city of Teos (on the Turkish coast) records that three dogs were to be purchased for sentinel duty at the garrison fort. In the fourth century BC, Aeneas the Tactician referred frequently to dogs as sentries and messengers in wartime, but he also warned that their instinct to bark could backfire.

Dogs also participated in combat. Perhaps the earliest evidence of dogs in war is an Assyrian stone relief from about 600 BC found at Birs

Nimrud (Iraq), depicting a warrior carrying a shield and leading a large, armored mastiff. According to Pliny, the king of the Garamantes of Africa had two hundred trained war dogs "that did battle with those who resisted him." The cities of Colophon and Castabala in Asia Minor also maintained troops of war dogs that fought ferociously in the front ranks. These canines were their most loyal allies, joked Pliny, "for they never even required pay." The Hyrcanians of the Caspian Sea and the Magnesians (a mountain tribe of northeastern Greece) were also feared for the large hounds with spiked collars that accompanied them on the battlefield (by the Middle Ages, war dogs would sport full coats of mail). "These allies were an advantage and great help to them," remarked Aelian, although he did not give any gory details.

Just as using poison arrows (originally intended for hunting) to kill humans tended to raise the hackles of classical Greeks and Romans, siccing hunting dogs on human quarry might have seemed brutal and inhumane to many. But Polyaenus, the strategist who advised the Roman emperors on how to beat the barbarian Parthians in the second

FIGURE 30. *Assyrian war dog on a sculptural relief from Birs Nimrud, about 600 BC.*

century AD, recounted with approval how the "monstrous and bestial Cimmerians" were driven out of Asia Minor in the sixth century BC by the vicious hounds of King Alyattes of Lydia (west-central Turkey). The Cimmerians of the steppes had been driven west by the Scythians and subsequently invaded Lydia. King Alyattes set his "strongest dogs upon the barbarians as if they were wild animals"—which is exactly how Polyaenus characterized the invaders. The king's war dogs, he wrote, "killed many and forced the rest to flee shamefully."

At the glorious Battle of Marathon in 490 BC, when the Athenians and their allies defeated the Persian army to the tune of 6,400 dead (only 192 Greeks perished), one Athenian dog received honors "for the dangers it faced," along with the greatest human heroes of the war. The dog had served as a "fellow-soldier in the battle," wrote Aelian, and it was featured in the famous paintings of the victory in Athens.

Dogs continued to participate in battles up to modern times, and the classical vignette of the trusty war-dog hero at ancient Marathon could serve as the original K-9 Corps tale. Many dogs went to war in World War I, but war-dog training in the U.S. armed forces began on a

FIGURE 31. *The heroic Athenian war dog at the Battle of Marathon (490 BC) during the defeat of the Persians.*

large scale during World War II. By 1945, nearly ten thousand dogs served in K-9 War Dog platoons in Europe and the Pacific. Dogs also worked as sentries, scouts, and pack animals in the Korean, Vietnam, and Gulf wars.

Canines and other mammals fall into the Defense Department's category of "Controlled Biological Systems" for waging war with the help of animals. The zoological scope of the program far exceeds Cambyses' military menagerie in the Persians' front ranks, used to stop the Egyptian artillery 2,500 years ago. Since the Vietnam War, the Pentagon has funded the classified training and deployment of numerous species of mammals, including dogs, skunks, rats, monkeys, sea lions, dolphins, and whales. For example, in the 1980s U.S. Navy-trained dolphins were sent to the Persian Gulf to patrol the harbor for mines and to escort Kuwaiti oil tankers. In 2003, sea lions, trained to pursue and capture enemy divers with leg clamps, were deployed to the Gulf. The Navy claims that no mammals have ever been trained to kill humans, in keeping with the ancient justification of biological weapons for defense only.[12]

*　　*　　*

The Greeks were astounded when they first encountered trained war elephants in action, at the battle on the Hydapses River, where Alexander the Great defeated King Porus in India, in 326 BC. The soldiers were able to rally their spirits and prepared to fight the strange, imposing beasts, but Alexander quickly realized that his cavalry horses were terrified and would not face Porus's two hundred elephants. He found ways to outmaneuver the elephants with his infantry, by boxing the elephants in and ordering his men to aim their long javelins to kill the mahouts. Hemmed in and without their drivers, Porus's elephants ran amok and trampled many of their own men. Alexander captured eighty of Porus's elephants and, seeing how useful they could be, he obtained one hundred more in subsequent campaigns in India.

According to legends that grew up around the figure of Alexander, he devised another brilliant plan to deflect the ranks of living tanks. As

FIGURE 32. *Indian war elephant, with tower of warriors and mahout, detail from a coin.*

they story goes, Alexander piled up all the bronze statues and armor that he had taken as booty during his conquests so far and heated them over a fire until they were red-hot. (In reality, the Greeks brought very little booty with them over the Khyber Pass.) Then he set up the statues and shields like a wall in front of the elephants. When Porus sent forth his elephants, they made straight for the heated statues, taking them for enemy soldiers. As the beasts smashed into the statues, "their muzzles were badly burnt" and they refused to continue the attack.

Alexander's Hellenistic successors, the Seleucids and Ptolemies, made heavy use of war elephants, which became *the* glamour weapon of the Hellenistic era. The elephants were carefully trained from birth by the traditional suppliers in India and they were very effective, especially against men and horses who had never set eyes on such creatures before. Elephants could also tear down wooden fortifications. Clanging bells were hung on the massive beasts; they were fitted with coats of armor and iron tusk covers, and carried crenellated "castles" with archers on top. An elephant could charge at fifteen miles per hour (but at that momentum, it had difficulty coming to a halt). The stampeding animals could plow through tight phalanxes of men, crushing them or causing them to scatter to avoid being trampled.

The Romans were first introduced to war elephants when Pyrrhus of Epirus invaded Italy in 280 BC with Indian war elephants. The "bulk and uncommon appearance" of Pyrrhus's twenty pachyderms, each one carrying a tower with one or two men with bows and javelins, undid the Romans, and their terrified cavalry horses refused to face the beasts. In the panic, many Roman soldiers were impaled by the elephants' tusks and crushed under their feet. Pyrrhus won, but with such excessive losses of his own men that he remarked that another victory would totally ruin him—thus the phrase "Pyrrhic victory." By 275 BC, Pyrrhus had lost many of his elephants and two-thirds of his original forces.

FIGURE 33. *War elephants could cause chaos in enemy ranks, but sometimes trampled their own men in the melee.*

Hannibal's elephants crossed the Alps in the winter of 218 BC, during the Carthaginian's invasion of Italy. The North African forest elephants were smaller than Indian elephants and carried only a single mahout—the beasts themselves were the weapons. In the alpine winter, however, all but one of the Carthaginian's thirty seven elephants died in the snow. He sent for more in 215 BC, but by then the Romans and their horses were not as terrified by the sheer sight of elephant phalanxes.

In the third century BC, the Hellenistic Seleucid king Antiochus routed the Galatians, Gauls who had invaded Anatolia. In the famous non-battle, the Galatians were overwhelmed by the bizarre sight and loud clamor of Antiochus's sixteen trumpeting elephants with gleaming tusks advancing on the distant plain. The Galatian cavalry horses reared and wheeled in fright, and the foot soldiers were trampled under their hooves. In the first century BC, the Britanni surrendered to the Romans at the sight of just one enormous elephant in gleaming armor. One of the advantages of biological weapons is the element of surprise and horror that can cause the challenged to capitulate without a fight—and elephants were no exception.

The war elephant could intimidate the enemy, but the cumbersome animal was so unpredictable that after a time it came to be regarded as a liability rather than an asset. The problems of friendly fire and collateral damage were serious. Apparently, drugs were frequently administered before battle to make the beasts more aggressive, and if the elephant's mahout was killed, or the elephant was badly wounded or disoriented by something untoward, or in rut, the crazed behemoth would crash out of control, squashing its own men. Contemplating such bloody disasters with elephants in the first century BC, the Roman philosopher Lucretius surmised that perhaps other wild animals, such as lions, were "once enlisted in the service of war" in very early times, with similarly catastrophic results. The "experiment of launching savage boars against the enemy failed," he speculated, as did "advance guards of lions on leashes." The brute beasts, "enflamed by the gory carnage of battle," must have slashed their own masters with tusks, talons, and teeth, "just as in our own times war elephants sometimes stampede over their own associates."

Safety procedures were developed to deactivate rampaging war elephants. Each mahout had a sharp chisel blade bound to his wrist, so that if his wounded elephant suddenly reversed direction he could drive it into the beast's neck with a mallet, killing it instantly. This expedient was said to have been invented by the Carthaginian general Hasdrubal.

"Elephants, like prudent men, avoid anything that is harmful," noted Aelian. Unlike insects, intelligent creatures such as dogs, horses, and elephants are subject to fear and rational instincts for self-preservation, which creates disadvantages and boomerang effects. It's an old problem that continued in modern times: in the Thirty Years' War (1618–48), the Swedish warhorses fled from swarms of stinging bees unloosed by the enemy; and during World War II, British scout dogs, unnerved by heavy artillery fire, lost their sense of direction and failed to smell out the enemy.

In antiquity, guard dogs barked at the wrong time, and cavalry horses were spooked by elephants, while wounded war elephants panicked and crushed their own armies. Horses stampeded at the exotic scent of camels—who, for their part, "possessed an innate hatred for horses." What if incompatible species, say camels and horses, actually met on the battlefield? Pandemonium ensued—and that could work to a clever general's advantage.[17]

*　　*　　*

Some animal species instinctively loathed other species or panicked at the presence of unfamiliar beasts, and an unexpected confrontation of incompatible or hostile animals could cause violent confusion during a skirmish. Drafting various members of the animal kingdom into human warfare, in order to take advantage of the antipathy between, say, horses and elephants, constituted a biological strategy, in the sense of manipulating natural forces against the enemy. These ingenious schemes had devastating consequences for an unprepared army, but animal ruses like these aroused few qualms about fairness in antiquity. An intelligent commander might anticipate, or even prepare for ploys based on the natural anagonism among animals. Nevertheless, a leader who understood which kinds of creatures would immediately send the enemy's trained war animals into a frenzy could often gain the upper hand. When inter-species conflict suddenly erupted during a military engagement, some spectacular reverses of fortune resulted.

In 546 BC, for instance, King Cyrus of Persia was about to meet the formidable cavalry of King Croesus, the son of Alyattes, in Lydia. At the sight of the ranks of skilled Lydian cavalrymen armed with long spears massing on the plain, however, the Persian king's confidence plummeted. Cyrus was sure his cavalry would be bested. Herodotus tells us that one of Cyrus's advisors came up with an emergency plan based on his knowledge of animal antipathy. Knowing that a horse naturally "shuns the sight and the scent of a camel," the Persians unloaded their baggage train of camels, and placed them in the front line, keeping their own camel-tolerant cavalry in the rear. Before the battle even began, Croesus's proud cavalry was "rendered useless." At the first sight and scent of the dromedaries, the horses turned and galloped away, snorting in disgust and fear. Many of the Lydian foot-soldiers were trampled in the melee. Ever since that battle, most ancient armies kept a few camels among their horses, to acquaint them with their rank odor.

A couple of generations later, King Darius of Persia was galled and frustrated by the hit-and-run guerrilla tactics of the mounted Scythian archers, who made raids and then melted away, refusing to meet the Persians face to face. Darius knew that the Scythian cavalry was superior to his own, but felt certain that he could beat the nomads with his infantry, if only he could force them to stay and fight. Herodotus reports that the Persians enjoyed only one small advantage over the Scythians in skirmishes. Donkeys were completely unknown in Scythia, and during the battles the harsh hee-hawing of these Persian pack animals "so upset the nomads' horses . . . that they would constantly stop short, pricking up their ears in consternation." Darius, exasperated and running short on supplies, finally used his asses to cover his ignominious retreat from Scythia. As he slunk away by night, he left behind his donkeys, whose braying tricked the nomads into thinking the Persians were still there.

* * *

As noted earlier, the sight, sound, and odor of elephants threw untrained horses into chaos, and ancient military history records several disastrous defeats caused by horses (and men) turning tail at the novel appearance of elephants. The most famous example occurred in Britain in 55 BC, when the Britannis' chariot-horses fled at the sight of Julius Caesar's monstrous war elephant covered in iron scales and clanging bells emerging from a river with a tower of archers balanced on its back.

By the Hellenistic period, when war elephants became all the rage for the Ptolemies and Seleucids, commanders tried to obtain at least some elephants in order to condition their cavalry horses. In the second century BC, however, Perseus, a son of the Macedonian King Philip V, came up with an alternative plan to prepare his cavalry for an invasion by Romans who were bringing African and Indian war elephants. Perseus had artisans build and paint wooden models to resemble elephants, so that their size and shape would not intimidate his horses. Then he had pipers hide inside the huge mock-ups and, as these were rolled toward the horses, the pipers played "harsh, sharp trumpeting sounds" on their pipes. By this means, the Macedonian horses "learned to disdain the sight and sound of elephants."[14]

Over time, elephants became less of a novelty and ever more creative gambits were discovered to neutralize them in battle. Alexander the Great was the first to discover a surefire way to repulse elephants —by making use of elephants' natural aversion to pigs. Elephants were admired in antiquity as intelligent and tasteful lovers of all things beautiful; they appreciated perfumes, lovely women, flowers, music, and so on. By the same token, these wrinkled, gray, lumbering beasts, capable of ear-piercing trumpeting, abhorred ugly things and were especially agitated by discordant sounds. Their highly developed aesthetic sensibilities could be turned against them in battle.

Legend has it that Alexander the Great learned this important bit of local knowledge from King Porus, who became Alexander's ally after Porus's defeat in 326 BC. Alexander had a chance to test the repellent effect of swine on elephants in India when his scout reported that about one thousand wild elephants were approaching the camp from the forest. On Porus's advice, Alexander ordered his Thracian horsemen to take some pigs and trumpets and ride out to meet the elephant herd. Porus assured Alexander that if the pigs could be caused to keep squealing they could overcome the elephants. Indeed, as soon as the great beasts heard the harsh sound of the pigs combined with the Thracian trumpets, they fled back into the forest.

The Romans discovered a similar technique in 280–275 BC, when Pyrrhus was wearily marching the surviving twelve of his original twenty war elephants across Italy. The Romans noticed that the pachyderms were unnerved by the sight of rams with horns and that they could not abide the high-pitched squeals of swine. Aelian says that both of these domestic animals were used to deflect the elephants of Pyrrhus, perhaps helping to account for his heavy losses of men and beasts.

In antiquity, the use of special sensory effects—sound, smell, and sight—to terrify war animals—or human foes—was considered an unconventional but fair tactic. For example, the Roman historian Tacitus described the psychological effects of the *baritus*, the hair-raising war-cry of the Germanic tribes intended to demoralize the enemy. The chanting warriors produced a "harsh, intermittent roar," which rose to a reverberating crescendo as they held their shields in front of their mouths to amplify the thunderous sound. Ways of producing "horrible sounds," optical illusions, and explosive noises to

FIGURE 34. *A squealing pig was an effective weapon against war elephants. Red-figure kylix, about 490 BC, detail.*

(University of Pennsylvania Museum)

disorient and frighten enemies were also described in ancient Indian and Chinese war manuals. As we've seen, assaults on sensitivity to odors—the stink of unfamiliar or hated species—could send an enemy's war animals into chaos, but offensive smells could be directed against humans as well. Strabo, for instance, described the overpowering reek of the poison arrows of the Soanes of Colchis as being injurious to victims even if they were not wounded.

The ancient experiments with unbearable noise and odors used against enemies and their war animals have been revived with modern research into "non-lethal" weapons directed against humans. Military scientists have created malordorants (repulsive smells to trigger incapacitating nausea) and very loud, low-frequency sounds, like the deafening rock music that was blasted day and night by U.S. Loudspeaker Teams during the siege of Panamanian general Manuel Noriega in 1989, and again, in Iraq, during the Gulf War of 1991. Even more damaging are new infrasound wave transmitters, which induce hallucinations and incapacitating nausea (and possibly internal injury and death).[15]

*   *   *

Alexander had used fire—red-hot bronze statues—and, in a separate incident, noisy pigs, against elephants. Not long after Pyrrhus's retreat from Italy in 275 BC, fire and pigs were combined in a single devilish plan to repel war elephants.

In about 270 BC, Antigonus Gonatus, the Macedonian ruler of Greece, massed his Indian war elephants to besiege the city of Megara (between Athens and Corinth). The resourceful Megarians knew the folk wisdom that elephants had a terror of squealing hogs but decided to take a further step. They smeared a bunch of pigs with flammable liquid pitch, set them on fire, and released them. These living torpedoes made a beeline for Antigonus's lines of war-trained elephants. As the shrieking, flaming pigs rushed the elephants, the behemoths panicked. Made frantic by the sight, the noise, and the smell of the desperate burning pigs, the elephants fled trumpeting in all directions, breaking the siege. Antigonus's confused rout at Megara must have been one of the most spectacular retreats on record. The sticky pitch-fueled flames that tortured the pigs at Megara were intended to maximize their squealing, rather than to burn the enemy forces. But one could say that the Megarian stratagem of setting pigs afire with combustible resin created the first hybrid biological-chemical weapon.

"In the future," commented Polyaenus, "Antigonus ordered his Indian suppliers to raise the young war elephants in the company of pigs," so the beasts would become accustomed to their appearance, smell, and shrill voices.

The last recorded use of a pig against an elephant occurred at the siege of Edessa, held by the Romans in the time of the Emperor Justinian (sixth century AD). Chosroes, king of the Persians, stormed the city, sending his biggest elephant with many soldiers on top right up to the circuit wall. Just as the Persians were about to clamber over the wall and capture the city, the quick-witted Romans grabbed a pig and suspended it directly in the face of the startled elephant. The dry-witted historian Procopius writes: "As the pig was hanging there, he very naturally gave vent to sundry squeals, and this angered the elephant so that he got out of control." Confusion swept back in waves through the entire Persian army and, panic-stricken, they fled in great disorder.[16]

Fire plus animals was a combination guaranteed to wreak havoc against the enemy, as Frontinus and Appian proved in their description of a Spanish strategy against Hannibal's father, Hamilcar Barca, in 229 BC. The Spanish front lines consisted of steer-drawn carts filled with combustibles: pitch, animal tallow, and sulphur. These carts of fuel were set afire and driven into the Carthaginian lines, causing screaming panic. Nine-year-old Hannibal went along with his father on the conquest of Spain. Perhaps he recalled the combination of steers and fire when he engineered his own rout of the Romans in 218 BC, by means of the cattle-horn torches, described earlier.

The use of animals as a delivery system to carry flammable materials occurred elsewhere in the ancient world. Chinese and Arabic military manuals, for example, suggested smearing crows and other birds with incendiary substances to set fire to enemy tents, and Kautilya's *Arthashastra* recommended attaching incendiary powders to birds, cats, mongooses, and monkeys. The flammable packages were lit and the creatures were dispatched to burn down thatched-roof structures and wooden forts. It's not clear how these involuntary suicide bombers were persuaded to zero in on the right targets (this is precisely the problem that has now been solved with the creation of remote-controlled rats and other species that can be directed to specific targets, described above). Kautilya anticipated the problem, though: he suggested capturing only vultures, crows, and pigeons that nested in the besieged city walls. They could be trusted to fly back to their nests with the flammable powders.

Genghis Khan relied on the same "homing" principle on a large scale during his conquest of China in AD 1211. During his siege of several fortified cities, it is said that he offered to lift the siege in exchange for "1,000 cats and 10,000 swallows. "These were duly handed over," writes the historian David Morgan, and the Mongols tied flammable materials to the tails of the birds and cats and ignited them. When the creatures were released, they fled home, setting each city on fire, and Genghis Khan easily stormed the burning cities.

In other cases, perhaps intelligent animals were trained beforehand, to offset the potential for serious backfire. In 2003, during the invasion of Iraq, it was reported that Morocco offered U.S. military two thousand monkeys from the Atlas Mountains trained to deactivate and detonate land mines. Trained primates also figure in a Chinese account from 1610 claiming that the General Tseh-ki-kwang trained several hundred monkeys from Mount Shi-Chu in Fu Tsing to shoot firearms. When the monkey militia was ordered to fire on Japanese raiders, the marauders were so terror-stricken that the general's soldiers hiding in ambush were able to slay them all. The animal guerrillas must have been taught not to shoot at their Chinese handlers.

Friendly fire accidents caused by confused creatures carrying incendiaries would fall into the category of medieval folklore and modern urban legends collectively known as "the revenge of the exploding animal." These tales recount the ironic consequences of tying dynamite, firecrackers, or other burning material to dogs, cats, or birds, or tossing live grenades at sharks, and so on, who inevitably circle back toward their tormentors. One Indian folktale, for example, about a flaming cat burning down a village, was collected in Kashmir. Another medieval European tale tells of a flock of birds set afire by besiegers to burn down a city. The actual use of such tactics in antiquity may be the origin of these folk motifs.

Perhaps the last instance of an animal-on-fire weapon was used by Tamerlane, the great conqueror from the East in 1398, to sack Delhi, which was protected by the Indian sultan's 120 war elephants. Tamerlane's warriors were usually mounted on war camels, but for this battle, Tamerlane loaded the camels with straw and ignited the bundles. As the flaming camels raced forward, the sultan's elephants fled in panic.[17]

The image of terrified burning pigs or awkward flaming camels may seem amusing in a macabre way, but it only takes a slight shift of perspective to imagine the terror and pain that would be experienced by human beings set afire with unquenchable, corrosive flames. And that brings us to the final chapter, about ancient chemical incendiaries, culminating in some of the most inhumane weapons ever devised.

Infernal Fire

> Attacked by a terrible stream of
> consuming fire, her flesh fell from her
> bones, like resin from a pine-torch,
> a sight dreadful to behold.
> —Euripides, *Medea*, 431 BC

THE PRINCESS DONNED the gown, a gift from the sorceress Medea, and twirled before the looking glass. Suddenly the gown burst into flames. Like Hercules in his envenomed tunic, the princess tried to tear off the flaming dress, but the material stuck to her skin, creating a fire so hot that it melted the flesh from her bones. Engulfed by "clinging streams of unnatural, devouring fire," she dashed outside and threw herself into a fountain. But water only made the fire burn more intensely. Her father, King Creon, tried to smother the flames, but he too caught fire. Both perished, burned alive. The blaze spread, destroying the entire palace and everyone inside.

This scene from Euripides' *Medea*, based on ancient Greek myth, was performed in Athens in 431 BC. It describes a terrible fire weapon concocted by Medea of Colchis, who had helped her lover Jason, and his Argonauts, find the Golden Fleece. When Jason abandoned Medea, she took revenge on his new love, the Corinthian princess Glauke. She treated a beautiful gown with secret substances that "stored up the powers of fire," sealed the gift in an airtight casket, and delivered it to the unsuspecting princess.

How did Medea create such an extraordinary conflagration? The graphic details—and the popularity of the story in Greek and Roman literature and art—suggest that some real but unusual fire phenomenon inspired the legend. The notion that materials could be made to suddenly combust in the presence of water or heat must have been plausible to audiences as early as the fifth century BC.

Some, like Diodorus of Sicily, speculated that Medea knew of a magical "little root" that, once set afire, was impossible to extinguish. But, according to Euripides, Medea combined special volatile substances which had to be sealed from air, light, moisture, and heat. The violent combustion resulted in flames that were clinging, corrosive, extremely hot, and unquenchable by water—much like modern napalm in its ghastly effects. The myth points to knowledge of chemical weapons more than one thousand years before the invention of Greek Fire in the seventh century AD.[1]

Fire itself has been a weapon "from the first time an angry hominid snatched a burning brand from a campfire and threw it at the cause of his wrath," writes historian Alfred Crosby in *Throwing Fire*. More than two millennia before Crosby, the Roman philosopher Lucretius had written that fire became a weapon as soon as men learned to kindle sparks. In Greek myth, the hero Hercules used burning arrows and torches to destroy the Hydra monster, and blazing arrows were shot by heroes of the great Indian epics, the "Mahabharata" and "Ramayana."

Fire arrows were a very early invention in human history and Assyrian reliefs from the ninth century BC show attackers and defenders exchanging volleys of burning arrows and firepots, apparently filled with local oil, over fortified walls. In ancient India, fire weapons were common enough to be forbidden in the *Laws of Manu*, which proscribed kings from using "weapons made red-hot with fire or tipped with burning materials," although Kautilya's *Arthashasta* and several other Indian treatises of the same era give many recipes for creating chemical fire projectiles and smoke weapons. Meanwhile, in China, during the Warring States period of feudal conflicts (403–221 BC), Sun Tzu's *Art of War* and other military treatises advocated ways to deploy fire and smoke to terrify foes.² The inventory of fire armaments devised in antiquity is impressive in its variety, beginning with burning arrows and progressing to chemical additives and sophisticated incendiary technologies.

*   *   *

The first incendiary missiles were arrows wrapped with flammable plant fibers (flax, hemp, or straw, often referred to as tow) and set afire. Burning arrows of these materials could be very effective in destroying wooden walls from a safe distance. Indeed, Athens was captured by flaming hemp arrows in 480 BC, when the Persians invaded Greece. Xerxes had already destroyed many Greek cities with fire and, as the grand Persian army approached Athens, the populace was evacuated to the countryside. A few priests and poor and infirm citizens were left behind to defend the Acropolis. These defenders put up barricades of planks and timber around the Temple of Athena and managed to hold off the Persians for a time by rolling boulders down the slopes of the Acropolis. But, in the first recorded use of fire projectiles on Greek soil, the Persians shot fiery arrows to burn down the wooden barricades.

FIGURE 35 *Greek warrior assaulting a city wall with a burning pine-resin torch. Campanian neck-amphora, about 375 BC.*

(The J. Paul Getty Museum)

The Persians then swarmed over the Acropolis, slaughtering all the Athenians in the temple and burning everything to the ground.

But simple flaming missiles of straw were "insufficiently destructive and murderous" to satisfy ancient strategists for long, notes Alfred Crosby. They were not much use against stone walls, and ordinary fires could be doused with water. "What was wanted was something that would burn fiercely, adhere stubbornly, and resist being put out by water." What kinds of chemical additives would produce fires strong enough to burn walls and machines, capture cities, and destroy enemies?

The first additive was a plant chemical, pitch, the flammable resin tapped from pine trees. Later, distillations of pitch into crude turpentine were available. Resinous fires burned hotly and the sticky sap resisted water. Arrows could be dipped in pitch and ignited, or one could set fires fueled with pitch to burn the enemy's equipment. Other mineral accelerants for making hotter and more combustible weapons were discovered, too.[3]

The earliest evidence that flaming arrows were used by a Greek army appears in Thucydides' *History of the Peloponnesian War*. In 429 BC, the Spartans besieged the city of Plataia, an ally of Athens, and used a full panoply of siege techniques against the stubborn Plataians. We know the Spartans used fire arrows, because the Plataians protected their wooden palisades with what would later become the standard defense against flaming projectiles—they hung curtains of untanned animal skins over the walls. Then, the Plataians lassoed the Spartans' siege engines, winching them into the air and letting them crash to the ground. With their machines smashed and with their archers unable to ignite the rawhide-covered walls, the Spartans advanced beyond mere flaming arrows, into the as-yet-unexplored world of chemical fuels. This event occurred just two years after Euripides' play about Medea's mysterious recipe for "unnatural fire."

The Spartans heaped up a massive mound of firewood right next to the city wall. Then they added liberal quantities of pine-tree sap and, in a bold innovation, sulphur. Sulphur is the chemical element found in acrid-smelling, yellow, green and white mineral deposits in volcanic areas, around hot springs, and in limestone and gypsum matrix. Sulphur was also called brimstone, which means "burning stone." Volcanic eruptions were observed to create flowing rivers and lakes of burning sulphur, scenes that corresponded to ancient visions of Hell with its lakes of fire. In antiquity, clods and liquid forms of sulphur had many uses, from medicine and pesticides to bleaching togas. Sulphur's highly flammable nature also made it a very attractive incendiary in war. "No other substance is more easily ignited," wrote Pliny, "which shows that sulphur contains a powerful abundance of fire."

When the Spartans ignited the great woodpile at Plataia, the combination of pitch and sulphur "produced such a conflagration as had never been seen before, greater than any fire produced by human agency," declared Thucydides. Indeed, the blue sulphur flames and the acrid stench must have been sensational, and the fumes also would have been quite destructive, since the combustion of sulphur creates toxic sulphur dioxide gas, which can kill if inhaled in large enough quantities. The Plataians abandoned their posts on the burning palisades. Much of the wall was destroyed, but then the wind reversed and the great fire eventually subsided after a severe thunderstorm. Plataia was saved by what must have seemed to be divine intervention against the Spartans' technological innovation. Notably, this also happens to be the earliest recorded use of a chemically enhanced incendiary that created a poison gas, although it is not clear that the Spartans were aware of that deadly side effect when they threw sulphur on the flames.

Defenders quickly learned to use chemically fed fires against besiegers. Writing in about 360 BC, Aeneas the Tactician's book on how to survive sieges devoted a section to fires supplemented with chemicals. He recommended pouring pitch down on the enemy soldiers or onto their siege machines, followed by bunches of hemp and lumps of sulphur, which would stick to the coating of pitch. Then, one used ropes to immediately let down burning bundles of kindling to ignite the pitch and sulphur. Aeneas also described a kind of spiked wooden "bomb" filled with blazing material that could be dropped onto siege engines. The iron spikes would embed the device into the wooden frame of the machine and both would be consumed by flames. Another defense strategy was to simply "fill bags with pitch, sulphur, tow, powdered frankincense gum, pine shavings, and sawdust." Set afire, these sacks could be hurled from the walls to burn the men below.

During the grueling year-long siege of the island of Rhodes by Demetrius Poliorcetes ("The Besieger") in 304 BC, both sides hurled resinous missiles—firepots and flaming arrows. On moonless nights during the siege, wrote Diodorus of Sicily, "the fire-missiles burned bright as they hurtled violently through the air." The morning after a particularly spectacular night attack, Demetrius Poliorcetes had his men collect and count the fire missiles. He was startled by the vast resources of the city. In a single night, the Rhodians had fired more than eight hundred fiery projectiles of various sizes, and fifteen hundred catapult bolts. Rhodes' resistance was successful, and Poliorcetes withdrew with his reputation tarnished, abandoning his valuable siege equipment. From the sale of his machines, the Rhodians financed the building of the Colossus of Rhodes astride their harbor, one of the Seven Wonders of the Ancient World.

Technological advances in fire arrows were reported by the Roman historians Silius Italicus and Tacitus, who describe the large fire-bolt (the *falarica*), a machine-fired spear with a long iron tip that had been dipped in burning pitch and sulphur. (The opening scene of the 2000 Hollywood film "Gladiator" showed the Roman *falarica* in action in a night battle in Germany). The burning spears were "like thunderbolts, cleaving the air like meteors," wrote Silius Italicus. The carnage was appalling. The battlefield was strewn with "severed, smoking limbs" carried through the air by the bolts, and "men and their weapons were buried under the blazing ruins of the siege towers."

Machine-fired fire-bolts and catapulted firepots of sulphur and bitumen were used to defend Aquileia (northeastern Italy) when that city managed to hold off the long siege by the hated emperor Maximinus in AD 236 (his own demoralized soldiers slew him in his tent outside the city walls). Later, incendiary mixtures were packed *inside* the hollow wooden shafts of the bolts. Vegetius, a military engineer of AD 390, gives one recipe for the ammunition: sulphur, resin, tar, and hemp soaked in oil.

Ammianus Marcellinus (fourth century AD) described fire-darts shot from bows. Hollow cane shafts were skillfully reinforced with iron and punctured with many small holes on the underside (to provide oxygen for combustion). The cavity was filled with bituminous materials. (In antiquity, *bitumen* was a catchall term for petroleum products such as asphalt, tar, naphtha, and natural gas.) These fire-darts had to be shot with a weak bow, however, since high velocity could extinguish the fire in the shaft. Once they hit their target, the fire was ferocious. They flared up upon contact with water, marveled Ammianus, and the flames could only be put out by depriving the blaze of oxygen, by smothering it with sand.[4]

The fire-dart sounds similar to the Chinese fire-lance, invented in about AD 900. This was a bamboo (later, metal) tube with one opening, packed with sulphur, charcoal, and small amounts of the "fire chemical" (explosive saltpeter or nitrate salts, a key ingredient of gunpowder). The tube was affixed to a lance with a kind of pump, which Crosby describes as "a sort of five-minute flame thrower." At first, they "spewed nothing but flame," but soon the Chinese added sand and other irritants like sharp shards of pottery and metal shrapnel, and many different kinds of poisons, such as toxic plants, arsenic, and excrement, to the saltpeter mixture. As Robert Temple, historian of ancient Chinese science, remarked, "Bizarre and terrible poisons were mixed together" to make bombs and grenades. "Practically every animal, plant, and mineral poison imaginable was combined," for "there hardly seemed to be a deadly substance unknown to them."

In India, a military manual by Shukra, the *Nitishastra* (dated to the beginning of the Christian era) describes tubular projectiles thrown by devices used by the infantry and cavalry. The tube, about three feet long, contained saltpeter, sulphur, and charcoal, with other optional ingredients, such as iron filings, lead, and realgar (arsenic). The tubes shot iron or lead balls by "the touch of fire" ignited "by the pressure of flint." Shukra remarked that "war with [these] mechanical instruments leads to great destruction."[5]

*　　*　　*

"In practice," speculates one modern historian of incendiaries, the earliest fire weapons were probably used "against large, inflammable targets at close range," such as wooden walls and ships. Indeed, the Spartans' great sulphur and pitch conflagration at Plataia was piled next to the walls of the fort. In a navel battle during the Hannibalic War, the Roman general Gnaeus Scipio fashioned early Molotov cocktails, by lighting jars filled with pitch and resin and hurling them onto the wooden decks of Carthaginian ships.

Lucan (a Roman writer of the first century AD) writes of casting burning torches dipped in oil and sulphur onto ships' decks and shooting arrows smeared with burning pitch or wax to ignite the flaxen sails. To make the arrows "burn even more vehemently," the archers soon learned to melt a mixture of varnish, oil and petroleum, colophon (dense black residue of turpentine boiled down with "sharp" vinegar), and sulphur. Lucan's description of one firefight at sea is harrowing. Fire, fed by chemicals and the extremely flammable wax caulking of the ships, coursed swiftly through the riggings. It consumed the rowers' wooden benches and spread everywhere, even over the water itself. Houses near the shore also caught fire, as wind fanned the conflagration. Such fire weapons were clearly intended to destroy the ship and the crew, and the victims faced the choice of burning or drowning. Some sailors clung to blazing planks in the waves, terrified of drowning, while others grappled with the enemy amid the burning wreckage, thinking it best to go down fighting.

Wooden ships were not just good targets, their flammability also made them attractive delivery systems for fire. During the ill-fated

Athenian attack on Sicily in 413 BC, for example, the Syracusans came
up with a creative deployment of resinated fire in a naval battle. They
loaded an old merchant ship with faggots of torch-pine, set it alight,
and simply let the wind blow the ship of fire toward the Athenians' fleet
of wooden triremes. Frontinus, the Roman strategist, reported that in
48 BC, the commander Cassius, also fighting in Sicily, copied the
Syracusans and filled several decrepit transport vessels with burning
wood, and "set them with a fair wind" to destroy the enemy fleet. Fire-
ship tactics required favorable winds, of course, or else the boomerang
effect could be disastrous.

The most stupendous fire ship of all was manufactured in 332 BC,
by the Phoenicians, during Alexander the Great's famous siege of Tyre
(an island city on the coast of Lebanon). The historians Arrian and
Quintus Curtius described the ship as a floating chemical firebomb. The
Phoenician engineers fitted a very large transport ship (originally used
for carrying cavalry horses) with two masts and yardarms. From these
they suspended four cauldrons brimming with sulphur, bitumen, and
"every sort of material apt to kindle and nourish flame." The foredeck
of the ship was packed with cedar torches, pitch, and other flammables,
and the hold was filled with dry brush liberally laced with more chemical combustibles.

Waiting until the wind was favorable, Phoenician rowers towed
the great fire ship right up to the offensive mole (a pier extending from
the shore to the fortified island) erected by Alexander's men. The mole
had two movable towers and many ballistic engines behind its palisades, all protected with curtains of raw hides in case of flaming
arrows. But the Macedonians were unprepared for the unstoppable
ship of flames. The Phoenicians ignited the transport and then rowed
like mad to crash the burning mass into the mole. They escaped by
jumping overboard and swimming to skiffs that returned them to
safety. On impact with the mole, the cauldrons on the burning ship
spilled their flammable contents, further accelerating the flames.
Propelled by the wind, the raging chemical fire incinerated Alexander's

palisades and his siege engines. The Macedonians on the mole were either consumed by flames or leaped into the sea. The Phoenicians chopped at the desperate swimmers' hands with stakes and rocks until the men drowned or were taken prisoner.[6]

The casualties and destruction of the mole did not end Alexander's siege, nor was the fire ship the last of the fiendish incendiary devices thought up by the Phoenician engineers of Tyre. The Phoenicians, noted Diodorus of Sicily, realized that the Macedonians possessed superior hand-to-hand fighting qualities. They needed an antipersonnel weapon to "offset such a courageous enemy." There is a clear sense of disapproval in Diodorus's account, deploring the cowardice of those who turn to chemical weapons to defeat honorable warriors.

The Phoenician engineers "devised an ingenious and horrible torment which even the bravest could not deflect," wrote Diodorus. They filled enormous shallow bowls of iron and bronze with fine sand and tiny bits of metal. These pans they roasted over a great fire until the sand glowed red-hot. "By means of an unknown apparatus" (a catapult of some sort), the Phoenicians cast the burning sand "over those Macedonians who were fighting most boldly and brought them utter misery." There was no escape for anyone within range of the sand. The molten grains and red-hot shrapnel "sifted down under the soldiers' breastplates and seared their skin with the intense heat, inflicting unavoidable pain." Alexander's men writhed, trying to pull off their armor and shake out the burning sand. "Shrieking like those under torture, in excruciating agony, Alexander's men went mad and died." The scene at Tyre brings to life in astonishing detail the mythic image of Hercules struggling to escape from his burning tunic.

The rain of burning sand at Tyre, created more than two millennia ago, also has an uncanny resemblance to the effects of modern metal incendiaries, such as magnesium and thermite. Burning particles of magnesium and molten iron are dispersed by the combustion of intensely hot metal bombs and splatter on victims, making myriad small but extremely deep burns. The high-temperature metallic embers, just like the red-hot sand, penetrate far into the skin and keep on burning, causing deep tissue injury and death.[7]

* * *

A century after Alexander's tribulations with burning weapons at Tyre, the Syracusans invented a long-range thermal weapon of amazing effectiveness. During the Roman siege of Syracuse in 212 BC, Archimedes, the brilliant philosopher-mathematician, was commissioned by King Hiero to develop ingenious ways of defending Syracuse. The elderly engineer developed an array of formidable weapons that were used against the Romans, from catapults that hurled burning fireballs to gargantuan grappling cranes that lifted warships completely out of the water and smashed them down with such force that they sank.

But the most celebrated weapon invented by Archimedes was essentially a heat ray used against the Roman navy commanded by Claudius Marcellus. According to ancient accounts, Archimedes had soldiers polish the concave surfaces of their bronze shields to a mirror finish. Then he assembled them to stand in a parabola shape and tip their shields to create a huge reflective surface to focus the sun's rays onto the Roman ships' riggings. Like burning ants or matchsticks with a magnifying glass, the intense heat of the concentrated rays caused the sails and wooden masts to catch fire instantaneously. Marcellus's fleet was reduced to ashes. He gave up the naval blockade and finally captured Syracuse "by thirst."

Marcellus ordered his men to capture Archimedes alive, thinking that the Romans could learn from him (this appears to be the first recorded instance of the practice of capturing or giving immunity to enemy biochemical weapons scientists). But the old man was killed during the brutal sack of the city. Marcellus buried the scientist with honor, decorating his tomb with a geometric cylinder and sphere. The grave was long forgotten, until it was discovered in a bramble patch outside the gates of Syracuse by the Roman orator Cicero, more than a century later. About seven hundred years after Syracuse, in AD 515, the philosopher Proklos was said to have used Archimedes' mirror technique to burn the ships sent by Vitalianus against the Emperor Anastasios.

Since the Enlightenment, many scientists have undertaken complex calculations and experiments to learn whether Archimedes' method could have worked. The first series of experiments, by Count Buffon of the Paris Museum of Natural History in 1747, used mirrors to instantly ignite a pine plank 150 feet away. The most recent test was carried out in 1975 by a Greek scientist, Dr. I. Sakkas. He lined up sixty Greek sailors each holding a mirror shaped like an oblong shield. In concert, they tilted the mirrors to direct the sun's rays at a wooden ship 160 feet away. It caught fire immediately.[8]

According to the Latin sources, Marcellus's Roman sailors were sent into deepening panic at each new weapon deployment, with many believing that the Syracusans were being aided by the gods or by magic. The burning ray that caused their ships to suddenly burst into flame must have seemed like a bolt from the heavens. Indeed, the impressive effects of long-range thermal-ray weapons continue to be sought by weapons designers today. A burning ray in the form of a laser gun that incinerated victims was apparently one of many sophisticated secret weapons tested by the United States during its invasion of Panama, in 1989, according to interviews with medical personnel and eyewitnesses. And a burning ray is the feature of another secret weapon recently developed by the U.S. military: in 2001, the Pentagon unveiled an antipersonnel weapon that fires a beam of intense heat more than a third of a mile. The painful burning sensation, caused by the same microwave energy used to heat food is, however, supposed to disperse crowds without actually cooking or killing anyone. The idea is to mount the microwave ray gun on a military vehicle and point it at individuals or groups. "It's safe, completely safe," said Colonel George Fenton, the director of the U.S. Joint Non-Lethal Weapons Directorate, in 2001. "You walk out of the beam [and] there's no long term effect, none, zero, zip." Critics point out, however, that severe burns could result if the beam is focused on someone long enough, say someone already incapacitated by other "nonlethal" weaponry such as tear gas or calmative mists—or immobilized in a crowd. That person might be as unable to escape as a Macedonian trapped in the range of the burning sand at Tyre, or a Roman sailor who happened to be in the riggings when Archimedes aimed his heat ray.[9]

*   *   *

Bows and arrows, Archimedes' mirrors, and burning ships proved to be good systems for delivering fire. Torsion catapult technology (based on the spring-tension of ropes made of elastic materials such as sinew or hair), invented in about 350 BC, greatly expanded the horizons for hurling fire-pots and fiery projectiles over the walls of cities, and onto vessels. An even earlier invention for propelling fire, a remarkable flame-blowing contraption, was created at a very early date, in 424 BC, by Sparta's allies during the Peloponnesian War, the Boeotians.

This device was built just four years after the Spartans had created the super-conflagration at Plataia, which had ultimately failed due to shifting wind. The design of the primitive Boeotian flamethrower got around the problems encountered by the Spartans at Plataia by creating man-made wind. The device had a large capacity but a short range, like modern flamethrowers. Thucydides described how the flamethrower destroyed the wooden fortifications at Delium, held by the Athenians. The Boeotians hollowed out a huge wooden log and plated it with iron. They suspended a large cauldron from the log by a chain attached to one end of the hollow beam, and an iron tube was inserted through the length of the hollow beam, curving down into the cauldron, which was filled with lighted coals, sulphur, and pitch. The apparatus was mounted on a cart and wheeled right up to the wall. At that point the Boeotians attached a very large blacksmith's bellows to their end of the beam and pumped great blasts of air through the tube to direct the chemical fire and gases in the cauldron at the wall. The walls and many defenders were incinerated as they attempted to flee their posts, and Delium was captured.[10]

A similar flamethrowing device—with the surprising addition of vinegar to the combustibles—was devised by Apollodorus of Damascus, the military engineer for Roman emperors in the second century AD. The addition of vinegar reputedly allowed the flamethrower to destroy stone fortification walls. Historians such as Dio Cassius and Vitruvius also reported that vinegar and fire in combination could shatter rock, but modern scholars have puzzled over how vinegar could accomplish this. The use of vinegar and fire for breaking up stone was first described by the historians Livy and Pliny, in their accounts of how Hannibal's engineers solved a logistics problem while crossing the Alps in 218 BC. To clear a landslide obstructing Hannibal's route in the mountains, the Carthaginians felled large trees into a pile on top of the rock slide, then set them on fire. When the huge bonfire had caused the rocks fall to glow red, they poured vinegar on the rocks, which instantly disintegrated.

The ancient claims that vinegar and fire could somehow destroy walls and the story of Hannibal's feat were long ridiculed as legends, until scientific experiments in 1992 proved that rocks heated to high temperatures will indeed fracture if a considerable quantity of acidic vinegar is splashed on the hot stone. Further experiments with sour red wine (the source of vinegar in antiquity) produced even more violent results, as the hot rocks sizzled and cracked apart. The scientists found that the chemical reaction worked best on limestone and marble, which happened to be the favorite building stone for ancient fortification walls.[11]

*   *   *

With the multitude of types of fire weapons proliferating through the ages, methods of defense against them were sought. Aeneas the Tactician advised that those fighting flaming weapons should shield their faces if possible. He also recommended covering wooden parapets or walls with felt or raw animal hides, the practice carried out by the

Plataians defending against Spartan fire arrows, and by the Macedonians besieging Tyre.

Alum (double sulphate of aluminum and potassium) was known as a fire retardant that could prevent wood combustion: it was mined in Egypt and Pontus. After the temple of Delphi burned down in 548 BC, for example, King Amasis of Egypt sent a large quantity (one thousand talents) of alum to fireproof the timber used for rebuilding. King Mithridates of Pontus fireproofed the wooden towers of his fortresses with alum in 87 BC, and in AD 296 the emperor Constantine fireproofed his siege engines with alum against Persian incendiaries.

Incendiaries containing sulphur, resins, tar, or petroleum would stick tenaciously to any surface and could only be put out with difficulty, using sand or dirt, wrote Aeneas. To protect siege machines from chemical fires or melted lead poured from above, he suggested that the housings should be covered with clay mixed with hair, or wet mud. Advice on protecting men from chemical burns is notably nonexistent in Aeneas and other ancient Greek and Roman military manuals. In India, however, it was believed that certain ointments rubbed on the skin could protect a soldier from burns and Kautilya's military treatise of the fourth century BC told how to make fire-resistant salves from sticky plant juices and frog skin. Muslim military books gave recipes for fire retardants that called for a paste of talc, eggwhites, gum, and "salamander-skin" (an early name for the fire-resistant mineral asbestos).

Another well-known fire retardant in antiquity was vinegar, despite its ability to shatter stone when heated. "If the enemy attempts to set fires with highly combustible materials" such as pitch and sulphur, water cannot soak into or wet the fire, wrote Aeneas. Only "vinegar will put it out and also makes it difficult to restart the fire." In 74 BC, the city of Cyzicus on the Black Sea successfully beat back Mithridates' siege and managed to extinguish his fire missiles with vinegar, just as Aeneas advised.

Defenders using vinegar to put out flames directed at their stone walls would have to take care lest they cause their own heated walls to crack, however, and the besiegers could also use vinegar to resist burning materials thrown on them by defenders. To protect siege equipment, Polyaenus recommended that vinegar, "particularly good at extinguishing every kind of fire," should be poured or sponged periodically onto wooden siege machines. Vinegar could also help neutralize choking fumes from fires: Pliny noted its beneficial effects on sneezing and other respiratory problems. Interestingly, in skirmishes between political dissidents and riot police today, the sharp odor of vinegar often hangs in the air; protestors routinely soak handkerchiefs in vinegar and hold them over their faces to counteract the pepper and tear gas sprayed by the police.[12]

*　　*　　*

Burning materials often produce toxic, asphyxiating smoke and this potentially useful aspect of incendiaries was not overlooked in antiquity. Aeneas, for example, advised defenders to build smoky fires and channel the smoke toward besiegers who were attempting to tunnel under walls. This "will be injurious to the men inside and may even kill many of them." A Chinese historical text, *Mo Zi,* written around the same time, told how to lower burning bundles of kindling, hemp, and reeds, by chains into tunnels to smoke out diggers: "The enemy will immediately die."

Smoke could be used by attackers, too, as the Spartans proved when they created the sulphur and resin fire at Plataia in 429 BC. To overtake Cromium in Sicily in about 397 BC, the Carthaginian general Himilco created a fire with thick black smoke that blew into the eyes of his enemies. Smoke from ordinary fires can be very harmful, even deadly, but sulphurous fumes from chemically activated fires, like at Plataia, would be even more toxic and lethal.

One could create choking, irritating gases by burning particularly noxious substances. The Chinese had created poisonous smoke clouds by burning sulphur and arsenic to fumigate insects as early as the seventh century BC, a practice that may have led to their interest in

FIGURE 36. *Noxious substances could be burned to create toxic smoke. Here, two men make a smoky fire. Attic vase painting, 510 BC.*

(Toledo Museum of Art, Libbey Endowment, Gift of Edward Drummond Libbey)

developing toxic gases for military use. Ancient Chinese writings contain hundreds of recipes for producing irritating fogs and fumes, and incendiary-weapons manuals also give directions for making poisonous smoke balls. One extremely effective smoke ball compound called for powdered aconite root and wolfbane (species of lethal monkshood), croton beans (a drastic purgative that also causes blisters and pustules), the poisonous mineral arsenic, hallucinogenic hemp, blister beetles, toxic sulphur, plus charcoal and resin.

In the fourth century BC, the *Arthashastra* provided formulas for creating burning powders whose fumes were supposed to drive enemies mad or blind, or cause them to sicken or perish immediately. Different smoke powders were concocted from the droppings of certain reptiles, animals, and birds, and mixed with genuine poisons and intoxicants. One lethal cloud was created by burning the bodies of venomous snakes and stinging insects along with the seeds of toxic plants and hot peppers. (Incidentally, hot peppers were used against enemies in the New World, too: in the sixteenth and seventeenth centuries, Caribbean and Brazilian Indians produced an early form of pepper spray against the

Spanish conquistadors by burning piles of ground-up hot pepper seeds.) In India, turpentine and tree resins, charcoal, and wax were the flammable components of smoke powders.

Poisonous smokes that combined magical and toxic ingredients intended to kill or disorient enemies also appeared in ancient Greek and early medieval alchemy treatises. For example, Hippolytus (AD 230) claimed that burning powdered magnets would produce a deadly smoke. The addition of weasel feces to the magnets was supposed to create the sensation of an earthquake to terrify the foe.

Noxious smoke was hard to control and direct, and therefore most effective when employed in confined spaces like tunnels. As early as the fourth century BC, defenders of fortresses in China burned toxic substances and plants such as mustard seeds in furnaces connected by pipes to ox-hide bellows to pump poison gases into tunnels dug by attackers. In western Greece in AD 189, during the long Roman siege of Ambracia, the defenders invented a smoke machine to repel the Romans attempting to tunnel under the city walls. The Ambracians prepared a very large jar equal in size to the tunnel, bored a hole in the bottom, and inserted an iron tube. Packing the giant pot with layers of fine chicken feathers (burning feathers were known to create nasty fumes) and smouldering charcoal, they capped it with a perforated lid. They aimed the lidded end of the jar at the tunnelers and fitted blacksmith's bellows to the iron tube at the other end. With this device—which calls to mind the primitive flamethrower at Delium—the Ambracians filled the passage with clouds of acrid smoke, sending the choking Romans hurrying to the surface. "They abandoned their subterranean siege," was Polyaenus's succinct comment.

Tunnelers mining under towers would employ wooden timbers to temporarily prop up the structure and then set them afire to cave in the tower. Opponents defending the fortresses dug countermines, and sometimes battles with incendiaries took place in the tunnels. A fascinating archaeological discovery in 1935 at Dura-Europos in Syria revealed evidence of such an underground battle. The Persians had besieged the Roman fort there in AD 265, and each side dug tunnels. The archaeologists found many weapons and skeletons (one in Persian armor) and a jar containing the telltale burnt residue of sulphur and pitch.

Plutarch (writing in about AD 100) described a chemical aerosol (particulates suspended in air) created by the Roman general Sertorius when he was trying to defeat the Characitani of Spain, in 80 BC. The Characitani lived in caves carved out of an impregnable mountainside. Frustrated, Sertorius rode around the hill "muttering empty threats." Then, he noticed that his horse was kicking up clouds of caustic dust from the fine white soil at the foot of the caves. The soil may have been soft limestone or gypsum, since Plutarch compared it to "ash or unslaked lime powder": limestone powder is a severe irritant. Sertorius also noticed that the prevailing winds blew each day from the north, and that the cave entrances faced north. Putting these natural facts together, Sertorius ordered his men to pile great heaps of the powdery soil in front of the caves. The next day as the north wind gathered force, the Romans stirred up the mounds and rode horses over the powder, raising great clouds that blew into the cave entrances. The Characitani surrendered after three days of enduring the choking, blinding dust.

In China, lime dust was used to make an early form of tear gas to quell riots. In AD 178, for example, an armed peasant revolt was quelled by horsedrawn "lime chariots" equipped with bellows to blow fine limestone dust "forward according to the wind." This very effec tive fog was accompanied by stampeding horses with burning rags tied to their tails, loud drums and gongs, backed up by ranks of crossbow-men. The revolutionary forces were blinded, thrown into chaos, and "utterly destroyed." When the dust interacts with the moist membranes of the eyes, nose and throat, the effect is corrosive. A poison aerosol described in the Byzantine emperor Leo's *Tactics* was based on the same principles: pots of powdered quicklime (burnt lime) were thrown to form a caustic cloud that blinded and suffocated the enemy as they inhaled the dust.

Obviously, the blowback problems of wind-borne weapons would be an issue. Those who made use of toxic powders and smoke had to beware of unpredictable, reversing winds. Kautilya was highly aware of the danger and, in his chapter on poison smokes, he warned that the army must keep their "eyes secure" with applications of protective salves before deploying chemical aerosols. Only after "having applied these remedies to ensure the safety of himself and his army, should the king make use of poisonous smokes and other mixtures" against an enemy.

An Islamic manuscript from the early Middle Ages suggested the use of "smokes, prepared liquids, and ill-smelling deadly odors for causing damage to forts and castles and horrifying the enemy." Noxious smokes have not gone out of style in modern arsenals. Dense clouds of smoke, chemicals weapons like mustard gas, pepper sprays, and tear gas still present blowback problems, however, requiring the users to don gas masks to avoid eye injury and inhalation.[13]

*　　*　　*

By the time of the Peloponnesian War, three combustible chemicals were known in the Mediterranean world—pitch, sulphur, and quicklime—and the first two were definitely used in warfare in during that era. Pitch, the highly flammable resin from pine trees, has a sticky consistency and burns hotly. Sulphur, a mineral characterized by corrosive combustion, burns at extremely high temperatures and creates sulphur dioxide gas. As it heats, sulphur liquefies, and also releases corrosive vitriol, sulphuric acid.

The choking effects of lime powder were apparently weaponized by Sertorius in the first century BC, but lime's ability to spontaneously burst into flame was known centuries earlier. As Pliny remarked, lime "possesses a remarkable quality: once it has been burnt, its heat is increased by water." Roasting limestone produces a crumbly residue called *calx*—caustic quicklime or calcium oxide. Sprinkled with water, quicklime becomes slaked lime (calcium hydroxide), which generates enough heat to cause spontaneous combustion—and more water feeds the blaze. Theophrastus, a natural philosopher of the fourth century BC, reported that ships laden with cargoes of new togas, which were commonly bleached by brushing them with lime and sulphur, sometimes went down in flames when water splashed on the treated wool. Such accidents were rare, but they would have demonstrated to observers the concept of mixing spontaneously combustible materials for use as weapons.

Sulphur, quicklime, and other substances were combined to make what was known in Latin as *pyr automaton,* "automatic or self-lighting fire." The combination was first used to produce pyrotechnic tricks staged by priests and magicians. In 86 BC, for example, the historian Livy watched a religious ceremony in which torches drenched in sulphur, tar, and quicklime continued to burn after being plunged into the Tiber River. Other Latin authors provided recipes for *pyr automaton* in which sulphur, pitch, quicklime, and naphtha were tightly sealed in containers and then ignited with a single drop of water. Naphtha is the highly flammable light fraction of petroleum, an extremely volatile, strong-smelling, gaseous liquid, common in oil deposits of the Near East. It was the quicklime that caused the mixture to ignite with a drop of water. In the Old Testament, a similar self-lighting fire trick was described as a miracle performed by Elijah to impress the priests of Baal, in about 875 BC.

The potential of combining these substances as an implement of warfare was not realized until much later. A remarkable automatic incendiary weapon, ignited by morning dew, appears in a compilation often attributed to Julius Africanus, a philosopher born in about AD 170 who wrote on magic and military tactics. The recipe calls for sulphur, salt, resin, charcoal, asphalt, and quicklime to be very carefully mixed into a paste during the day, and then tightly sealed in a bronze box, protected from moisture and heat. In the evening, the paste was to be surreptitiously smeared on enemy siege engines. At sunrise, the paste was supposed to combust, ignited by heavy dew or light mist. Such an unpredictable weapon with serious backfire issues was "probably not viewed with favor by military commanders," commented the British historian of ancient incendiaries, James Riddick Partington, but the elaborate combination of the chemical reactions of sulphur, petroleum, and quicklime hydrated by the natural condensation of dew was one of many experiments that eventually led to the development of complex incendiary weapons.

Perhaps a paste like the one attributed to Julius Africanus could have been used by Medea to turn Princess Glauke's gown into a murder weapon. By the first century AD, Roman authors familiar with "automatic fire" magic tricks and the destructive properties of petroleum had begun to speculate on Medea's formula. In his version of the Medea legend, the Stoic philosopher Seneca named "the fire that lurks in sulphur" as one of the components that ignited Glauke's gown, and he also referred to Medea's knowledge of "fire-breathing" natural petroleum wells in Asia Minor. Meanwhile, Pliny and the historian Plutarch both concluded that naphtha must have been one of Medea's secret ingredients.[14]

* * *

The extraordinary conflagration created by Medea, which adhered to the victims' clothing and skin and burned them alive, has striking similarities to modern napalm. A mixture of a volatile naphtha (or gasoline, another petroleum derivative) and a thickening agent to make it jell, napalm burns at more than five thousand degrees Fahrenheit. Invented in the 1940s at Harvard, napalm was used widely against combatants and civilians by U.S. and South Vietnamese forces in the Vietnam War. One of the most unforgettable images of that war was the 1972 photograph of a naked girl fleeing an aerial napalm attack on South Vietnamese villagers. The jellied, liquid fire consumed her clothes and clung to her body, as she and the other victims ran away in pain and terror. The searing, sticky flames burned down to the bone, and water was of no avail. The ghastly scene could have been written by Euripides 2,500 years ago. Just as the use of napalm was an emotional issue during the Vietnam War and "came to symbolize the horrific nature" of advanced war technologies, so the fate of Glauke burned alive by liquid fire symbolized for the ancients the horrors of nefarious toxic weapons.[15]

The connection between the fate of the young Vietnamese girl and the Corinthian princess suggests that the myth of Medea was based on arcane knowledge of the destructive burning nature of petroleum. Medea hailed from Colchis, a region between the Black and Caspian Seas known for the rich oil deposits of Baku, where burning gas wells were worshipped as early as the sixth century BC. In antiquity, the Greek name for petroleum—Medean oil—could refer either to Medea or to the land of the Medes (Persia), which also has abundant oil deposits.

Petroleum hydrocarbons come in many forms—all combustible—from the vaporous light fractions and volatile natural gas and liquids like naphtha, to heavier crude oils and tarry bitumen or asphalt. A few rare deposits of petroleum exist in the Mediterranean, but very rich petrochemical resources exist throughout the Middle East (some deposits occur in China and India, too). In the deserts, oily and highly flammable liquid petroleum wells up from the sand and seeps from bedrock (*petroleum* means "rock-oil" in Latin), and natural gas wells send up cascading flames and burn under water.[16]

Ancient texts from Mesopotamia show that spontaneously burning lakes and fountains of fire—fire that behaved like water and was unquenched by any liquid—evoked awe from earliest times. Persians, Babylonians, Jews, and other people of the ancient Near East had special reverence for the mystifying phenomena of "liquid fires." As in Baku by the Caspian Sea, the ancient worshippers in Persia and Babylonia built temples at sites where natural gas wells burned perpetually. For example, the so-called Eternal Fires, a naphtha fountain at Baba Gurgur (near Kirkuk in northern Iraq), had burned continuously since 600 BC before it was tapped by the first modern oil well in Iraq in 1927. Naphtha figured in Jewish religion, too. Elijah's self-lighting fire was described earlier, and in about 169 BC, Nehemiah gathered a

FIGURE 37. *This burning petroleum fountain at Baba Gurgur (in modern Iraq) has been worshipped since 600 BC.*

thick liquid from Persia, called *nephthar*, to create another miraculous self-lighting fire that astounded witnesses. Nehemiah's trick was ana-lyzed by Partington, who pointed out that spontaneous combustion would occur if naphtha and water were poured over quicklime, or if water was poured onto wood soaked in petroleum and quicklime, or onto sulphur and quicklime. All these components were known and available for experimentation from earliest times. This simple chemical reaction could have produced the effects of Medea's mythical murder-ous gown.

Archaeological evidence shows that surface deposits of oil in the Near East were exploited—for lamps, torches, pigments, waterproof-ing, cleaning, magic fire rituals, and weapons—as early as 3000 BC, and evidence from cuneiform tablets and inscriptions indicates that even the dangerously volatile liquids and gases were used. Ancient Assyrian texts indicate that burning petroleum was used to punish criminals, and *naft* (naphtha) was apparently a siege incendiary in Mesopotamia at an early date, as shown in Assyrian reliefs of flaming firebombs of the ninth century BC.[17]

It took longer for the early Greeks and Romans to understand the origins and uses of the petroleum of exotic lands. Herodotus was the first Greek historian (about 450 BC) to refer to the awesome powers of the "dark and evil smelling oil the Persians call *rhadinace.*" Around the same time, Ctesias, the Greek physician who lived in Persia and wrote often garbled accounts of wonders from the strange lands further east, described a curious fire weapon of India. The method of gathering this combustible substance was surrounded by fable, probably to keep it a state secret. Only the king of India was allowed to possess the special oil that derived from giant "worms" lurking in the Indus River, reported Ctesias. The power of the oil was marvelous: "If you want to burn up a man or an animal, just pour some oil over him and at once he is set on fire." With this weapon, Ctesias heard, the Indian king captures cities without the use of battering rams or siege engines. He simply fills clay vessels with the oil, seals them up, and slings them against the city gates. Upon impact, the oil oozes down and fire pours over the doors. The miraculous oil consumes enemy siege machines and covers the fighting men with fire. Water cannot put it out; the only hope is to smother the flames with dirt.

Apollonius of Tyana, a Greek sage who traveled to India in the first century AD, also heard about something resembling a "white worm" in the River Hyphasis in Punjab that was melted down to render a flammable oil, which could only be kept in glass vessels. Once ignited, it was virtually inextinguishable, and it was the king's exclusive secret weapon against enemy battlements.

The mystical "worm" oil of India was obviously some form of petroleum, ignited by various means. Other reports about the remarkable effects of liquid fire from the East filtered back to Greece and Italy, but the true sources and ways of controlling the substances remained shrouded in mystery until Roman armies began besieging cities in the Middle East to expand their empire and encountered weapons made from local naphtha.[18]

* * *

Alexander the Great was introduced to the wonders of petroleum "magic" after he captured Babylon in 324 BC. *Naft* was the most singular of these, wrote Strabo, for "if it is brought near fire it instantly catches fire; and if you pour the liquid on a body and bring a flame near, the person will burst into flames. It is impossible to quench those flames with water, which makes them burn more violently." The only resort is to suffocate the fire with mud, vinegar, alum and glue, or enormous volumes of water. To impress Alexander, one night his hosts at Ecbatana sprinkled a street with naphtha and set fire to one end— the flames flashed instantaneously to the other end.

Intrigued, Alexander, "for an experiment," poured some naphtha on a young singer named Stephanus and then brought a lamp near him. Sure enough, the boy was immediately enveloped in flames and would have burned to death, like Glauke in the myth, had not bystanders quickly smothered the fire. Even so, the boy was severely burned.

For Alexander and the Greeks of the fourth century BC, naphtha was an exotic marvel of Babylonia, not a weapon. Although bituminous materials were used in the fire ship at Tyre, no ancient historian recorded the use of petroleum weapons against Alexander in Mesopotamia or India. Recently, however, archaeologists have recovered a bit of evidence indicating that Alexander may have encountered some kinds of incendiary weapons during his campaign in India. At the site of Gandhara (Pakistan), besieged and sacked by Alexander in 327 BC, a strange object was found in the defensive ditch. It was a charred, man-made ball composed of the minerals barite and sulphur, and organic pitch. Its form resembles incendiary balls of bituminous materials found in ancient Mesopotamian sites.

The archaeological team proposed that the sphere was a surviving specimen of fireballs that had been ignited and propelled by slingers at the Macedonian invaders. And indeed, among the incendiary formulas in the *Arthashastra*, the Indian manual written during the time of

FIGURE 38 *In antiquity the deposits of seeping, gushing, and flaming oil deposits from Baku to Persia were known as the "lands of the naphtha fountains." Here, Alexander's Greek soldiers watch local people gathering naphtha in Babylonia.*

(Painting by Bob Lapsley/ Aramco Services/PADIA)

Alexander's invasion, there are instructions for preparing "small balls" to be hurled at the enemy, along with fire arrows. The balls and arrows were made flammable from a paste of powdered plant fibers mixed with resins, dung, charcoal, zinc, "red metals" (perhaps the red mineral realgar, the source of arsenic), lead, and wax. Other Indian recipes for making naphtha arrows and fireballs included magical herbs and ground-up reptiles and worms—as well as the very effective pitch, charcoal, and petroleum. There was even an interesting method of painting the walls of an enemy's chamber with a mysterious explosive substance—which may have been saltpeter.[19]

*   *   *

Burning naphtha could easily destroy siege engines, but unlike fire arrows aimed at wooden walls, liquid petroleum incendiaries seem to have been chiefly intended to burn humans alive, re-creating the mythical deaths of Hercules, Glauke, and Creon, and causing extreme suffering and injury for real-life soldiers. Plutarch, Pliny, and Seneca, the historians who identified naphtha as Medea's secret weapon, based their speculation on firsthand accounts of liquid-fire weapons from Roman army veterans who had seen action in Asia in the first century BC. The armies that pursued Mithridates and his allies, from the Black Sea to Mesopotamia, were the first Romans to experience naphtha attacks, which continued over the next two centuries as the emperors attempted to maintain their rule in the Middle East.

Hatra was one of many Mesopotamian strongholds that relied on nearby petroleum seepages to defend itself against Rome. Ammianus Marcellinus described the lakes of naphtha found in the region (now the rich oil fields of northern Iraq). The liquid was prodigiously sticky, he said, with heavy, "mortally noxious fumes." Once it begins to burn, "human intelligence will find no other means of quenching it other than covering it with earth."

In AD 199, as we saw in chapter 6, Severus's soldiers at Hatra were assailed by a gauntlet of terror weapons, including scorpion bombs and streams of burning naphtha. Because of its invisible but highly flammable fumes, the naphtha appeared to jump toward any spark, igniting the intervening air, and it was so sticky that it pursued anyone who tried to flee. Once again, water offered no hope, but fed the flames of intense heat. According to Dio Cassius, at Hatra the cascades of burning naphtha "inflicted the greatest damage, consuming the engines and all the soldiers on whom it fell." A horrified Severus gave the order to retreat even as his men breached Hatra's walls.[20]

Conventional weapons of antiquity—arrows, spears, and swords—wounded or killed by penetrating the skin and damaging internal organs. One could depend on skill, courage, and armor for protection. But there was almost no way to prepare for or deflect weapons of fire. Ordinary fire was bad enough, causing severe injury or death from smoke inhalation and the destruction of skin—measured in degree (depth) and extent of burns over body surface. But fire weapons fueled by exothermic chemicals, because of their adhering nature and extremely high temperatures, intensified the degree of destruction of skin, deep tissue, and even bone, and prolonged the victim's death or else inflicted torturous pain and lifelong injuries. For all these reasons, incendiary weapons have been considered exceptionally cruel and abhorrent.[21]

*   *   *

By the time of Muhammad, in the seventh century AD, naphtha projectiles had become favored siege weapons in the Middle East. Interestingly, in some Arabic, Persian, and Mongol traditions and treatises on military incendiaries, Alexander the Great (and his "grand vizier," the philosopher Aristotle, Alexander's teacher and friend) was credited with the invention of several infernal naphtha fire weapons. Two of those naphtha legends were recounted in the *Shahnama* epic by the Persian poet Firdawsi (AD 940–1020).

According to one legend, while in India Alexander forged thousands of life-sized horses and riders of hollow iron on wheels, each filled with naphtha. When these were rolled toward Porus's war elephants, the eerie black metal figures spewed streams of fire (apparently ignited by a fuse or quicklime and water, since naphtha alone is not self-lighting). A dramatic color illustration of this battle appears in the elaborate Mongol version of the *Shahnama*. The tale is a curious combination of the old Homeric myth of the Trojan Horse and the later Greek legend of Alexander's red-hot bronze statues deployed against Porus's war elephants. In the other illustrated legend of Alexander's ingenious inventions of chemical weaponry, Alexander constructed an invincible double wall of iron and copper, and filled it with charcoal, sulphur, and naphtha. When savage tribes attacked,

FIGURE 39. *According to legend, Alexander the Great created a naphtha-spewing iron cavalry, to rout King Porus of India and his war elephants. This illustration is from the Great Il-Khanid* Shahnama *manuscript, AD 1330-40.*

(Courtesy of the Arthur M. Sackler Museum,
Harvard University Art Museums, Gift of Edward W. Forbes)

the naphtha inside the wall could be ignited, to produce a shield of awesome flames and heat.[22]

The first use of catapulting naphtha by an Islamic army reputedly occurred during one of Muhammad's last campaigns, in AD 630. At the siege of Ta'if, a fortified city in the mountains east of Mecca held by the pagan Thaqif tribe, Muhammad ordered a catapult attack with fire.

The Thaqif responded with catapult fire that rained red-hot scraps of metal on Muhammad's army, a reprise of the catapult loads of red-hot sand and shrapnel first used by the Phoenicians against Alexander the Great's men besieging Tyre, more than a thousand years earlier.

In the civil wars after the death of Muhammad (AD 632), a specialized siege machine for delivering naphtha bombs was mentioned for the first time by name in Muslim annals. Created for the Umayyad caliph in Damascus (Syria), the *manjaniq* or mangonel was a heavy-duty catapult designed to bombard cites with blazing naphtha. Prototypes were reportedly first manned at the siege of Alexandria in AD 645, but the mangonels saw massive use in AD 683, when the Umayyad army set out to take Medina and Mecca. In Damascus, the soldiers loaded a camel caravan with great numbers of the heavy catapults and many containers of volatile naphtha, and accomplished the astonishing feat of crossing the searing Nafud Desert in high summer to make surprise attacks on the two holy cities.

In AD 813, Baghdad, the Islamic capital, was totally destroyed by a new type of special forces—naphtha troops called *naffatun,* who manned hundreds of mangonels catapulting thousands of barrels of liquid fire. By AD 850, every Islamic army maintained regular *naffatun* units, and they were now protected by special fireproof uniforms and padding. Their gear was woven of the mysterious substance they called *hajar al-fatila*, asbestos, the fibrous rock impervious to flame that had been discovered by Muslims, in Tajikhstan, in the 800s. The invention of the fireproof uniforms led to a novel form of Islamic psychological warfare that brought Alexander's legendary naphtha-filled iron horses and riders to life. In an innovation worthy of today's Hollywood stuntmen on fire, Muslim riders and horses were covered with asbestos padding and then doused in naphtha and set afire to terrify the enemy cavalry.

In AD 1167, an extreme example of the "scorched earth" policy of denying resources to an invading army occurred. In this case, when Cairo faced attack by Frankish Crusaders, the Muslims used their petroleum weapons to destroy their own city. As the Crusaders advanced

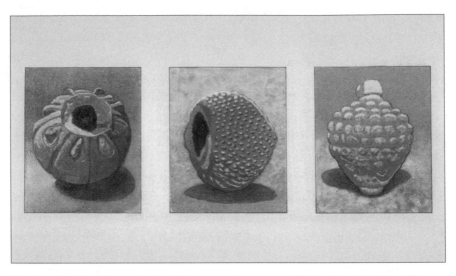

FIGURE 40. *Naphtha grenades. These ceramic pots were filled with volatile naphtha, lit with a fuse, and hurled at the enemy.*

(Painting by Bob Lapsley/Aramco Services/PADIA)

across Egypt, the Islamic ruler turned the entire city into a raging inferno in order to leave nothing but rubble for the Christians. As the terrified populace fled, twenty thousand naphtha pots and ten thousand petroleum bombs were ignited and flames engulfed the city for fifty-four days.

This historical incident shows that enormous stockpiles of volatile petrochemical weapons were stored in military warehouses in the Middle East at a surprisingly early date. The actions of desperate Cairo during the Crusades set a precedent for the threat, anticipated by U.S. intelligence in 2003, that Saddam Hussein might torch Iraq's fifteen hundred oil wells, in order to deny them to U.S. invaders. In the 1991 Gulf War, Saddam's retreating Iraqi troops had set fire to 650 oil fields in Kuwait, creating fires of stupendous magnitude that burned for eight months.

Archaeological evidence of the destruction of Cairo by its own chemical weapons surfaced in 1916, when French and Egyptian archaeologists began to uncover troves of the ceramic, fist-sized naphtha pots in the ruins of the old city. The grenades were of astonishing sophistication: they had been filled with volatile jellied naphtha (similar to napalm) and a crude gunpowder made of nitrates and sulphur.[23]

*　　*　　*

The dangers of backfire for the early users of weaponry based on pyrophoric chemicals were daunting. As Kautilya remarked in his discussion of how to use incendiaries to capture cities: "Fire cannot be trusted." In the case of quicklime, sulphur, and petroleum, ensuring safety in collecting and storing the combustible substances was difficult, because volatile vapors and liquids had to be kept away from moisture, oxygen, heat, and sparks. (Notably, Medea had followed these precautions in treating the combustible gown, by sealing it in an airtight container.) During the chaos of battle, one had to mix the unstable, sticky materials, and ignite and aim them at the enemy, without allowing the rapacious flames to leap back toward the source of the spark or toward combustible fuel or water in the vicinity of the user.

One precaution when using combustibles, advised by Aeneas the Tactician in 360 BC, was to hurl or otherwise emplace the unlit fuel first and then fire a blazing arrow or throw a burning pot to ignite it. That technique was used in AD 1190 by Arabs besieging the Crusader castle at Acre. The Muslims tossed pots of naphtha without fuses against the towers. When nothing happened, the Christians crowded onto the towers and mocked the besiegers. The Muslims held their fire and waited for the naphtha to soak in. Then they threw a lighted pot, and the whole edifice and all the Christians exploded in flames.

With vaporous naphtha and other combustibles, the chances of accidental explosions were very high, as acknowledged in Byzantine warfare manuals. Preparations of volatile compounds were always done outdoors for fear of fire. Chinese texts warned that heating sulphur, arsenic, carbon, and saltpeter indoors had resulted in severe burns to the alchemists' hands and faces, and even burned down the buildings where they were working. Naphtha bombs were especially difficult to aim and control, as the Umayyad Muslims learned during their siege of the holy city of Mecca in AD 683. As they catapulted naphtha projectiles into the city, they tried to avoid the Ka'aba, the sanctuary of the Black Stone worshipped by Muslims, but the covering was struck and caught fire. The intense heat split the sacred Black Stone into three pieces.

And of course, wind could also betray wielders of liquid fire. In a famous military disaster on the Yangtze River in AD 975, the Chinese admiral Chu Ling-Pin watched in horror as the liquid fire his troops were propelling toward the enemy fleet of the Sung emperor was suddenly swept up by a strong contrary wind. The "smoke and flames were blown toward his own ships and men," immolating more than 150,000 sailors and soldiers. "Overcome with grief," the admiral "flung himself into the flames and died."

Petroleum bombs and naphtha flamethrowers posed hazards to the users because of the low viscosity and vaporous light fractions: the fuel tended to explode prematurely. The use of soaps and other agents to thicken and stabilize naphtha and/or gasoline in the 1940s is what led to the formulation of napalm, and allowed it to adhere to targets and burn at very high temperatures over a prolonged time. In antiquity, it was discovered that liquid naphtha could be somewhat stabilized with heavier oils, tar, or pitch, but those additives are themselves flammable. Handlers of such weapons always had to exercise great caution, even after the discovery of distillation techniques to remove the flammable vapors, a technique that led to the creation of the weapon known as Greek Fire.[24]

* * *

According to evidence that survives in Islamic and Byzantine chronicles, the weapon known as Greek Fire was based on the development of effective distillation and siphon pump technologies which enabled a flammable mixture to be propelled under pressure from boats, thus introducing the deployment of "something new, dreadful, launchable, and flammable," in the words of the historian Alfred Crosby.[25]

Greek Fire's origin is surrounded by fable. According to one legend, an angel whispered the formula to Constantine the Great, the first

Christian emperor in AD 300. But Greek Fire did not suddenly burst on the scene out of nowhere. Centuries of observations, discoveries, and experiments with combustible sulphur, quicklime, and naphtha—in formulas known by various names such as liquid fire, *maltha, pyr automaton* or automatic, artificial, or prepared fire, sea fire, wild fire, flying fire, *oleum incendiarium*, fierce fire oil, water-white *naft abyad*, and so on—ultimately led to the invention of the naval incendiary that was dubbed "Greek Fire" by the Crusaders in the 1200s. Naphtha had been a tool of siege-craft since Assyrian times and with Islamic mangonels and *naffatun*, naphtha weaponry reached its peak performance in land engagements. Further inventions in Syria and Constantinople (modern Istanbul) perfected naphtha armaments for battles at sea.

What exactly was the "terrible agent of destruction" known as Greek Fire? The story of how the Byzantine and Islamic formulas, once heavily guarded state secrets, were lost, and the evolution of similar weapons in Indian and Chinese warfare, has been recounted in detail in modern military literature. Basically, Greek Fire was a *weapon system* for blasting ships in naval engagements: the weapon consisted of a refined chemical *ammunition* and an ingenious *delivery system* of cauldrons, siphons, tubes, and pumps.

The main ingredient of the ammunition was naphtha, originally used as an incendiary poured over or hurled at besiegers in Mesopotamia, and later in firebombs catapulted by mangonels invented in Damascus and used by Muslims to bombard fortifications, as described earlier. The Byzantines had used small siphons and syringes to squirt petroleum incendiaries as early as AD 513, but the new technology of pumping pressurized, distilled naphtha through bronze tubes aimed at ships was achieved through brilliant chemical engineering by a "petroleum consultant" named Kallinikos. Fleeing the Muslim occupation of Syria, Kallinikos sought refuge in Constantinople in about AD 668 and taught the Byzantines about his invention. Greek Fire was first used to break the Muslim navy's seven-year siege of Constantinople in AD 673 and it saved the city again from the Muslim fleet in AD 718.

Kallinikos's formula and delivery system are lost to modern science, and historians and chemists who try to reconstruct how the device worked disagree on the exact composition of the naphtha ammunition and the system design. Greek Fire burned in water and may have been ignited by water, and it adhered to victims. Besides distilled naphtha, the ingredients may have included thickeners such as resin or wax, quicklime, sulphur, turpentine, and saltpeter. The exact formula matters less than the amazing delivery system, which was capable of shooting liquid fire from swiveling nozzles mounted on small boats without the benefit of modern thermometers, safety valves, and pressure gauges.

The only recourses available to crews facing Greek Fire—draping ships with masses of heavy, wet hides; only sailing in stormy weather; and attempting rapid, evasive maneuvers—were rarely successful and dangerous in themselves. "In short," writes military historian Alex Roland, "there was no adequate countermeasure to Greek Fire." From the seventh century on, the Byzantines and Arabs formulated variations on Greek Fire, which resembled napalm in the way "it clung to everything it touched, instantly igniting any organic material—ship's hull, oars, sails, rigging, crew, and their clothing. Nothing was immune," and even "jumping into the sea failed to quench the flames." The weapon caused enemies to "shiver in terror" and capitulate in despair.

Greek Fire was the ultimate weapon of its time. "Every man touched by it believed himself lost, every ship attacked with it was devoured by flames," wrote a crusader in AD 1248. Partington, the historian of Greek Fire, compared the ancient reaction of horror to the modern dread of the atomic bomb. In 1139, the Second Lateran Council, following Western ideas of chivalry and honorable war, decreed that Greek Fire or similar burning weapons were "too murderous" to be used in Europe. The council's decision was respected for centuries, but the issue may have been moot since the formula for Greek Fire seems to have been lost by the thirteenth century. The recipe was rekindled in a treatise published for Napoleon, with the chilling title "Weapons for the Burning of Armies."[26]

FIGURE 41. *An artist's conception of naval battle with Greek Fire.*

(Painting by Bob Lapsley/Aramco Services/PADIA)

Centuries before the invention of Greek Fire, however, naphtha was already a weapon of devastating destructive power. The early precursors of Greek Fire, first described so graphically in the ancient Greek myth of Medea and Glauke, and then experienced in real battles during the Roman Empire, were the most dreaded, fearsome weapons of their day. There was no adequate countermeasure, no way to withstand such infernos. Neither extraordinary valor nor a suit of bronze armor could save a soldier enveloped by cascades of corrosive flames that melted both metal and flesh. The experiences of Lucullus and his Roman legions in the first century BC serve as a compelling case study of the effects of liquid fire.

*   *   *

Veterans who served with Licinius Lucullus were among the first Romans to undergo naphtha attacks and they had nightmarish tales

FIGURE 42. *Licinius Lucullus, the Roman general who pursued Mithridates and encountered biochemical attacks in the Near East in the first century* BC.

(From Harry Thurston Peck, *Harper's Dictionary of Classical Antiquities*, 1898)

to tell of their campaigns in Asia. The story of Lucullus's campaign is a fitting conclusion to this chapter on infernal fire weapons—and it also draws together a full range of the biochemical weapons described in the preceding chapters. Lucullus's army faced a panoply of bioterrors, from poisoned arrows, stinging bees, and savage bears to burning mud.

For eight years, in 74–66 BC, Lucullus was one of a series of generals who unsuccessfully pursued King Mithridates, the master of terror tactics and an arch-poisoner whose dream was to create the ultimate personal antidote to biotoxins. Mithridates and his allies invented a stunning array of terror strategies directed at the Romans. He had begun his challenge to Roman power in 88 BC, with a shocking atrocity. He secretly ordered the massacre of every Italian man, woman, and child living in the new Roman Province of Asia, to take place on a specified date. So hated were the imperial colonists that more than eighty thousand Romans were reportedly slaughtered on a single day. Mithridates then swept west through Greece and threatened to invade Italy, while his client princes took control of significant cities in Rome's Asian Province.

The Roman army's first battle with Mithridates in Bithynia ended very badly for the Romans. When Mithridates' vicious scythe-bearing chariots plowed at high speed through the ranks, the legionaries were overwhelmed by the sight of their companions "chopped in halves but still breathing, and others mangled and cut to pieces" by the whirling blades. It was the "hideousness of the spectacle," not the losses, that sent the Romans fleeing in horror, commented the historian Appian.

Next, Mithridates captured the Roman legate Manius Aquillius, the son of the brutal Roman commander who had been criticized for poisoning wells in Asia in an earlier war (chapter 3). Mithridates paraded the official on an ass, and then executed him for bribe-taking in a particularly horrid way—by pouring molten gold down his throat. These acts ushered in the long Mithridatic Wars (90–63 BC), in which a succession of Roman generals achieved victory after victory on land and sea against the monarch and his allies, but failed to capture Mithridates, who eluded their grasp like quicksilver.

Beginning in 74 BC, Lucullus relentlessly attacked and sacked the monarch's allied kingdoms from Pontus to Mesopotamia and back again. After difficult sieges of several cities near the Black Sea, where the defenders let loose swarms of bees and rampaging bears to assault the Roman tunnelers, Lucullus tracked Mithridates south, to Armenia. There, Lucullus laid siege to Tigranocerta on the Tigris (in eastern Turkey), where Mithridates had taken refuge with his son-in-law King Tigranes. The new fortifications were only half-built and the city was captured, but the two monarchs slipped out of Lucullus's hands, and began to gather up new armies.

Despite his victory at Tigranocerta, "the barbarians did Lucullus serious injury" with a new weapon of unexpected savagery. Dio Cassius described how the Tigranocertans poured streams of fire on the

Romans and their siege engines. The extraordinary fire flowed over and consumed everything, wood, leather, metal, horses, and human bodies. "This chemical," marveled Dio Cassius, "is full of *bitumen* and is so fiery that burns up whatever it touches, and cannot be extinguished by any liquid." The weapon was naphtha, from the rich local petroleum deposits. This event and similar attacks on Roman armies in the region counter the suggestion by biochemical warfare historian Eric Croddy that "the combustible properties of naphtha and its utility as a weapon" only came to the Romans' attention with the invention of Greek Fire in AD 668.[27]

In the Armenian countryside, the Romans suffered another kind of bio-attack by Mithridates' allies. In skirmishes with mounted barbarians, Lucullus lost a great many men to the skilled archers, who shot arrows backwards as they galloped away from the pursuing Romans. The men's wounds were "dangerous and incurable," wrote Dio Cassius, for the archers used "double arrow-points of iron and moreover, they poisoned them." The missiles had a loosely attached second point that broke off deep inside the wound when the shaft was pulled out. With so many dead and dying from the poison arrows, Lucullus retreated.

After facing these weapons of extraordinary brutality in battles of dubious outcome in 69–68 BC, Lucullus's legionaries began to revolt. But Lucullus forged on, intending to conquer another ally of Mithridates, the Kingdom of Commagene in the oil fields along the Euphrates (on the border of southeastern Turkey and Syria). Samosata, the wealthy fortified capital of Commagene, guarded the Euphrates river traffic, the strategic crossroads from Damascus to Pontus, and the east-west trade routes.

When Lucullus stormed the fortified city in 69 BC, he was unaware that the Samosatans had a secret weapon to defend their walls. They had collected "a flammable mud called *maltha* that exudes from nearby marshy pools," wrote Pliny, who described the battle. *Maltha* was apparently a very viscous form of naphtha skimmed from great pools of asphaltum, petroleum tar that oozes from fissures in sandstones in the region.

When the Samosatans poured the flaming mud over the Roman soldiers, the effect was horrendous. *Maltha's* ravenous appetite makes it "cling stubbornly to anyone who tries to flee," Pliny declared, "and water only makes it burn more fiercely." Only covering the flames with earth could have extinguished the blaze, a fact discovered by later experiments, noted Pliny. At Samosata, the voracious flames burned up the men in their armor, and the extreme heat even turned the Romans' own armaments against them. "They were repeatedly burned by their own weapons," wrote Pliny.

In later times, other besieged populations in the region would capitalize on the unique ability of high-temperature incendiaries to turn an attacking soldier's weapons and armor against him. We already saw how the Phoenicians, with a rain of hot sand, had turned the bronze chestplates of Alexander's Macedonians into red-hot torture devices. And in AD 630, during the siege of Ta'if near Mecca, Muhammad's army advanced on the walls under a "testudo" (turtle-shell) of interlocking shields held over their heads to deflect the arrows of the defenders. But they were unprepared for the rain of molten metal that heated their shields to intense temperatures. As they dropped the burning shields, the men were cut down by a barrage of arrows.

The terror of the burning *maltha* at Samosata forced Lucullus to withdraw again. His army, never very loyal, now began to mutiny and desert in significant numbers. And Samosata, like Hatra, remained an independent desert stronghold for another century. [28]

Mythic parallels were beginning to accumulate for Lucullus, eerie reminders of the old stories of Hercules and Medea. First, the poison arrows of the Armenians caused torturous death and incurable wounds like those suffered by Hercules' victims, and then the burning mud coated the soldiers, like the corrosive tunic that tormented Hercules. The scene at Samosata also replicated the deaths of Glauke and Creon and the Corinthians in the palace, in the unnatural conflagration engineered by Medea. Pliny was certainly struck by the coincidence, for in his description of the Roman disaster at Samosata, he suggested that some form of *maltha* must have been Medea's secret weapon.

FIGURE 43. *Hercules struggling to tear off the burning, poisoned tunic. Bronze sculpture by Pierre Puget, 1680.*

(Jules Bache Collection, The Metropolitan Museum of Art)

During his campaign in the region, Lucullus discovered an art treasure with haunting mythical resonance: a large bronze statue of Hercules, showing the mighty hero contorted in pain, trapped in the garment that turned his own weapons against him. Lucullus wrapped the magnificent bronze in a linen shroud and brought it back to Rome. The statue was paraded along with the rich booty he had raided from Mithridates' kingdoms, and then placed on permanent public display, next to the Temple of the Divine Julius. About a century later, Pliny recorded the layers of inscriptions that had been carved into the base of the "highly valued" art work by the unknown sculptor of Asia Minor. Known as *Hercules in the Burning Tunic*, it was admired by the Romans as a powerful evocation of the hero's "final agony."[29]

Yet another event with mythic implications occurred during Lucullus's campaign. After capturing a string of cities loyal to Mithridates, Lucullus chased Mithridates' navy—led by three of the king's major allies, Varius, Alexander, and Dionysius—down the coast of Turkey. The historian Appian described how, at the same harbor where the Greeks had landed to attack Troy in Homer's *Iliad*, Lucullus captured thirteen of Mithridates' ships, and overtook the rest of the fleet on a small, barren island near Lemnos. The trio of captains escaped, but Lucullus discovered them hiding in a cave on the small island. Varius, he killed; Alexander, he captured; but Dionysius, a true follower of Mithridates, drank the poison that he always carried with him and died by his own hand.

As Appian pointed out, the tiny island was none other than Chryse, the desert isle where, according to myth, Philoctetes had suffered an accidental wound from Hercules' Hydra-venom arrows. Philoctetes was marooned in misery for ten years in a cave on the island, perhaps in the very cave where Mithridates' allies took refuge. Chryse was a well-known landmark, where many travelers stopped to pay their respects to Philoctetes' shrine. A learned scholar of Greek mythology, Lucullus would certainly have been aware of the island's fame, and it was common for Roman commanders to visit mythological landmarks during their campaigns. In 191 BC, for example, after his victory over Antiochus in Greece, Manius Glabrio sought out the sacred site of Hercules' pyre, where Philoctetes had inherited the poison arrows. Lucullus probably paid a visit to the shrine on the isle of Chryse after his major victory there, to admire Philoctetes' bow and breastplate and the bronze serpent symbolizing the envenomed arrows.

Ancient authors describe Lucullus as a compassionate and generous man (early in his campaigns, for example, he had burst into tears at the site of a city he had reduced to ashes). Perhaps his war experiences with poison arrows and all-consuming fire gave a him a unique appreciation for Philoctetes' and Hercules' sufferings. On the other hand, maybe the beleaguered commander wished that Philoctetes could miraculously appear with a quiverful of Hydra arrows to turn the tide against Mithridates. Had Lucullus been able to peer into the future, he would have seen his successor Pompey sabotaged by poison honey and his arch-enemy Mithridates done in at last by his own reliance on poisons. Lucullus's own end came in 57 BC, after a descent into insanity brought about by poison—deadly drugs administered by his freedman.

There is no evidence that Lucullus or other Roman commanders ever fought "fire with fire," or retaliated with naphtha in Meso-potamia—probably because their enemies controlled the petroleum resources there. Eventually, however, the Romans found an even more morally repugnant use for the chemical weapon. In the Roman arena, one could witness the spectacle of prisoners condemned to reenact the fiery fate suffered by so many Roman soldiers at Tigranocerta and Samosata, and later at Hatra and other Mesopotamian cities. Perhaps inspired by the celebrated statue of Hercules displayed in Rome after Lucullus's campaign and by veterans' tales of burning *maltha*, public executions by the *tunica molesta*, a naphtha-soaked "shirt of torture," became a popular diversion. The gruesome death sentence was first devised by the emperor Nero in AD 64, as one of many inventive exe-cution methods designed to re-create mythic death scenes. Executions "à la Hercules" continued to be staged for the amusement of Roman audiences through the third century AD.[30] Meanwhile, in distant Mesopotamia, Rome's own soldiers, pursuing the imperial agenda demanded by their emperors, were compelled to endure the very real ordeals of poison and hellfire.

AFTERWORD:
THE MANY-HEADED HYDRA

> Chopping off the immortal head of the
> venomous Hydra, he buried it alive,
> and placed a heavy rock over it.
> —*Myth of Hercules*

LICINIUS LUCULLUS and his Roman soldiers were not the first army to face weapons of poison and hellish fire, nor were they the last. But theirs is a story brimming with mythic parallels. Not only did they encounter biological and chemical weapons on their campaigns, but they discovered the celebrated statue of the dying Hercules and visited the famous desert island of Philoctetes, two mythic warriors who exemplified the unforeseen consequences of toxic weapons. Lucullus's experiences help show how the ongoing history of biochemical weapons continually harks back to its mythological beginnings.

From antiquity onward, the annals of toxic weaponry form a widening gyre of myth reflecting history, and history mirroring myth. And just as the Hydra's heads multiplied at a drastic rate, so human ingenuity in waging biochemical warfare has proliferated at a dreadful pace. "And so," wrote the philosopher Lucretius, contemplating that murderous progression in his own lifetime (the first century BC), "tragic discord gave birth to one invention after another and added daily increments to the horrors of war." In the race to develop more and more fearsome weapons to intensify psychological dread and ensure agonizing death, suffering, and destruction on a scale far beyond that wrought by the simple sharp and blunt weapons of old, the terse words of Appian, historian of the Mithridatic Wars, are fitting: "They left nothing untried that was within the compass of human energy."

The basic concepts of the diverse biochemical weapons that were wielded in historical battles—from poisons and contagion to animal allies and hellish fire—were first imagined in ancient mythology. The archaic myths even anticipated the moral and practical quandaries that have surrounded biological and chemical armaments since their invention. Far from fading over millennia, the age-old problems of controlling toxic agents of war and avoiding unintended consequences have intensified with the advance of science in the service of war. Hercules thought he could control the poisoned arrows he created from the Hydra's venom, but they brought death and tragedy to his friends and ultimately destroyed Hercules himself. The poison weapons were inherited by Philoctetes and dealt him great misfortune, too, even though they turned the tide in favor of the Greeks at Troy.

Once created, toxic weapons take on a life of their own, resistant to destruction and threatening harm over generations. Tons of still-active chemical weapons from World Wars I and II lurk in long-forgotten dumping areas, releasing toxins and posing grave risks to unwitting finders. These weapons, and the countless vials of smallpox, anthrax, and other super-pathogens stored in laboratories around the world, ripe for weaponization, have their antecedents in the "plague demons" imprisoned in jars buried under the temple in Jerusalem, and the pestilence locked inside the golden casket in Babylon. Centuries later, those containers were broken open during wartime, and plague spread over the land.

Long before the invention of Greek Fire, and two millennia before the invention of napalm and nuclear bombs, the Greeks and Romans confronted new chemical fire weapons whose awesome powers of destruction could not be checked by normal means. Over and over, the ancient historians repeated the refrain: the only hope of quelling such ghastly fire was to cover it with earth. That solution echoed Hercules' method of getting rid of the monstrous Hydra's head by burying it under the earth. Now, those desperate attempts to bury poison and fire weapons seem to foreshadow our own efforts to dispose of dangerous weapons underground, out of sight but never completely out of mind.

As the myths forewarned, a tragic myopia afflicts those who resort to poison weapons. Even as modern adversaries threaten to attack and retaliate with terror weapons that would bring mass destruction of innocents, the United States and other nations are forced to seek safe ways to dispose of the stockpiles of biochemical arms and radioactive nuclear waste they have already brought into being. But every method that has been proposed, from burning to burying, poses contamination hazards for present and future generations. Sites where biochemical and radioactive weapons have been buried, tested, or accidentally released remain deadly to all lifeforms. The menacing situation recalls the ancient dread of places corrupted by *miasma*, exhalations of deadly vapors.

The Soviet stores of anthrax and other super-germ weapons that were dumped into pits on Vozrozhdeniye Island in the Aral Sea, for example, now poison the air and water of Uzbekistan and Kazakstan. The human cost of this, the world's largest bioweapons testing ground, is incalculable. But of the environmental disasters in the region that have been made public, the sudden death of 500,000 steppe antelopes in just one hour in 1988 was one of the most striking. The Aral Sea itself is shrinking at a fast rate, which means that sometime in the future rodents and humans could contract and spread the hyper-virulent plagues buried on what was once an island.[1]

In the United States, plans to incinerate tons of obsolete chemical weapons are going forward, in spite of the serious safety hazards and accidents that have already been documented at furnace sites in the Pacific and United States. Meanwhile, the search for other options for the disposal of nuclear weapons—such as chemical neutralization or vitrification (encasement in glass)—continues. "Geological disposal"—

FIGURE 44. *The Many-Headed Hydra, a symbol of the proliferating dilemmas of biological warfare. Caeretan hydria, about 525 BC.*

(The J. Paul Getty Museum)

entombing lethal, indestructible weapons under mountains of rock—is the most often proposed solution. In 1999, the world's first underground repository for the "safe and permanent disposal" of radioactive weapons material was dug in a salt bed more than 2,000 feet deep, in the Chihuahuan Desert near Carlsbad, Mexico.[2]

Hercules hit upon his own "geologic" solution to dispose of the Hydra's immortal head, after he had created his poison weapons. He buried the evil thing alive in the ground and placed a massive boulder over the spot, to warn away future generations. The serpent's head with fangs eternally dripping poison into the earth is a perfect symbol for indestructible biochemical and radioactive armaments emitting moral and physical pollution in the world today.

A geologic solution on a massive scale was proposed in 2002, when plans were developed to bury a huge cache of radioactive material deep under Yucca Mountain in Nevada, in the desert about one hundred miles northwest of Las Vegas. The seventy-seven thousand tons of nuclear material are expected to remain dangerously radioactive for one hundred thousand years. The government hopes to make the toxic sepulchre impregnable for at least ten thousand years, until the year AD 12,000.

Scientists who oppose the plan point out that the man-made containers, seals, and barriers buried under the rock cannot safeguard the material against seismic faulting, volcanic activity, erosion, ground water seepage, and climate changes over ten thousand years. Ominous evidence at Rocky Mountain Arsenal near Denver, Colorado, where chemical weapons were disposed of in deep wells in the mid-twentieth century, suggested that the deep dispersal of toxic fluids actually caused earthquakes in the area.

But beyond the grave problems of trying to imprison perilous materials of mass destruction under rock for one hundred centuries, there is also the necessity of preventing "inadvertent human intrusion" into such storage sites. Most obvious are the immediate problems of keeping uninformed people or terrorists away from deadly weapons burial grounds.

Since the Russians abandoned the biochemically contaminated Vozrozhdeniye Island in 1992, for example, people living around the Aral Sea continue to salvage tons of military equipment and valuable scrap materials despite the health risks. In Denver, the Rocky Mountain Arsenal National Wildlife Refuge is contaminated with napalm, mustard gas, sarin, and other biochemical weapons dumped in the 1940s and '50s. Public access to the popular wildlife refuge had to be suspended in 2000, while ways to deal with the pernicious miasma are investigated.

Since 1993, several caches of live munitions containing viable mustard gas were unearthed in a luxury housing development in Washington, DC, and in 2003, an archaeological discovery with disquieting echoes of the vessels of plague in ancient temples occurred in San Francisco when, during excavations of the historic fort at the Presidio, archaeologists unearthed a cache of glass vials. The strange "artifacts" turned out to contain still-toxic mustard gas buried by the U.S. military during World War II. These examples are only the tip of the iceberg: it is estimated that hundreds of thousands of deteriorating chemical munitions lie in unmarked burial sites around the world.[3]

But at sites like that proposed for Yucca Mountain and already in existence in New Mexico, the enormity of the geologic scale and vast time frame of toxicity take on cosmic proportions. In other words, the authorities must face the ramifications of their act on future generations in mythic terms. To that end, the government has turned to mythic solutions. Panels of folklorists, anthropologists, linguists, archaeologists, and other scholars and scientists were convened to figure out how to ensure that the buried Hydra's head of radioactive doom will remain undisturbed by human beings over time measured in many thousands of years.

What if, over the ages, Yucca Mountain takes on a mysterious allure? What if the site comes to be seen as a place where treasure was hidden in the deep past, like the Pyramids of Egypt or the secret tomb of Genghis Khan? How can future treasure hunters, archaeologists, scientists, prospectors, and other explorers, be prevented from breaking the seals of the Pandora's box inside the mountain and unwittingly releasing the "spirits of death," as occurred in the ancient temples where plague was once stored?

Some experts have suggested that frightening legends be disseminated about the doomsday weapons, in the hope that these tales will become long-lasting oral traditions, like Homer's *Iliad* or biblical stories. Inspired by Babylonian inscriptions carved on stone in the eighteenth century BC, archaeologists proposed that stone tablets inscribed with warnings in seven languages be randomly buried in the surrounding desert. These messages would explain what is under Yucca Mountain and why it should never be disturbed. But it is doubtful that present-day languages and cultures will exist ten thousand years from now.

To back up verbal warnings in what will surely become dead languages, other consultants suggest surrounding such places with "menacing earthworks," such as gigantic concrete thorns or jagged lightning bolts emerging from the ground to convey a sense of menace. Another plan calls for a "spike field," tall towers of polished granite, engraved with ominous symbols. Human faces expressing horror and nausea (along the lines of Edvard Munch's *The Scream*) and pictographs indicating mass death and destruction have been proposed. Backfiring

FIGURE 45. *Landscape of Thorns, one of the designs intended to warn future civilizations away from nuclear materials burial sites like Yucca Mountain. Concept by architect Michael Brill, art by Safdar Abidi.* (SAND92-1382. Sandia National Laboratories)

potentials loom, however. And with the tombs of the pharaohs, grandiose warnings, elaborate boobytraps, and terrifying curses could attract adventurers. As with the golden casket in the ancient Babylonian temple, valuable materials like titanium or marble would lure looters.

As an anthropologist on the team remarked, the essential concept is to identify the place itself as an urgent message for future civilizations. "We considered ourselves to be a powerful culture. But this place is not a place of honor." What lies buried here "was dangerous and repulsive to us."[4] Such a message would have struck a chord with ancient Greeks and Romans who visited the shrine where Philoctetes had dedicated his poison arrows, or with those who marveled at the tragic statue of Hercules in the burning cloak, listened in awe to the story of Glauke's death, or pointed out the rock marking the place where Hercules had entombed the Hydra's head.

If only it were so easy to extinguish the poisonous miasma of bio-toxic weapons, invented so long ago, by hiding them under mountains of solid rock. If only mythology really does possess the power to warn against the relentless advance of the dark sciences of war. Perhaps there is a ray of hope in the myth of Philoctetes, in his decision to dedicate the dreadful bow and arrows to a memorial of divine healing rather than pass the weapons on to a new generation of warriors. His act anticipates modern efforts to forge treaties in which nations could agree to halt the proliferation and deployment of biochemical and nuclear arms, and turn technological efforts to alleviating human suffering.

One can only hope that a deeper understanding of toxic warfare's mythic origins and earliest historic realities might help divert the drive to transform all nature into a deadly arsenal into the search for better ways to heal. Then Appian's sorrowful words about war, "They left nothing untried that was within the compass of human energy," could refer to human ingenuity striving to turn nature's forces to good.

Notes

Introduction

1. The chimerical adjective "biochemical" is often used as a catchall term to denote biological and chemical agents in general. Poupard and Miller 1992, 9. Other historians of biochemical warfare accept the common assumption that there is very little ancient evidence for biological and chemical strategies. "Given the potential advantage that could accrue from biological weapons," comments the historian of biological and chemical warfare Mark Wheelis (1999, 8), "it is surprising that there are so few recorded instances of their use." The noted biological and chemical warfare authority Julian Perry Robinson (2002) remarks that "the exploitation of disease as a weapon of war is exceedingly rare in the historical record," as were the uses of poison and chemicals. In her study of smallpox in Colonial America, Fenn 2000, 1573, is typical in claiming that ancient Greeks lacked technical knowledge for carrying out bio-war. According to biological and chemical warfare scholar Cole, 1996, the frequency of poison weapon use antiquity was "minimized" because of ancient taboos.

2. It is asserted in some histories of biological warfare (e.g., Miller 1998) that the ancient Assyrians (whose civilization began around 2400 BC in modern Turkey, Iran, Syria and Iraq) poisoned enemies' wells with LSD-like ergot, a fungus of rye, wheat, and other grains. It appears that ergot is referred to in Assyrian texts, but there is no basis for the notion that the hallucinogen was deliberately used against foes.

3. Definitions of biological and chemical warfare: The 1972 bio-weapons convention bans "microbial or other biological agents, or toxins whatever their origin or method of production, of types or quantities that have no justification for prophylactic, protective, or other peaceful purposes." This includes living agents such as insects, and toxins produced from them. For a comprehensive definition of biological weapons, see Federation of American Scientists "Special Weapons Primer," www.fas.org. Definitions of chemical weapons: Stockholm International Peace Research Institute (SIPRI) 1971 and 1975, 202–6. See also history and definitions of biological and chemical weapons at www. cbwinfo.com. Robertson and Robertson 1995, 369, exclude forcing enemies into "unsanitary" areas and bio-terrorism from their definition of bio-war. Poupard and Miller 1992, 9, separate biological weaponry which uses "viable organisms," from "bacterial toxins and related chemical derivatives of microorganisms," which they believe should be categorized as chemical weapons (CW). Biological warfare is defined as "the use of pathogens, . . . disease-causing bacterial and viral agents, or biologically derived toxins against humans, animals, and crops," according to Croddy 2002, 219; on 130 Croddy notes that "while purists would not consider Greek Fire" and ancient incendiaries as "true CW, these early flame- and smoke-producing techniques have direct [and indirect] connections with the modern use of toxic substances on the battlefield."

4. Every arms innovation in antiquity was regarded as inhumane and dishonorable at first. When the new catapult technology of the fourth century BC was demonstrated to the Spartan general Archidamus, for example, he exclaimed, "Now what will become of valor?" Plutarch, *Moralia* "Sayings of Spartans" 219. In the 1100s, the crossbow was singled out as inhumane; gunpowder raised similar criticism in the 1300s. But "today's secret weapons had the nasty habit of becoming tomorrow's universal threat," notes O'Connell, "Secret Weapons" in Cowley and Parker 1996, 417–19.

5. Criteria for evaluating attempts to deploy disease as a weapon since the Middle Ages are discussed by Wheelis 1999, 9, who restricts his dis-

cussion of biological warfare before 1914 to the intent to transmit contagion, leaving out the use of toxins and pollution of wells.

6. Poison weapons have "long been regarded as peculiarly reprehensible [and] subject to express prohibition since ancient times," in Greece, Rome, India, and in the Koran, remarks Robinson 2002. He suggests that this "ancient taboo" reflects a "human impulse against the hostile use" of disease and chemicals that is "multicultural, multiethnic, and longstanding." Banning biochemical arsenals today "goes to the roots of what humankind finds acceptable and unacceptable." Indeed, the ancient "taboo may be our one remaining hope" as science and commerce push biotechnology still more deeply into developing "immensely threatening new weapons." Leonard Cole, discussing the ancient "poison taboo," proposed that the "moral repugnance [and] deep-seated aversion" to such weapons going back thousands of years helps explain their rarity in the past. But Cole's claim that "the Greeks and Romans condemned the use of poison in war as a violation of . . . the law of nations," projects a seventeenth century concept ("law of nations") into antiquity (see note 9, below). "Poisons and other weapons considered inhumane were forbidden [in] India around 500 BC and among the Saracens 1,000 years later," continues Cole 1996, 64, 65. Neufeld 1980, 46–47.

7. Creveld 1991, 23, points out that what is "considered acceptable behavior in war is historically determined, neither self-evident nor unalterable." See also Fenn 2000, 1573–74. Strabo, 10.1.12–13. For differing views of the development of Greek conventions of war and military protocols from Homeric epic to the Peloponnesian War, see Ober 1994 and Krentz 2002.

8. Krentz 2002, 25. Nostalgic notions of the ancient "poison taboo" were evident in the late Middle Ages. A pledge taken in about 1650 by German artillery gunners vowed never to employ poison projectiles on the grounds that "the first inventors of our art thought such actions as unjust . . . as unworthy of a man of heart and a true soldier." From the SIPRI Web site, www. projects.sipri.se/cbw/docs/cbw-hist-pledge.html. Ober 1994, 14; on hoplite battle, 14–17. Hansen 1989. Sallust, *Jugurthine War*, chapter 11, 101.

9. Creveld 1991, 27, points out that "war by definition consists of killing, of deliberately shedding the blood of fellow creatures." Killing cannot be tolerated unless it is "carefully circumscribed by rules" defining what is permissible and what is not. The line between murder and war is essential but never precise. Hugo Grotius, considered the originator of international law (1625–31), condemned the use of poison in warfare as a violation of what he called the Laws of Nations and Natural Law. He argued, citing various ancient Greek and Roman writers (Livy, Claudian, Cicero, Gellius, Valerius, Florus, and Tacitus), that by general consent war is murderous enough without making it more so by poisons. On Grotius and ancient rules of war, see Penzer 1952, 5–6. Drummond 1989 notes that "laws of war are currently recognized as customary practices which are intended to reduce the amount of suffering in wartime to a minimum and to facilitate the restoration of peace." There is a modern sense that the level of destruction in wartime should be limited to "minimum necessary force." On Western laws of war from ancient Greece to the late twentieth century, see Howard et al. 1994; SIPRI 1975, 18–20. On ethics of war, see Nardin 1996.

10. Righteous warfare, *dharmayuddha,* was opposed to *kutayuddha,* crafty, ruthless strategies. *Laws of Manu* 7.90; 92; and 195. *Arthashastra*: Kautilya 1951, 436–37; Kautilya 1992. Ishii: Lesho et al. 1998, 516. China: Cowley and Parker 1996, s.v. "Sun Tzu" and see review by Sienho Yee, of Zhu Wen-Qi, *Outline of International Humanitarian Law* (Shanghai: International Committee of the Red Cross, 1997, in Chinese, with an English abstract).

11. Deuteronomy 19–20. Jericho: Joshua 6.21, 24. On ancient Jewish rules of war, see Nardin 1996, 95, 97–98, 106–9. The ten plagues in Exodus are discussed in chapter 4.

12. Koran 2.11–12; 2.190–94; 3.172; 22.19–22; 22.39–40; and later Islamic traditions in the Hadith. John Kelsay, personal correspondence, February 2, 2003. Sheikh Hamza Yusuf interviewed by Goldstein 2001. See also Nardin 1996, 129–33, 161–64, 166 notes 25 and 26. Hashmi forthcoming. History of Muslim fire weapons: Bilkadi 1995.

13. Polybius 13.3.2–6. Krentz 2002, 25. Strabo 10.1.12–13. See chapter 3 for the story of the destruction of Kirrha by poison. Ober 1994, 12, 14. Drummond 1989, introduction. Herodotus on Queen Tomyris, see chapter 5. Thucydides, *History of the Peloponnesian War* 1.49; 3.82–83, atrocities against noncombatants and children, e.g., 3.81–82; 7.29–30. For Aeneas, see chapters 3 and 7.

14. Cicero discussed just war in *On Duties* 1.34–6, esp. 21–25, and in his *Republic,* which only survives in paraphrases in later sources. According to Cicero, war was justified for self-defense, defense of allies, and vengeance. Ovid and Silius Italicus, see chapter 2; Florus, chapter 3. Tacitus, *Germania* 43. Vegetius, *On Military Matters* 3. On changing rules of war in the Roman Empire, see Drummond 1989, a case study of the period AD 353 to 378.

15. Self-defense in extremity and last resorts: Nardin 1996, 28–29, 86–88. Roman Stoic commanders idealized Odysseus: Krentz and Wheeler introduction to Polyaenus, 1:vi–xxiv, esp. vii, xii. On use of inhumane weapons against "cultural others," see Mayor 1995b; Fenn 2000, 1574. On challenges to rules of war through history, and situations that encourage violations, see chapter 12 of Howard et al. 1994.

16. "Greek mythology, always a good source of insight," depicted warriors punished for breaking conventions of war or committing excessive brutalities, notes Creveld in his article on changing rules of war since the Gulf War of 1991 (1991, 27). Whirlwind: O'Connell, "Secret Weapons," in Cowley and Parker 1996, 419.

Chapter 1

1. Dioscorides' statement appears in book 6 of the *Materia Medica,* an extensive collection of medical and pharmacology texts attributed to the physician Dioscorides. Majno 1991, 145, 147 and note 38. Pliny the Elder 16.51 gives the folk etymology associating yew and poison: see Harrison 1994. See also Reinach 1909, 70. Thanks to Joshua Katz for linguistic advice.

2. Hercules' struggle with the Hydra is one of earliest myths depicted in Greek art, appearing as early as the eighth century BC. The Hydra myth is recounted in Ovid, *Metamorphoses* 9.62–75; Apollodorus, *Library* 2.5.2; Diodorus of Sicily 4.11, and other sources. For a full discussion of the myth in ancient literature and art, see Gantz 1993, 1:23, 384–86. On pitch from trees in antiquity, see Pliny 16.52–61.

3. The deaths of Chiron and Pholus, and wounding of Telephus: Apollodorus, *Library* 2.5.4; *Epitome* 3.17–20, and see Frazer's notes 1 and 2, 2:186–89. Centaurs dying of Hercules' poison arrows were featured in many famous sculptures and paintings in antiquity. Places where they had died, polluting waters with the poison, were also pointed out. Telephus's wounding was the subject of several ancient plays and paintings. Pliny 25.42; 34.152. Gantz 1993, 1:147, 390–92, see also 2:579. Telephus's infected wound was healed by rust scrapings from Achilles' spear; see chapter 2.

4. Death of Hercules: Apollodorus, *Library* 2.7.7, with Frazer's note 1, 1:270–71; Sophocles, *Trachinian Women* 756ff.; Diodorus of Sicily 4.38; Ovid, *Metamorphoses* 9.100–238. See Gantz 1993, 1:458. For the burning, corrosive symptoms of the bite of the *dipsas* viper, see Scarborough 1977, 6, quoting Lucan, *Civil War*.

5. On Troy, and the cycle of stories about the Trojan War, see *Oxford Classical Dictionary*, entries for "Troy" and "Homer"; Gantz 1993, 2:576–657; Rose 1959, 230–53.

6. Homer, *Iliad* 1.50–70, 376–86; 2.731–33; 4.138–219; 11.812–48. Reinach 1909, 70, points out other linguistic hints of empoisoned arrows in Homer, who often uses words that evoke the imagery of snakebites to describe arrows, such as "biting, burning, and bitter." See Majno 1991, 145–47 and note 35, on "sucking out of snakebite wounds" in antiquity; see also 271, on black blood indicating poisoned arrows; for ancient treatment of snakebite by sucking out the venom and cautery, see 280. See Scarborough 1977, 6, 8–9, for vivid and accurate ancient descriptions of the sequelae of snake envenomation.

7. Homer, *Iliad* 2.725–39. That Philoctetes' ships were rowed by

archers was considered historical by the fifth-century BC Greek historian Thucydides 1.10. Gantz 1993, 1:459–60; 2:589–90, 625–28, 635–38, 700–701 surveys the Philoctetes stories in literature and art. Apollodorus, *Epitome* 3.26–27, 5.8–10, and see Frazer's note 2, 2:194–97, and note 1, 2:222–23. See Sophocles' play *Philoctetes* (409 BC); Euripides, Aeschylus, and two other playwrights also wrote *Philoctetes* tragedies, now lost. Quintus of Smyrna, *Fall of Troy* 9.334–480. Philoctetes' suffering was depicted in vase paintings and other art works, with the earliest known art dating to 460 BC. The shrine to Philoctetes on Chryse could be visited through the first century AD, but in about AD 150, the island was submerged by earthquakes. Appian, "Mithridatic Wars" 12.77; Pausanias 8.33.4. Scarborough 1977, 7, 9.

8. Quintus of Smyrna, *Fall of Troy* 3.58–82 and 148–50; 9.353–546. Ovid, *Metamorphoses* 12.596–628.

9. On the ideal of fighting up close, not "at long range" (i.e., with arrows), in the "front ranks for action and for honor," and avoiding blows "from behind on nape or back, but [taking them] in the chest or belly as you wade into . . . the battle line," see, e.g., Homer, *Iliad* 8.94f; 12.42; 13.260–300; 16.791, 806f. See Salazar 2000, 156–57, for a good discussion of the criticism of archers and the ideals of fighting face-to-face and avoiding wounds in the back. On ancient negative opinions about projectiles in war, see *Oxford Classical Dictionary*, s.v. "archers." The bow and arrow as "unheroic weapon": Faraone 1992, 125.

10. Virgil, *Aeneid* 9.770–74. Philoctetes after Troy and his last years: Gantz 1993, 2:700–701. Philoctetes' dedication of the weapons: Euphorion cited by Apollodorus, *Epitome* 6.15b; Pseudo-Aristotle, *On Marvelous Things Heard* 107 (115), says that Philoctetes dedicated the weapons in the Temple of Apollo at Macalla, near Krimissa, and that the citizens of Croton later transferred them to their own temple of Apollo. Ancient vases, coins, gems, and sculptures depicted Philoctetes receiving Hercules' quiver, wounded and abandoned, taking arrows from his quiver, shooting birds, fanning flies from his unhealing wound, shooting Paris, and so on.

11. Homer, *Odyssey* 2.235–30; 1.252–66. On the moral and historic meaning of this passage, see Dirlmeier 1966. Gantz 1993, 2:711–13; 732 (Circe). Ovid, *Metamorphoses* 7.406–25 (Cerberus), 14.41–68, 264–302 (Circe). Birds killed by fumes: Pliny 4.2. The stingray spear was made by Hephaestus, at Circe's request. The ray, perhaps a marbled blue stingray common in the Mediterranean, had been killed by Phorkys, a Triton, and the thorny, serrated spine was forged onto a shaft inlaid with adamantine and gold. See chapter 2 for evidence of the actual use of stingray spines as weapons.

12. Sophocles, *Trachinian Women* 573–74. The paradoxical figure of Hercules is discussed by Faraone 1992, 59.

13. The "poisoner poisoned" folk motif is a widespread and ancient theme: for examples see the standard folklore reference work, Stith Thompson's *Motif-Index of Folk-Literature*, motifs K1613. The reason for the deaths at Bari was covered up by the U.S. military: Harris and Paxman 1982, 77–79, 119–25. The U.S. troops' health problems have also been attributed in part to vaccinations against biochemical arms in 1991. On the origins of Iraq's biological weapons, see note 4, chapter 5, and Shenon 2003.

14. Faraone 1992, 125 on combined plague and fire imagery. Poisons and incendiaries combined: see chapter 7 and Partington 1999, 149, 209–11, 271, 273, 284–85.

15. Quintus of Smyrna, *Fall of Troy* 9.386–89. On Greek atrocities during the sack of Troy see Gantz 1993, 2:650–57; for ancient sources, see note 3 in chapter 3. Painting on the Acropolis: Pausanias 1.22.4. Ovid, *Metamorphoses* 9.170–204; and Ovid, *Tristia*.

Chapter 2

1. Galen (second century AD) cited in Scarborough 1977, 3 and note 1. See Scarborough's discussion of the ancient dread of venomous snakes and the many Greek and Roman treatises on plant and animal poisons and antidotes, some effective and some bizarre. Homer, *Iliad* 3.35–47.

2. Aelian, *On Animals* 9.40, 1.54, 5.16, 9.15. Pseudo-Aristotle, *On Marvelous Things Heard* 844 b 80 (140), claims that wasps that have feasted on poisonous adder's flesh have a sting worse than the adder's bite.

3. Quintus of Smyrna, *Fall of Troy* 9.392–97. Pausanias 2.37.4. Diodorus of Sicily 4.38. On symptoms of snakebites and Nicander, see Scarborough 1977, 6–9. *Dipsas, seps, aspis, kerastes,* and *echis* are a few of the names for Viperidae in ancient texts. *Vipera ammodytes, Cerastes* species, *Vipera berus,* and *Echis carinata* are some of the poisonous snakes known to Greeks and Romans.

4. Quintus of Smyrna, *Fall of Troy* 9.392–97. Hercules shooting the deer, the Centaurs, and the man-eating Stymphalean birds: Gantz 1993, 1:387–88; 390–92, 394. According to Grmek 1979, 143, and Reinach 1909, 56, classical Greek authors felt that using weapons intended for hunting animals in battles with men was an odious practice, rather than an acceptable military stratagem. This attitude explains why Homer had King Ilus refuse to give Odysseus poison for "murdering men." See Lesho et al. 1998, 512, on the psychological terror of biological projectiles.

5. Galen and Paul of Aegina referred to Dacian and Dalmatian arrow poisons, Salazar 2000, 28. Hellebore: Majno 1991, 147, 188–93. Pliny 25.47–61. Pseudo-Aristotle, *On Marvelous Things Heard* 837 a 10 (86). Hadzabe tribe of Tanzania: Martin 2001. For a survey of Celtic and other ancient arrow poisons and antidotes, see Reinach 1909.

6. Ovid, *Metamorphoses* 7, origin of aconite. Aelian, *On Animals* 9.18, 4.49. Pliny 6.4 (the town of Aconae on the Black Sea was of "evil repute for the poison called aconite"); 8.100; 22.18 (nature's weapons); 27.4–10; for antidotes see 20.132; 23.43, 92, 135; 25.163; 28.161; 29.74, 105. Aconite in India: Penzer 1952, 11. Moors and aconite: Partington 1999, 231 note 103. Aconite bullets: Harris and Paxman 1982, 61. On septic bullets, see Wheelis 1999, 34. Henbane: Aelian, *On Animals* 9.32. Pliny 23.94; 25.35–37. See also Majno 1991, 387.

7. Poison-arrow frogs: Lori Hamlett, Nashville Zoo, Tennessee, www.nashvillezoo.org. Psylli: Pliny, 25.123; Aelian, *On Animals* 1.57; 16.28. Curare: Economic Botany Web pages of University of California,

Los Angeles, www.botgard.ucla.edu. In North America, the Iroquois, Apaches, Navajos, and other tribes used poison arrows: Reinach 1909, 52–53 and note 1. Hemlock: Aelian, *On Animals* 4.23. Rolle 1989, 65.

8. Aelian, *On Animals* 9.27. Pliny 16.51; 21.177–79. Majno 1991, 488 note 38. Also see Harrison 1994. Lucretius, *On the Nature of the Universe* 6.780–86, may have been speaking of yew when he mentioned a tree whose "shade was so oppressive as to provoke a headache in one who lies under it." Arrow poisons can be very long-lived. Recent toxicological analysis of desiccated poison paste on arrows collected in the 1900s in Assam, India, and Burma, in the Victoria and Albert Museum, London, revealed that the longevity of the toxin was thirteen hundred years! Victoria and Albert Museum Web site: vam.ac.uk. Rhododendron honey as a weapon: chapter 5.

9. Aelian, *On Animals* 4.41; Ctesias Fragment 57.17. As a safety precaution to avoid pricking themselves with the lethal toxin, the San Bushmen place the insect guts on the shaft just behind the arrowhead: Robertson 2002. Aristotle and Nicander on toxic beetles: Scarborough 1979, 13–14, 20–21, 73–80. The powerful toxin *pederin* is now being tested as an anticancer drug. Frank and Kanamitsu 1987 (thanks to Robert Peterson for this reference).

10. Aelian, *On Animals* 1.56; 2.36 and 50; 8.26. Pliny 9.147 on the "burning sting" of jellyfish and sea urchins. For ancient sources for the story of the stingray spear, see Apollodorus, *Epitome* 7.36–37 and Frazer's note 2, pp. 303–304. Thanks to Dolores Urquidi, Austin, Texas, for sharing her research into the use of stingray spines as arrowheads in Central and South America. Schultz 1962, 130, 132. For facts about aconite, henbane, belladonna, curare, and stingrays, see "Poisonous Plants and Animals," copyright Team C007974, www.library.thinkquest.org.

11. Ancient writers on poison archery: Reinach 1909, 54–56 and notes. Hua T'o removed a poisoned arrow that pierced the arm of General Kuan Yu, about eighteen hundred years ago: Majno 1991, 249–51, Fig. 6.19. Bradford 2001, 160. Strabo 16.4.10. Silius Italicus, *Punica* 1.320–415, 3.265–74. Ancient Greek and Roman authors who mention

arrow poisons: Salazar 2000, 28–30. Poisoned arrows were reportedly used in violent uprisings in Kenya in August 1997, according to CNN news reports. Lesho et al. 1998, 512, notes that the use of "biological projectiles . . . persisted into the 20th century during the Russian Revolution, various European conflicts, and the South African Boer wars."

12. On the history of the bow and arrow and advances in archery technology, see Crosby 2002, 37–39, and his chapter 5. Herodotus's book 4 describes the Scythians, see esp 4.9. Rolle 1989, 65. For example, a Corinthian vase of 590 BC (Antikenmuseum, Basel, Switzerland) shows Athena holding out a phial for the Hydra poison. Akamba poison arrows: information from Timothy F. Bliss, former resident of Kenya; and descriptions of Akamba bow, quiver, and poison arrows from the 1970s offered for sale in 2002 by the Krackow Company, New Wilmington, Pennsylvania, specializing in traditional, worldwide archery equipment.

13. The recipe in Pseudo-Aristotle, *On Marvelous Things Heard* 845 a 5 (141) states that human blood was buried in a dunghill until it putrefied, then the contaminated blood was mixed with the rotten venom. Aelian, *On Animals* 9.15, citing a lost work by Theophrastus. Dioscorides also mentions the *toxicon pharmacon* of the Scythians, 1.106, 2.79. See Reinach 1909, 54–55. Unless it was collected separately, the venom itself would probably lose neurotoxicity if allowed to decompose in the snake.

14. Plutarch, *Artaxerxes*. Pungee sticks: Christopher et al. 1997, 412. Strabo 11.2.19 (first century BC). Modern stench weapons are based on the finding that excrement and rotting corpses are the two universally intolerable odors for humans across cultures—and with good reason, since corpses and feces are sources of potentially lethal pathogens. The logic was evident in the prescientific era, when foul odors or miasmas were thought to actually cause disease: Wheelis 1999, 11 note 10; Creveld 1991, 25; and see *New York Times Magazine*, December 15, 2002, 126. U.S. military scientists are developing stench and colored smoke weapons that target racial groups: "When Killing Just Won't Do" 2003. Rolle 1989, 65. Excrement as weapon in prescientific era: In China (AD 800–1600) defenders of cities poured boiling urine and feces on attackers: Wheelis 1999, note 4, and see

Temple 1991, 223, for the use of poison arrows and 216 for excrement explosives in early China. In 1422, two thousand cartloads of excrement were hurled at foes at Carolstein: Eitzen and Takafuji 1997. Parts of this section on Scythian arrow poison appeared in different form in Mayor 1997a. Thanks to herpetologist Aaron Bauer, Villanova University, for information on poisonous snakes of Scythia and India and the feasibility of venom arrows. On tetanus in domestic animal dung and death from tetanus after arrow wounds, see Majno 1991, 199–200. Ancient descriptions of gangrene and tetanus: Salazar 2000, 30–34.

15. Ovid, *Tristia* 3.10.64; *Letter from Pontus* 1.2.17; 4.7.11 and 10.31, cited in Reinach 1909, 55, note 5. Armenian arrows: see chapter 7. Rolle 1989, 65. Barbed arrows in antiquity: Salazar 2000, 18–19, 49, 232–33. Superfluous injury: Unlike the blade of a Greek hoplite's javelin or Roman soldier's sword, which passed cleanly through a body and could be easily pulled out, the use of long-distance projectiles and missiles with hooked shapes caused more tissue damage and loss of blood. Modern analogies to the misgivings evoked by such arms are evident in the 1899 Hague Convention's Declaration Concerning Expanding Bullets, prohibiting the newly developed "manstopping" dumdum bullets that expanded on impact and left gaping, ragged wounds instead of penetrating cleanly at high velocity like streamlined metal-jacketed bullets. The expanding bullets were invented at Dum-Dum Arsenal in India in the 1890s to stop fanatical fighters in Afghanistan and India. Current U.S. and NATO copper-jacket, lead-core bullets do fragment on impact, but still cause less damage than exploding bullets. One might compare the Greek hoplite's spear to the metal-jacket bullet as ancient and modern icons of "clean" warfare "by the rules," whereas a hooked arrow coated with venom was the ancient equivalent of a dumdum bullet combined with a bio-toxin. See 1907 Hague Convention IV, also 1977 additions to the 1949 Geneva Convention. As early as 1868, the Saint Petersburg Declaration prohibited exploding bullets on the rationale that such weapons are contrary to the laws of humanity because they "uselessly aggravate the sufferings of disabled men, or render their death inevitable." Howard et al. 1994, 6–7,

120–21 (1899 Hague rules). Thanks to Mark Wheelis for helpful information on dumdum bullets.

16. Rudenko 1970, 217–18, and color plates 179–80. For patterns of poisonous snakes of Scythian territory, see Phelps 1981, 97–102, 162–64, Figs. 26–30, color plates 16 and 17.

17. Mining gems with arrows: Pliny 37.110–12. Rolle 1989, 65–66; *Oxford Classical Dictionary*, s.v. "archers." Modern ethnological parallels suggest the rate of twenty arrows a minute, but the expert Scythians may have been faster.

18. Aelian, *On Animals* 4.36 describes death by ingestion of tiny amounts (the size of a sesame seed) of the Purple Snake poisons placed in wine, but the sticky residue would serve very well as arrow poisons. For an ancient account of men killed by drinking from a spring poisoned by snake venom, see Aelian, 17.37; and on similar fears in Libya, see Lucan, *Civil War*, 9.605–20. Thanks to Aaron Bauer and Robert Murphy, senior curator of herpetology, Royal Ontario Museum, Toronto, for help in identifying the Purple Snake. Kautilya 1951, 449.

19. Strabo 15.2.5–7. Majno 1991, 283, citing the ancient historian Arrian, *Indica* 8.15. Other sources for Alexander's campaign in India are Quintus Curtius Rufus, Justin, Diodorus of Sicily. See Polyaenus 4.3.22 for Alexander's strategies against Porus. On Chandragupta: Bradford 2001, 125–27. About fifteen thousand people die annually from snakebite in India today: Majno 1991, 283.

20. Alexander and contemporary historians referred to the "Brahmans" of Harmatelia as an ethnic group, unaware of the Hindu caste system. Diodorus of Sicily 17.102–103. Strabo 15.2.7. Quintus Curtius 9.8.13–28. Viper constipation: Angier 2002. Aelian, *On Animals* 12.32, remarks that Indian doctors knew which herbs counteracted the "very violent and rapid spread" of snake venom. Symptomology of viper and cobra envenomation from discussions with Aaron Bauer and Scarborough 1977, 8–9.

21. According to Reinach 1909, 55–56, note 9, the Rigveda epic of India contains references to poison arrows. *Laws of Manu* 7.90, see Buhler 1886, 230. Majno 1991, 264. The *Arthashastra*, attributed to Kautilya

(also known as Chanakya), in its surviving form also contains material from the first to fifth centuries AD. Kautilya 1951, 442–455, 449 (terror effects), and Book 14. Indian Defence Ministry experiments at University of Pune and National Institute of Virology: Rahman 2002. U.S. military research into pharmaceutical and genome-based anti-sleep agents: Onion 2002; and see the DARPA Web site: www.darpa.mil.

22. Pliny 34.152–54; 25.33, 42, 66–69, 99. The rust treatment is mentioned by Apollodorus and Ovid, too: Gantz 2:579. The effect of rust on poison arrow wounds is unknown, but myrrh has antiseptic properties. Majno 1991, 218, 370, 387–389, and Fig. 9.25. Aelian, *On Animals* 1.54. Scarborough 1977, 11, 12–18. Salazar 2000, 29.

223. Immunity to venom and poisons: Aelian, *On Animals* 5.14; 9.29; 16.28. Pliny 7.13–14, 27; 8.229; 11.89–90. Strabo 13.1.14. See chapter 5 on Mithridates.

24. Aelian, *On Animals* 9.62. Strabo 13.1.14. Cato and the Psylli: Lucan, *Civil War* 9.600–949. Pliny 11.89–90.

25. On treating poisoned arrow wounds, see Salazar 2000, 28–30; black blood of poison wounds; 29; removing barbed projectiles; 48–50. Majno 1991, compares Greek and Indian arrow wound treatments in the fourth century BC. See 142–45 on treating arrow wounds in Homer: of 147 wounds, the survival rate was 77.6 percent (quote, 143). See 171 (red vs. black blood); 193–95, 266, 271–72 (treating arrow wounds); 279–80 (sucking out venom); 359–61 (removing barbed arrows); 381 (Celsus on the Psylli). "Gloom": Scarborough 1977, 3.

Chapter 3

1. Thucydides, *History of the Peloponnesian War* 7.84. Strabo 15.2.6. Poupard and Miller 1992, 10, on thirst and poisoning water. Wheelis 1999, 9 note 3, agreed with military historian Milton Leitenberg that contaminating water in antiquity was intended to deny potable water rather than to spread disease. But the examples in this chapter and chapter 4 show that

poisoning water was often deliberately intended to cause illness.

2. Aeschines, *Against Ctesiphon* 3.107–24, curse 109. Frontinus, *Stratagems* 3.7.6. Polyaenus 6.13. Kirrha was also known as Krisa. Strabo 9.3.3–4 recounts the destruction of Kirrha and mentions the profusion of hellebore at Anticyra, but omits mention of the poison's role in the city's demise.

3. Pausanias 10.37. Ulrich's find: Peter Levi's note 259 in vol. 1 of the Penguin edition of Pausanias (1979). See also Plutarch, *Solon* 11. Slaughter of children and old people, and rape during the sack of Troy: Quintus of Smyrna, *Fall of Troy* 13.78–324; Apollodorus, *Epitome* 5.21–23, and Frazer's notes 1–2, pp 238–39. On Greek atrocities during the sack of Troy in ancient literature and art, see Gantz 1993, 2:650–57.

4. Thessalos, *Presbeulicos* is included in the corpus of Hippocratic texts cited by Grmek 1979, 146–48. Churchill and Iraq: Simons 1994, 179–81. Gas was prohibited by the 1899 Hague Convention, Howard et al., 7, 121, 123. Churchill's willingness to use gas against the Germans in World War II is discussed by Harris and Paxman, 1982, chapter 5. The British used mustard gas against rebels in Afghanistan in 1919, praising its effectiveness on ignorant and unprotected tribesmen (43–44). Similar lethal effects of deploying a supposedly "nonlethal" gas indiscriminately during a hostage crisis in Moscow in 2002 resulted in more than one hundred deaths of the innocent hostages: see chapter 5.

5. Doctors were accused of propagating pestilence in the Middle Ages, and suspicions continued in early modern times: see Bercé 1993. Examples of Italian, American, French, and Japanese doctors involved in biological warfare are discussed by Lesho et al. 1998, 513; Robertson and Robertson 1995, 370 (Civil War). The army physician who rose to the rank of general in World War II, Dr. Shiro Ishii, is one of the most notorious medical war criminals of the modern era. As director of Japan's extensive biological war effort, the doctor was responsible for many thousands of deaths from a vast array of biochemical agents in China and has been accused of creating "the most gruesome series of biological weapons experiments in history." His staff included more than three thousand entomologists, botanists, and

microbiologists, and fifty physicians. Harris and Paxman 1982; Robertson and Robertson 1995, 371; Christopher et al. 1997, 413; Williams and Wallace 1989. South African "doctors of death": "The Science of Apartheid" 1998; Finnegan 2001.

6. The Geneva Convention resulted in the Geneva Protocol of 1925, prohibiting the use, but not the production, of biochemical agents. Harris and Paxman 1982, 45–48. Grmek 1979, 147, 141–42. Poupard and Miller 1992, 13 on 1925 Geneva Convention, "Protocol for the Prohibition of the Use in War of Asphyxiating, Poisonous or Other Gases, and of Bacteriological Methods of Warfare." Isocrates, *Plataicus* 14.31. Whitehead 1990, commentary on Aeneas the Tactician 8.4, p 115, cites the Athenian orator Aeschines, *On the Embassy* 2.115, on the vow by Delphi's Amphictionic League never to totally destroy any league city or interfere with "flowing water." See also Ober 1994, 12. "As old as the weapons themselves": Lesho et al. 1998, 515. *Laws of Manu* 7.90, see Buhler 1886, 230, 247; see also Maskiell and Mayor 2001, 25.

7. Athenians fouling their own wells: Whitehead 1990, 115, commentary on Aeneas the Tactician 8.4, citing Francis and Vickers 1988. Thucydides, *History of the Peloponnesian War* 2.47–55; 3.87. Aeneas's shocked British commentators: see Whitehead's commentary, 1990, 115, citing Hunter and Handford. Iroquois: Wheelis 1999, 27. Historical and recent examples of poisoning wells: Christopher et al. 1997.

8. Frontinus, *Stratagems* 3.7.4–5. Diverting the Euphrates was attributed to Cyrus by Xenophon, *Cyropaedia* 7.5, and Polyaenus 7.6.5, 8.26 (Semiramis inscription). Philostratus, *Apollonius of Tyana,* 1.25, credited Medea with the engineering feat. See Polyaenus 1.3.5. Lesho et al. 1998, 512. Causing massive flooding that indiscriminately killed noncombatants involved ethical issues for early Islamic scholars: Hashmi (forthcoming) cites "numerous records of flooding as a battlefield tactic by Muslim armies" and notes "the many instances in which it backfired against its perpetrator, sweeping away his own besieging troops along with his enemies."

9. Frontinus, *Stratagems* 4.1.36. Florus 1.35.5–7. Tacitus *Annals* 3.1.59–68; 5.2.84. Aulus Gellius, *Attic Nights* 3.8. Virgil, *Aeneid* 9.770–74.

10. Penzer 1952, 3–5, citing Kautilya's *Arthashastra*. Kautilya 1951, 432–433, 435, 441–45, 455–57. Date of *Susruta Samhita*, Majno 1991, 511 note 26.

11. On deadly, sulphurous exhalations from bodies of water or the earth: Pliny 2.207–208; 2.232 (deadly springs); 31.26 and 49; 35.174. See also Virgil, *Aeneid* 6.236–42, and Healy 1999, 246. Lucretius, *On the Nature of the Universe* 6.738–79, 6.817–38. Foul odors and disease or poison: Poupard and Miller 1992, 10.

12. Strabo 8.3.19 (marsh poisoned by Hydra poison). Quintus of Smyrna, *Fall of Troy* 2.561–66. Empedocles and draining malarial marshes: Diogenes Laertius, *Lives of the Philosophers* 8.70; Grmek 1979, 159; Faraone 1992, 64. Thanks to Philip Thibodeau for pointing out Varro's *De Re Rustica* 1.12.2. Lucretius, *On the Nature of the Universe* 6.1091–1286. Livy 5.48; 25.26. Diodorus of Sicily 12.45.2–4; 14.70–71. Vegetius, *On Military Matters*.

13. Xenophon, *Cyropaedia* 1.6.15. Military disasters due to malarial swamps and the "strategic uses of insalubrious terrain": Grmek 1979, 149–63, 151 ("particular measures"), citing Thucydides *History of the Peloponnesian War* 6–7, esp. 7.47.1–2; Plutarch, *Nicias*; and Diodorus of Sicily 13–14. Grmek 149–50.

14. Frontinus, *Stratagems* 2.7.12. Plutarch, *Moralia* 202.4. Bradford 2001, 201. Pliny 25.20–21. Tacitus, *Annals* 3.1.58–70.

15. Grmek 149–50. Polyaenus 2.30. Robertson and Robertson 1995, 369.

16. Grmek 1979, 161–63, believes that the grim story of Clearchus is true, based on many historical accounts that were available to Polyaenus but are now lost. Saddam's attack on Kurds: Simons 1994; Hashmi 2004. As the George W. Bush administration prepared to attack Iraq to destroy its stores of biochemical arms in 2002, reports emerged that suppliers in the United States had provided many of the raw materials for Iraq's biological and chemical weapons program during the Reagan administration of the 1980s; those reports were confirmed in 2003. Some U.S. troops who destroyed Iraq's biochemical munitions in the Gulf War of 1991

now suffer a cluster of health problems that stem in part from the very agents created by the United States and sent to Iraq. Acknowledging the age-old rebound problems for those involved with biochemical armaments, one U.S. senator critical of the attack on Iraq asked in 2002, "Are we now facing the possibility of reaping what we have sown?" Origins of Iraq's bio-weaponry: CBS News, and *New York Times*, August 18, 2002; Kelley 2002; Shenon 2003. Controversial allegations of poisons used against political insurgencies in Ethiopia and Southeast Asia between 1975 and 1981 are discussed by Eitzen and Takafugi 1997, chapters 18 and 34; Lesho et al. 1998, 515; and Christopher et al. 1997, 415. South Africa: "Science of Apartheid" 1998; Finnegan 2001. Widely discussed examples of U.S. government bio-weapons and nuclear tests endangering American citizens during the Cold War have been documented. For example, the release of supposedly harmless pathogens in San Francisco Bay in 1950 caused an outbreak of infections with at least one fatality, and in 2002, the U.S. government acknowledged secret releases of bio-toxins and chemical agents (nerve agents and hallucinogens being developed as offensive weapons) aboard Navy ships, and in several U.S. locations in 1949–71. Lesho et al. 1998, 513–14; Christopher et al. 1997, 414; Aldinger 2002; "Sailors Sprayed with Nerve Gas in Test," 2002. Japanese dissemination of cholera among the Chinese in 1941 resulted in about seventeen hundred fatalities of unprotected Japanese troops, besides the targeted ten thousand Chinese victims: Christopher et al. 1997, 413. Grmek 1979, 149–50.

Chapter 4

1. Today the word "plague" usually connotes bubonic or Black Plague, but in antiquity, "plague" was used for all epidemics. The Mongols (Tatars) at Kaffa: Wheelis 2002; Derbes 1966; Robertson and Robertson 1995, 370; Christopher et al. 1997, 412; Lesho et al. 1998, 512. Poupard and Miller 1992, 11. Hasdrubal: Livy 27.43–50. Hannibal catapulting vipers, see chapter 6.

2. Communicable disease mechanisms were established by Louis Pasteur, Robert Koch, and other scientists in the nineteenth century, but disease transmission was observed and remarked upon very early in human history. Neufeld 1980, 32–34, discusses evidence for ancient intuitions about contagion. "Miasmas": Livy 25.26. Cyzicus: Appian, "Mithridatic Wars" 12.76; see also "Punic Wars" 73 for a similar corpse-borne plague that struck the Carthaginian army in 150 BC.

3. Livy 25.26 ("contact with the sick spread the disease"); Diodorus of Sicily 14.70.4–71.4 ("those who tended the sick were seized by the plague"). Thucydides, *History of the Peloponnesian War* 2.47–55; 3.87. Zinsser 1963, 119–27; McNeill 1976, 105–6. Sophocles, *Trachinian Women* 555–1038 (lines 956, 1038 *anthos*, "pustulant efflorescence"). Cedrenus cited in Zinsser 1963, 138. Chinese awareness of fomites in clothing: Temple 1991, 215.

4. Cuneiform tablets about contagion, found in the archives of Mari: Sasson 2000, 1911–24 and personal correspondence, November 2002; also Neufeld 1980, 33. On early understanding of smallpox contagion, inoculation, quarantine, and long-term virulence of desiccated smallpox matter, see Fenn 2000, 1561, 1563–64; McNeill 1976, 253. On political assassinations by gifts of smallpox-infected clothing in Mughal India: Maskiell and Mayor 2001. Smallpox-infected blankets and missiles in early Colonial American military history: Fenn 2000, 1577–79; Poupard and Miller 1992, 11–13. See Mayor 1995b for a cross-cultural survey of disease-infected items as bio-weapons, such as smallpox blankets given to Native Americans, from antiquity to the present. Articles of clothing laced with nerve poisons absorbed through the skin were created to kill anti-apartheid activists, according to testimony before the Truth and Reconciliation Commission, reported in "The Science of Apartheid" 1998; and in Finnegan 2001, 62.

5. Hittite plague rituals: Faraone 1992, 99, 109 notes 37–39; see also 41–42, 44, 47, 59–73.

6. On Hittite and Babylonian plague gods, Faraone 1992, 61, 120–21, 125–27, and see 128–32, esp. 130 on rodents bringing pestilence. On pestilence

and warfare through history, Zinsser 1963, esp. 139, 141; 125–26 on the epidemic that struck the Carthaginians. See also McNeill 1976, 115–27.

7. Exodus 1 and 7–12, and *New Oxford Annotated Bible* 1973, commentary. Poisoning fish with chemicals: Pliny 25.98. Homer, *Iliad* 1.50–70. On intention to spread contagion, see Wheelis 1999, 9. Tetrahedron, a New Age–survivalist company based in Idaho, sells "Bible-recommended" essentials oils to protect against biological warfare, including one called Exodus II supposedly concocted by Moses "to protect the Israelites from plague" (see chapter 5, on attempts to immunize against bio-attack).

8. Army troops in Burma (Myanmar) carried out systematic rape as a "weapon of war" to crush ethnic rebellion: *New York Times,* December 27, 2002. In 1975, a U.S. military manual alluded to the theoretical possibility of developing ethnic biochemical weapons to selectively incapacitate or kill specific population groups by taking advantage of genetic knowledge, and in the 1980s, the Soviets repeatedly accused the United States, Israel, and South Africa of seeking to develop "ethnic weapons," allegations denied by U.S. authorities as "preposterous [and] out of the question." Wick 1988, 14–21. South Africa's "Project Coast": Finnegan 2001, 58, 61–63. The possibility of ethnic "genetic bombs" is discussed by Harris and Paxman 1982. According to "Nonlethal Weapons: Terms and References," a recent report published by the U.S. Air Force Institute for National Security Studies, proposals are being considered for "genetic alteration" weapons that would create long-term birth defects over generations among enemy populations: reported in "When Killing Just Won't Do" 2003.

9. "Pharaoh's orders, see Exodus 1; Herod's orders, see Matthew 2. Rose 1959, 234–35; *Oxford Classical Dictionary* s.v. "Sabini"; Polyaenus 8.3.1. *Arthashastra*: Bradford 2001, 127.

10. Man-made pestilence: Grmek 1997, 148–50. Seneca, *On Anger* 2.9.3; Livy 8.18; Orosius, *Histories against the Pagans* 3.10. Dio Cassius, *Epitome* 67.11 and 73.14. Panic induced by modern bio-terror fears in the United States: Meckler 2002. On plagues in antiquity, see *Oxford Classical Dictionary*, s.v. "plague"; and Faraone 1992, 128–32.

11. Kautilya 1951, 443–46. Mousepox virus is discussed in Preston's *Demon in the Freezer* (2002). Synthetic virus discovery: "Do-It-Yourself Virus Recreated from Synthetic DNA," *Science News,* July 13, 2002, 22; see also *Newsweek* July 22, 8. Microbiologists point out that the polio virus is a relatively simple virus. "It is still a formidable challenge to synthesize in vitro one of the more complicated viruses (such as the pox viruses)." Mark Wheelis, personal correspondence, February 4, 2003.

12. On cross-cultural ancient and modern legends about "bottling up" plague and releasing it against enemies, see Mayor 1995b and Maskiell and Mayor 2001. The Ark: 1 Samuel 4–7; 2 Samuel 6.6–7 (Uzzah). For further discussion of the Ark-related plague, see chapter 6.

13. Plague demons kept in the temple at Jerusalem, *Testament of Solomon* manuscripts and *Testimony of Truth,* Nag Hammadi library. Dating and text analysis, Johnston 2002 and James Harding and Loveday Alexander, Biblical Studies, University of Sheffield, "Dating the Testament of Solomon," May 28, 1999. Conybeare 1898. Quotes from Bonner 1956, 5–6. (Faraone 1992, 72 note 84, cited Bonner, but mistook Solomon for Samuel and Babylonians for Assyrians.) Bashiruddin Mehmood was accused in 2001 of ties to Islamic terrorists, after plans for anthrax balloons were found in the offices of an organization he headed in Afghanistan: reported in the *New York Times,* November 28, 2001. Islamic scientists on the legend of Solomon: Aftergood 2001, citing a *Wall Street Journal* article on "Islamic Science," September 13, 1988, and *Islam and Science* (1991) by Pakistani physicist Pervez Hoodbhoy. The plague during Titus's reign (AD 79–81) occurred about nine years after he destroyed the temple, according to Suetonius, *Titus.*

14. Faraone 1992, 61–64. The two ancient sources for the great plague of AD 165–80, sometimes called the Plague of Antoninus, are the biography of Lucius Verus, by "Julius Capitolinus" in *Lives of the Later Caesars* (*Historia Augusta*) 7–8; and Ammianus Marcellinus, 23.6.24. Zinsser 1963, 135–37. McNeill 1976, 116–17.

15. Diodorus of Sicily 14.70.4. Appian, "Illyrian Wars" 4. Hamaxitus: Strabo 13.1.48–49. Aelian, *On Animals* 12.5; 4.40; 9.15; 10.49; 12.20;

14.20. Faraone 1992, 61–62. "Cures" for rabies are given by Pliny 29.98–102. Kautilya 1951, 444. Rabies "bombs": Robertson and Robertson 1995, 370. The Polish general was Casimir Siemenowicz, author of *The Grand Art d'Artillerie* (1650): see Lesho et al. 1998, 512–13; Partington 1999, 168. In about 1500, Leonardo da Vinci envisioned a bomb made from mad-dog saliva, tarantula venom, toxic toads, sulphur, arsenic, and burnt feathers. Temple 1991, 218. On the long viability of smallpox matter and aerosols: Lesho et al. 1998, 512. On archaeologists' concerns that smallpox could be accidentally released during excavations of ancient sites, see Fenn 2000, 1558 note 9.

16. Harris 1995. Catapults: See *Oxford Classical Dictionary*, s.v. "artillery." Greek Fire stored in Byzantine churches: Partington 1999, 25 and note 218. Myra: Forbes 1964, 19.

17. Quotes from Faraone 1992, 63, 65, 66 (Hercules can only offer defensive aid to armies). The temple at Chryse was dedicated to Apollo the god of pestilential mice, notorious carriers of disease, and it was not far from the temple of Apollo at Hamaxitus, which actually kept hordes of mice. In a striking coincidence in the ancient history of biological warfare, Chryse was also the name of the desert island where Philoctetes suffered a poison-arrow wound.

18. Partington 1999, 21 and note 191. Louis XIV, Hitler, Nixon, treaties: Robertson and Robertson 1995, 369, 371, 372. Christopher et al. 1997, 413–16. Lesho et al. 1998, 513–15. Many military scientists use the circular logic that biochemical weapons must first be invented so that they can prepare countermeasures. Harris and Paxman 1982, chapter 3, esp 42. In 1956, the United States "changed its policy of 'defensive use only' to include possible deployment of biological weapons in situations other than retaliation": Poupard and Miller 1992, 14–15. On last-resort strategies and extremities of war, see Nardin 1996, 28–29, 86–88, 133.

19. Booby-trapped chests: Partington 1999, 170. Modern examples: Robertson and Robertson 1995, 371; Christopher et al. 1997, 413–14; Lesho et al. 1998, 513. Ishii's chronic illness: Harris and Paxman 1982, 75–79. In 1971, a smallpox outbreak in Aralsk, Kazakhstan, may have

resulted from the release of a strain of weaponized smallpox tested on an island in the Aral Sea, an island that is contaminated by anthrax and other germ weaponry buried by the Soviet military. Miller 2002b. Faraone 1992, 66, 120–21.

20. Poison Maidens: Penzer 1952, 3, 12–71. Poison Sultan: Maskiell and Mayor 2001, 165. Fears of "smallpox martyrs," infected individuals who could be dispatched by terrorists to spread contagion, rose in 2002: *New York Times Magazine,* December 15, 2002, 122. Grafton 1995, 181.

Chapter 5

1. Xenophon, *Anabasis* 2.5; 4.8. Diodorus of Sicily 14.26–30. Pliny 21.74–78 (on poison honey); see 25.37 on antidotes from poisons. On toxic honey in antiquity and modern times, see Mayor 1995a. Interview with T. C., February 1986. Ambrose 1974, 34.

2. Pliny 25.5–7. Agari snake-venom doctors: Appian, "Mithridatic Wars" 12.88. Mithridates' animal bodyguard: Aelian, *On Animals* 7.46. *Laws of Manu* 7.218, see Buhler 1886, 251. Knowledge of Indian medicine in the Roman era, see Majno 1991, 374–78.

3. Celsus, a physician during the reign of Tiberius, listed thirty-six *theriac* ingredients. Majno 1991, 414–17.

4. Julius Capitolinus, *Lives of the Later Caesars, Marcus Antoninus* 15.3. Kautilya 1951, 443, 455–57. Saddam seeks antidote for nerve gas: Miller 2002a. One of Tetrahedron's "Essential Oils for Biological Warfare Preparedness" was allegedly "used by Moses to protect the Israelites from plague." The oil contains cinnamon, cassia, calamus, myrrh, hyssop, frankincense, spikenard, and galbanum in olive oil: www.tetrahedron.org. The existence of Gulf War Syndrome, a cluster of physical and psychological symptoms, has not been acknowledged by the U.S. government. The syndrome has been attributed in part to the vaccinations and in part to poisoning that occurred when U.S. troops destroyed chemical and biological

munitions in Iraq during the Gulf War of 1991. Sarah Edmonds, "Grisly U.S. Crimes Raise Questions on Gulf War Illness," Reuters, Washington, DC, November 15, 2002. Germans and typhus: Christopher et al. 1997, 413. Marcus Aurelius: Majno 1991, 414–15.

5. Pliny 25.5–7, 37, and 62–65; 29.24–26. Mithridates: Dio Cassius 36–37; Appian "Mithridatic Wars" 12; Strabo 12.3.30–31.

6. Pompey: Strabo 12.3.18. Mayor 1995a.

7. Aelian *On Animals* 5.29. Aeneas the Tactician 16.5–7. Kautilya 1951, 441. Hannibalic wars: Bradford 2001, 178–89. Frontinus, *Stratagems* 2.5.13–14, and 23.

8. Dio Cassius, *Epitome* 67.5.6.

9. Polyaenus 1.1.1; 1.1 and 1.3; 1.preface.1–3; 8.25.1.

10. Polyaenus 8.28; 31.18. Herodotus 1.199–216. Strabo's version, 11.8.4–6, substituted another Scythian tribe, the Sacae (neighbors of the Massagetae) as the victims.

11. Polyaenus 5.10.1; 8.23.1. See *Oxford Classical Dictionary* s.v. "Himilco." Mandrake: Pliny 25.147–50. Frontinus, *Stratagems* 2.5.12. A Theopompus fragment and Polyaenus 7.42 recounted the Celts' plan.

12. Leprosy wine: Grmek 1979, 147. Anthrax candy: Lesho et al. 1998, 513; and on Ishii see Harris and Paxman 1982, 75–79. "Science of Apartheid" 1998, 19, 24; Finnegan 2001. See Poupard and Miller 1992, 13, and Eitzen and Takfuji 1997, on the Nazis allegedly distributing infected toys and candy in Romania.

13. "Magical" biological and chemical weaponry was devised by "harnessing natural forces" in ancient India: Kokatnur 1948, 270. In modern times, the scientists who develop biological and chemical weapons usually work in secrecy, and their names are rarely publicized.

14. Polyaenus, *Stratagems* 8.43. See Faraone 1992, 99, sighting Burkert 1972, 59–65, 73–75, on "aggressive use of *pharmaka* in war." Faraone and Burkert both relate the Chrysame story to the ancient Hittite practice of sending poisoned or contagious animals toward the enemy. On modern strategies of poisoning enemy livestock in World War I, see Christopher et al. 1997, 413; Robertson and Robertson 1995, 370.

15. Quotes from Susan Levine, Joint Non-Lethal Weapons Directorate (JNLWD) research director, in *Navy News and Undersea Technology,* May 10, 1999; Col. George Fenton, director of JNLWD, in *New Scientist,* December 16, 2000; *New York Times* editorial, October 30, 2002, respectively. Ancient Indian recipes for calmatives and disorienting agents were delivered by hollow darts: Kokatnur 1948, 269.

16. Information on modern calmative and other nonlethal weapons: Sunshine Project, www.sunshine-project.org; and the Federation of American Scientists position papers and links at www.fas.org/bwc/non-lethal.htm; see also "When Killing Just Won't Do" 2003; Broad 2002. The JNLWD has a Web site: www.jnlwd.usmc.mil. Hallucinogen BZ records were declassified in October 2002: "Some Soldiers in Chemical Tests Not Fully Informed" 2002. Hitler: Moon 2000, 95 (thanks to Flora Davis). Polyaenus 7.6.4 recounts an ancient tactic by the Persians to "feminize" their enemies, the Lydians.

17. The gas used by the Russians in 2002 was identified as an aerosol version of the anaesthetic Fentanyl. After that event, a spokesman for the JNLWD "denied that it was conducting research on nonlethal chemical weapons," despite the JNLWD's publicized 2002 budget of $1.6 million to develop such weapons: *New York Times,* October 28–31 and Broad 2002. Eumenes quoted by Justin 14.1.12, cited in Penzer 1952, 6. On Hannibal's plan to catapult snakes, see chapter 6.

Chapter 6

1. Herodotus 2.141. The Egyptian god Ptah was recognized in Greece as Hephaestus, god of invention and fire. Bad omens of mice eating leather military gear: Pliny 8.221–23. Faraone 1992, 42–43, 65–66, 128–31. 2 Kings 19.35. Josephus, *Jewish Antiquities* 10.15–27. Bradford 2001, 44. Zinsser 1963, 194, believes that the rodents that attacked the Assyrians were rats rather than field mice. The pestilence that struck the Assyrians was the subject of a famous poem by Lord Byron, "The Destruction of Sennacherib," 1815.

2. When "mice" are mentioned in ancient texts, "rats" may be meant: Zinsser 1963, 190–91; and see his chapter 11 on rats and mice. Apollo's cult of pestilential mice and the temple of Hamaxitus with white mice: Aelian, *On Animals* 12.5; Polemon of Troy (190 BC) fragment, cited in Faraone 1992, 128. Faraone, 41–42 ("faulty reasoning") "hemorrhoids" theory, 50 note 39, 128–31. Strabo 13.1.46–48; 3.4.18. 1 Samuel 5–6. Commentary in the *Oxford Annotated Bible* identifies the Philistine pestilence as bubonic plague. The plague appeared in each Philistine town visited by the Ark, raising the question of fomites or insect vectors associated with the sacred chest: see chapter 4. Rats in "countless hordes" were a periodic plague in northern Iran and Babylon: Aelian, *On Animals* 17.17.

3. Neufeld 1980, 30–31. Ambrose 1974, 33–34. Aelian, *On Animals* 17.35. "Some authorities state that 27 hornet stings will kill a human being," wrote Pliny 11.73. Maya: *Popul Vuh,* lines 6800ff. Mayor 1995a, 36.

4. Neufeld 1980, 30–39, 43–46, 55. Exodus 23.28, Deuteronomy 7.20, Joshua 24.12, Isaiah 7.18–20. On the many species of venomous insects in the Near East, see Neufeld 51–52.

5. Ambrose 1974. Development of weapons based on marking enemies with pheromones to induce attack by bees: "When Killing Just Won't Do" 2003.

6. Neufeld 1980, 54–56. Harris and Paxman 1982, 49–50. Mayor 1995a, 36. Aeneas the Tactician 37.4; Appian, "Mithridatic Wars" 12.78.

7. Japanese flea bombs: Lesho 1998, 513; Christopher et al. 1997, 413; Robertson and Robertson 1995, 371; Lockwood 1987, 77. Kahn 2002.

8. The defense of Hatra: Herodian 3.9.3–8 and commentary by C. Whittaker. The Hatra debacle is also described by Dio Cassius 68.31–75.10.31.2, *Epitome* 75.10–13 and 76.10–12. Ammianus Marcellinus 25.8.2–6 visited the abandoned city of Hatra in AD 363, and described the desert as a "wretched" wilderness with no water and few plants. Scorpions: Pliny 11.87–91; 27.6. Aelian *On Animals* 6.20, 6.23, 8.13, 9.4, 9.27, 10.23, 15.26, 17.40 (a plague of scorpions in the Mideast). Strabo 15.1.37. Leo, *Tactica* 19.53, cited in Partington 1999, 18 and note 174. Scorpions in antiquity, see Scarborough 1979, 9–18; on winged scor-

pions, 14–15 and notes 146, 147, and 170. Assassin bugs: Ambrose 1974, 36. Thanks to entomologist Robert Peterson for information about assassin bugs. See Campbell 1986, "What Happened at Hatra?" for scholarly opinions on the puzzle of Severus's defeat.

9. Assassin or cone-nose bug in Vietnam: Ambrose 1974, 38. On the history of U.S. research and production of offensive insect weapons see Lockwood 1987, 78–82. The "Controlled Biological Systems" project to create sophisticated weapon technologies based on entomology and zoology is overseen by the Defense Sciences Office (DSO) of the Defense Advanced Research Projects Agency (DARPA): www.darpa.mil/dso. Remote-controlled rats were created by SUNY scientists funded by the Defense Department. *New York Times Magazine,* December 15, 2002, 116; and Meek 2002, citing *Nature,* May 2, 2002. Revkin 2002.

10. Cornelius Nepos, *Hannibal* 23.10–11; see also Justinius 32.4.6–8; Orosius 4.20; and Frontinus, *Stratagems* 4.7.10–11 who says the trick was played by Hannibal and again by Prusius, King of Bithynia. Neufeld 1980, 54–55.

11. *Greek Alexander Romance,* Stoneman 1991, 101. Polyaenus 15.6, 7.9.

12. Aeneas the Tactician 22.14, 22.20, 23.2, 38.2–3; and Whitehead's commentary pp 156–57. Aelian, *On Animals* 7.38. Pliny 8.142–43. Polyaenus 7.2. Ambrose 1974, 33. Dolphins: PBS Frontline Report, "A Whale of a Business," 1997. Sea lions: Williams 2003.

13. On elephants in antiquity: Scullard 1974. Livy 27.46–49; Ammianus Marcellinus 25.1.4. At Alexander's defeat of King Darius in 331 BC at Gaugamela, there were fifteen war elephants in the Persian forces. Alexander versus Porus: Quintus Curtius 8.13–14. Zonarus 8.3. Stoneman 1991, 129–30. Caesar's elephant: Polyaenus 8.23.5. Lucretius, *On the Nature of the Universe* 5.1298–1349. Aelian, *On Animals* 8.15; 8.17. Pliny 8.68.

14. Herodotus 1.80–82; 4.130–36. Polyaenus 7.6.6; Frontinus *Stratagems* 2.4.12. Aelian, *On Animals* 11.36 (he confused Lydians with Persians). Polyaenus 4.21. Zoological tricks help clarify the difference between acceptable biologically based ruses of war, like creating shields

against enemy cavalry with ranks of evil-smelling camels, and more reprehensible deployments of bio-toxins against human soldiers. The imaginative range of ancient low-tech animal strategies make one wonder what sorts of counterploys will be developed to subvert the high-technology bio-defenses using insects and animals being created today.

15. Aelian, *On Animals* 1.38; 16.14; 16.36. Alexander legend: Stoneman 1994, 11–12. Pliny 8.27 notes that elephants are scared by pigs' squeals, and when elephants are frightened or wounded they always give ground. Tacitus, *Germania* 3. Ancient Indian methods of producing disorienting aural and optical effects: Kokatnur 1948, 269. Modern aural, optical illusion, and odor weapons: Sunshine Project; and "When Killing Just Won't Do" 2003.

16. On flammable pitch and resin from trees and tar from crude petroleum deposits in the ancient world, see references cited in Whitehead's commentary at Aeneas the Tactician 11.3, p 129; and Forbes 1964. Procopius, *History of the Wars* 8.14.30–43.

17. Frontinus, *Stratagems* 2.4.17. Partington 1999, 46, 210. Kautilya 1951, 433–34. Morgan 1990, chapter 2. Monkeys: reported in the *Washington Times* (UPI), March 24, and the *World Tribune*, April 8, 2003, citing *Al Usbua Al Sisyassi* magazine, Rabat, Morocco. Jennison 1971, 38. Folklore motifs for burning animals: J2101.1; K2351.1 in the *Motif-Index of Folk-Literature*. The Tamerlane (Timur) legend comes from the University of Calgary Applied History Research Group, "Islamic World to 1600," copyright 1998.

Chapter 7

1. Medea's deadly gift to Glauke was described in Euripides' tragedy *Medea* (431 BC): the burning scene (1136ff) takes place offstage but is vividly described by horrified eyewitnesses. The story of Medea's fire weapon was retold in numerous versions by Greek and Latin authors, see for example Diodorus of Sicily 4.54; Apollodorus, *Library* 1.9.28. The princess in the burning gown was a favorite subject in vase paintings and sculpture. The

fountain where Glauke sought relief was a landmark in antiquity and is still pointed out to tourists in ancient Corinth. Mayor 1997b.

2. Crosby 2002, 87–88. Lucretius, *On the Nature of the Universe* 5.1243–46; and 5.1284–86. Partington 1999, 1, and 211 (*Laws of Manu*). SIPRI, *Incendiary Weapons* 1975, 15. According to Kokatnur 1948, 268–70, "chemical warfare or something similar thereto is strongly suggested" in the oral Indian epics of 2000–650 BC, written down in about the first century AD. Sun Tzu: Bradford 2001, 134–36. Temple 1991, 215–18.

3. Herodotus 8.51–53. Crosby 2002, 88. On early methods of distilling wood pitch, discussed by Pliny, Dioscorides, and Arabic sources, Forbes 1964, 33–36, 38–39; Partington 1999, 4; on the last uses of blazing arrows, 5.

4. Crosby 2002, 88. Thucydides, *History of the Peloponnesian War* 2.75–78. Sulphur and pitch: Healy 1999, 248–49, 257; Pliny 35.174–77; 16.52. On sulphur fires in sieges in Roman times, see Healy, 249 notes 228–29, citing Martial, *Epigrams* 1.41.4 and 42; 12.57.14. Aeneas the Tactician 33.1–3; 35.1. Rhodes: Diodorus of Sicily 20.48, 86–88, 96–97. Tacitus, *Histories* 4.23. Silius Italicus, *Punica* 1.345–67 (Hannibal). Vegetius 4.1–8, 18. Herodian 8.4. Ammianus Marcellinus 23.4, 14–15. See Partington 1999, 2–3. On petroleum weapons in antiquity, see Forbes 1964, chapter 7.

5. See Temple 1991, 217–18, 224–29, 232–37, 241–48, for Chinese discoveries and military uses of saltpeter and gunpowder. On the experimental weapons leading to the development of gunpowder guns and bombs in China and India, see Crosby 2002, 93–129; quotes on 98. James Riddick Partington 1999 is the authority on the early discoveries and formulas for Greek Fire and gunpowder. His work, originally published in 1960, is updated in the Introduction to the 1999 edition, see esp. xxi–xxiii. Poisons added to Chinese incendiaries: Partington 270–71; Temple 216–18. Indian fire projectiles: Kokatnur 1948, 269.

6. Lucan, *Civil War* 3.680–96; 10.486–505. Thucydides, *History of the Peloponnesian War* 7.53. Frontinus, *Stratagems* 4.7.9. and 14. Arrian, *Alexander* 2.19. Quintus Curtius 4.2.23–4.3.7. Partington 1999, 1.

7. Diodorus of Sicily 17.44–45. Quintus Curtius 4.3.25–26. SIPRI, *Incendiary Weapons* 1975, 150–51.

8. Dio Cassius, fragments of book 15 preserved by John Zonaras, *Epitome* 9.4; and John Tzetses, *Book of Histories* 2.109–28. Plutarch, *Marcellus.* Partington 1999, 5 and note 56. Modern experiments with Archimedes' invention: see *Applied Optics* special issue 1976. Capture or immunity for enemy scientists: After World War II, German nuclear scientist Wernher von Braun was given asylum in the United States, and Dr. Ishii of Japan was granted immunity in exchange for his records of bioweapons experiments. Poupard and Miller 1992, 16 (on the U.S. coverup of Japan's bio-weapons). In 2002, the U.S. government suggested a plan to "identify key Iraqi weapons scientists and spirit them out of the country" in exchange for information about Saddam Hussein's biochemical arsenals. *New York Times*, December 6, 2002.

9. Laser guns were allegedly used during the U.S. military's Operation Just Cause according to "Panama Deception," the Academy Award–winning documentary film directed by Barbara Trent, 1992. Colonel Fenton described the microwave gun on NPR, Morning Edition, March 2, 2001, "New Crowd-Control Weapon that the Pentagon Is Developing."

10. Catapults: Crosby 2002, 81–87; *Oxford Classical Dictionary*, s.v. "artillery." Spartan flame-hrower: Thucydides, *History of the Peloponnesian War* 4.100; Crosby 2002, 89. On Chinese flamethrowers, see Temple 1991, 229–31. On modern flamethrowers, SIPRI, *Incendiary Weapons* 1975, 106–11.

11. Apollodorus, *Poliorcetica* cited by Partington 1999, 2, and see 199 for later medieval recipes for burning stone castles combining vinegar, sulphur, naphtha, and the urine of children (urine contains combustible phosphates). Pliny 23.57; 33.71 and 94. Livy 21.37, and skeptical commentary by the translator B. O. Foster. Juvenal 10.153. Dio Cassius 36.18 reported that vinegar poured repeatedly to saturate a large brick tower weakened it and made it brittle enough to shatter. Vitruvius 8.3.1 noted that fire and vinegar dissolved flint rock. Modern vinegar experiments: Healy 1999, 131–33.

12. Aeneas the Tactician 33–35, and Whitehead's commentary pp. 197–98. Partington 1999, 5, 201. For fire-extinguishing methods in prac-

tice, see Diodorus of Sicily 13.85.5; 14.51.2–3; 14.108.4. Appian, "Mithridatic Wars" 12.74. Polyaneus 6.3.3; excerpts 56.3.6. The "powers of vinegar": Pliny 23.54–57.

13. Aeneas the Tactician 37.3. China: Temple 1991, 215–17 (fumigants and poison gases for military use). Croddy 2002, 127, citing Joseph Needham's encyclopedic *Science and Civilisation in China*. Croddy claims that Thucydides reported arsenic smoke used by the Spartans, but there is no mention of arsenic by Thucydides. Neufeld 1980, 38 and note 26. Creveld 1991, 25, on smoke in tunnels. Plutarch, *Sertorius*. Rahman 2002. Kautilya 1951, 434, 441–45, 457. Polybius 21.28.11–17. Polyaenus 5.10.4–5; 6.17. Partington 1999, 18 (quicklime dust); 149 (weasels and magnets); 171 and note 154 (Dura–Europos); 209–11 (*Arthashastra*); 263, 284–85 (poison smokes in China and the New World). Islamic smoke weapons: Hashmi forthcoming. Chemical smoke from burning sulphur or arsenic was used as pesticide in antiquity (against lice, mites, fleas, wasps, etc) by the Egyptians, Sumerians, and Chinese (2500–1200 BC), and burning sulphur and tar was used to repel insects in ancient Greece and Rome, according to Homer and Cato (thanks to Anne Neumann for the idea of looking into the history of pesticides). Ancient Chinese fumigation techniques led to military uses of poison gases: Temple 1991, 215.

14. See Forbes 1964, 96 on *pyr automaton*. On ancient knowledge of these chemicals, Bailey 1929–32, 1.111, 199, 209–10, 244–45; 2.121, 251–56, 272–77. See Mayor 1997b on combustible formulas in myth and history. Livy 39.13. Some date the recipe in the compilation attributed to Africanus to the sixth century AD. Partington 1999, 6–10. Seneca, *Medea* 817–34. See also Rose 1959, 204 1 Kings 18.23–38. Pliny 2.235–36; 35.178–82; 36.174.

15. The Pulitzer Prize-winning photo, by Associated Press photographer Nick Ut, was taken in 1972 at Trang Bang, Vietnam. The full story is told in Chong 2000. Napalm (naphthene thickened with palmitate) canisters were ignited by superhot white phosphorus. On napalm's invention and its various formulas and uses from World War II through the 1970s, see SIPRI, *Incendiary Weapons* 1975, 39–67, 91–97, 122–55 (effects of chemical burns); Perry 2001; Taylor 2001.

16. On geography of petroleum, see Partington 1999, 3–5. For classifications, definitions, and locations of bituminous petroleum surface deposits in the ancient world, see Forbes 1964, who also surveys ancient references to petroleum and archaeological evidence for its uses.

17. Forbes 1964, see 91 for Assyrian criminals punished with hot petroleum, and 29, 40–41 for oil deposits in India. Baba Gurgur: Bilkadi 1995, 25. Nehemiah: 2 Maccabees 1.19–30. Partington 1999, 6.

18. Herodotus 6.119. Ctesias quoted by Aelian, *On Animals* 5.3. Philostratus, *Apollonius of Tyana* 3.1.

19. Strabo 16.1.4 and 15 described fountains of burning naphtha and other forms of petroleum in Babylon, and Alexander's experiment, which was also reported by Plutarch, *Alexander* 35. Forbes 1964, 23–28; Classical scholar David Sansone 1980 sees Plutarch's narrative of the dangerous experiment with naphtha as an extended metaphorical commentary on Alexander's "fiery temperament." Incendiary missile at Gandhara from Taj Ali et al., "Fire from Heaven? Small Find no. 1513 and Southern Asia's Oldest Incendiary Missile," unpublished paper, Dept. of Archaeology, University of Peshawar, Pakistan, September1999. *Arthashastra*: Partington 1999, 209–11. Kautilya 1951, 434. Shukra's *Nitishastra* also describes incendiary balls flung at foes in ancient India: Kokatnur 1948, 269.

20. Ammianus Marcellinus 23.6.15. Dio Cassius, *Epitome* 76.10–12. Naphtha's ability to combust air, burn in water, and pursue fleeing victims: Pliny 2.235–41.

21. On burn injuries and smoke inhalation from fire weapons, see SIPRI, *Incendiary Weapons* 1975, chapter 3, and 187–99.

22. Arab legends of Alexander's inventions of incendiaries: Partington 1999, 47, 58, 198, 200–201; on petroleum weapons in India, 209–11. Illustration of the "Naphtha wall," *Shahnama*, Iran, 1330s, Arthur Sackler Gallery, S1986, 104, Smithsonian, Washington DC.

23. Thaqif: Hashmi forthcoming. Bilkadi 1995, 23–27. Partington 1999, 189–227. Asbestos was known to Pliny 36.139: "Asbestos looks like alum and is completely fireproof." Ancient Persians imported from India a "stone wool," magic cloth cleansed by fire, used for magic tricks. Asbestos in war:

Forbes 1964, 100; see also Partington 1999, 22, 201, 207 and Fig. 11 (burning riders in Islamic armies). Iraq: Miller and Vieth 2003. According to Crosby 2002, 91, the Mongols used trebuchets to hurl naphtha bombs.

24. Partington 1999, 24–25, 28–32, 45. Kautilya 1951, 434. Accidental explosions of Greek Fire mixtures: Forbes 1964, 96, citing Leo's military handbook of the ninth century AD. Crosby 2002, 89, 96–97. SIPRI, *Incendiary Weapons* 1975, 91, 106–7. Mecca: Bilkadi 1995, and see Nardin 1996, 164–65 on the Koran's ban on fighting near the Ka'aba, 2.191. Chinese warnings and naval disaster: Temple 1991, 228, 230; and see Croddy 2002, 130, quoting historian Shi Xubai, cited by Needham. In the thirteenth century AD, the Chinese defended against specially trained "naphtha troops" of the Mongol Hulagu Khan, Kublai Khan's predecessor, by covering dwellings with roof mats of grass coated with clay.

25. Crosby 2002, 89–92, quote 92.

26. Petroleum weapons: Forbes 1964, 33–41, 99–100; Byzantine hand-syringes for squirting Greek Fire, 96 and figs. See Partington 1999, 21 and 26; 10–41, 44; for modern chemists' reconstruction of Greek Fire, see Bert Hall's Introduction, xxi–xxiii. See also Roland 1990, for a clear and concise history of Greek Fire; quotes 18; and see diagram on 19 for a reconstruction of the Greek Fire system. For the development of Muslim oil weapons, see Bilkadi 1995. On early medieval Muslim-Asian exchange of naphtha weapon knowledge, Croddy 2002, 128–30. According to Healy 1999, 121, Pliny anticipated the basis for process of modern fractional distillation, in *Natural History* 31.81. On the question of whether Pliny described saltpeter, see Healy 134, 198–99; and Partington 298–306. The first military use of gunpowder was linked (as the ignition source) to Greek Fire deployed by Chinese warships in about AD 900. Croddy 2002, 129, citing the Chinese *Gunpowder Epic*. The Byzantine historian Theophanes wrote that enemies "shivered in terror, recognizing how strong the liquid fire was." Crosby 2002, 90. Forbes 1964, 98 for capitulation to Greek Fire: a Russian fleet of one thousand ships retreated from fifteen Byzantine ships carrying Greek Fire in AD 941.

27. Appian, "Mithridatic Wars" 12.18–23. Dio Cassius 36.4–6; and Xiphilinus 36.1b. Croddy 2002, 128.

28. Dio Cassius 36.4–6. Pliny 2.235. Muhammad at Ta'fiq: Hashmi forthcoming. The strategic open oil pits near Hatra, Samosata, and Tigranocerta were guarded by early Muslim "oil czars," see Bilkadi 1995, 25. The ruins of Samosata (Samsat, Turkey), the ancient capital of Commagene, were inundated in the late twentieth century by the Ataturk Dam. These rich petroleum fields now produce tens of thousands of barrels of oil in northern Iraq and southeastern Turkey.

29. Dio Cassius, Xiphilinus 36.1b. Appian, "Mithridatic Wars" 12.77. Pliny 2.235; 34.93; see also 35.178–82. The ancient statue of Hercules in the tunic has not survived. Ironically, in the second century BC, before Roman armies had experienced attacks by fiery naphtha, Roman soldiers desecrated the famous painting of Hercules dying in the poison robe, painted in 360 BC by the Greek artist Aristeides. During their sack of Corinth, it was among the fine paintings that the soldiers pulled to the ground and used to throw dice on. Strabo 8.6.23.

30. Plutarch, *Lucullus*. Mayor 1997b, 58. Seneca, *Epistle* 14.4–6. Martial, *Epigrams* 4.86, 10.25. Juvenal 1.155, 8.235 and notes. Coleman 1990, 60–61.

Afterword

1. Lucretius, *On the Nature of the Universe* 5.1295–1308. Appian, "Mithridatic Wars" 12.74. Vozrozhdeniye Island in the Aral Sea: "Poisoned Island" 1999; Pala 2003. On worst-case scenarios posed by biochemical weapons, see Miller et al. 2001. Numerous incidents of bio-weapon accidents between 1915–46 are given in Harris and Paxman 1982, 15–19, 28, 42, 56–57, 77–79. For a survey of U.S. bio-weapons accidents up to 2003, see Piller 2003. Thanks to Flora Davis for helpful comments.

2. Incinerating and burying biochemical weapons: Leary 2002; Wald 2002. Vitrification of nuclear weapons material is carried out at Savannah River, South Carolina. Burial of transuranic (high–level radioactive) materials from nuclear weapons in the Waste Isolation Pilot Plant (WIPP) near

Carlsbad began in 1999. Early boreholes in the salt beds were rejected because of fears of potential leakage due to geologic deformations and pressurized brine, but the present site is said to have been "stable for more than 200 million years," so the weapon materials are deemed to be safely stored forever. WIPP Web site: www.wipp.carlsbad.nm.us. Office of Civilian Radioactive Waste Management information on Yucca Mountain: www.ocrwm.doe.gov.

3. Pala 2003. Denver: "Nerve Gas" 2000. The U.S. Geological Service determined that leakage of toxic fluids from chemical weapons buried in deep wells at Rocky Mountain Arsenal reduced friction and allowed slippage along fault planes, resulting in earthquakes. Thanks to Will Keener, Sandia National Laboratories, personal correspondence, February 10–14, 2003, for facts and helpful comments about Rocky Mountain Arsenal and the Carlsbad WIPP and Yucca Mountain sites. Washington, DC and other chemical munitions dump sites: Tucker 2001. Presidio: "Vile Finds" 2003.

4. The plans for Yucca Mountain primarily anticipate burial of radioactive waste from nuclear reactors, with the possibility of including nuclear weapons materials. The suggestions of the expert panels were solicited beginning in 1993 by the U.S. Department of Energy (DOE) and Sandia National Laboratories in the planning for the Carlsbad weapons burial site, but the concepts, updated with the latest technologies, would also be applied at Yucca Mountain and similar sites. Pollon 2002; Hutchinson 2002; Pethokoukis 2002. Anthropologist Ward Goodenough quoted in Forest 2002. Detailed DOE information on proposals for warning succeeding generations ten thousand years into the future, based on Trauth et al. 1993, was provided by Steve Casey, WIPP Carlsbad Field Office, February 12, 2003.

BIBLIOGRAPHY

Ancient Greek and Latin Sources

Unless otherwise noted, the Greek and Latin texts are available in translation in the Loeb Classical Library, published by Harvard University Press, Cambridge, Mass. (Ancient Chinese, Indian, and Islamic works are listed in Other Sources.)

Aelian, *On Animals*

[Aeneas] Aineias the Tactician, *How to Survive under Siege*. Trans. and comm. David Whitehead. Oxford: Clarendon Press, 1990.

Aeschines, *Against Ctesiphon; On the Embassy*

Ammianus Marcellinus, *Roman History*

Apollodorus, *Library; Epitome*

Appian, *Roman History*

Arrian, *History of Alexander*

Aulus Gellius, *Attic Nights*

Cicero, *On Duties*

Cornelius Nepos

Dio Cassius, *Roman History*

Diodorus of Sicily, *Library of History*

Diogenes Laertius, *Lives of the Philosophers*

Euripides, *Medea*

Florus

Frontinus, *Stratagems*

Herodian

Herodotus, *Histories*

Historia Augusta: Lives of the Later Caesars. 1976. Trans. Anthony Birley. Harmondsworth: Penguin.

Homer, *Iliad; Odyssey*

Isocrates, *Plataicus*

Josephus, *Jewish Antiquities*

Juvenal

Livy, *Roman History*

Lucan, *Civil War*

Lucretius, *On the Nature of the Universe*

Martial, *Epigrams*

Ovid, *Metamorphoses; Tristia; Letters from Pontus*

Pausanias, *Description of Greece.* 2 vols. Trans. Peter Levi. Harmondsworth: Penguin.

Philostratus, *Apollonius of Tyana*

Pliny the Elder, *Natural History*

Plutarch, *Moralia; Lives of Alexander; Artaxerxes; Lucullus; Marcellus; Nicias; Sertorius; Solon*

Polyaenus, *Stratagems of War.* 2 vols. Ed. and trans. Peter Krentz and Everett Wheeler. Chicago: Ares, 1994.

Polybius, *Histories*

Procopius, *History of the Wars of Justinian*

Pseudo-Aristotle, *On Marvelous Things Heard*

Quintus Curtius Rufus, *History of Alexander*

Quintus of Smyrna, *Fall of Troy*

Sallust, *Jugurthine War*

Seneca, *On Anger; Epistles; Medea*

Silius Italicus, *Punica*

Sophocles, *Philoctetes; Trachinian Women*

Strabo, *Geography*

Suetonius, *The Twelve Caesars.* Trans. Robert Graves. Harmondsworth: Penguin, 1979.

Tacitus, *Annals; Germania; Histories*
Thucydides, *History of the Peloponnesian War*
Varro, *De Re Rustica*
Vegetius, *On Military Matters*
Virgil, *Aeneid*
Vitruvius, *On Architecture*
Xenophon, *Anabasis; Cyropaedia*

Other Sources

Aftergood, Steven. 2001. "Djinn Energy." Federation of American Scientists Secrecy News, www.battl.nl/Djinn301001.html, October 30.

Aldinger, Charles. 2002. "Bioweapons Tested in U.S., Records Say." Reuters news story, Washington, DC, October.

Ambrose, John. 1974. "Insects in Warfare." *Army* (December): 33–38.

Angier, Natalie. 2002. "Venomous and Sublime: The Viper Tells Its Tale." Science Times, *New York Times,* December 10.

Bailey, K. C. 1929–32. *The Elder Pliny's Chapters on Chemical Subjects.* London: Edward Arnold.

Bercé, Yves-Marie. 1993. "Les semeurs de peste." In *La vie, la mort, le temps: Mélanges offerts à Pierre Chaunu,* ed. J. P. Bardet and R. M. Foisil. Paris: P.U.F, pp. 85–94.

Bilkadi, Zayn. 1995. "The Oil Weapons—Ancient Oil Industries." *Aramco World* (January–February): 22–27.

Bonner, Campbell. 1956. "The Sibyl and Bottle Imps." In *Quantulacumque: Studies Presented to Kirsopp Lake,* ed. R. P. Casey et al. London: n.p., pp. 1–8.

Bradford, Alfred. 2001. *With Arrow, Sword, and Spear: A History of Warfare in the Ancient World.* Westport, CT: Praeger.

Broad, William J. 2002. "Oh, What a Lovely War. If No One Dies." *New York Times,* November 3.

Buhler, Georg, trans. 1886. *Laws of Manu.* Oxford: Oxford University Press.

Campbell, Duncan B. 1986. "What Happened at Hatra?" In *Defence of the Roman and Byzantine East,* ed. P. W. M. Freeman and D. L. Kennedy. Oxford: Oxford University Press, pp. 51–58.

Chong, Denise. 2000. *The Girl in the Picture: The Story of Kim Phuc, the Photograph, and the Vietnam War.* New York: Viking Press.

Christopher, George; Theodore Cieslak; Julie Pavlin; and Edward Eitzen. 1997. "Biological Warfare: A Historical Perspective." *JAMA* 278: 412–17.

Cole, Leonard. 1996. "The Specter of Biological Weapons." *Scientific American* 275, no. 6 (December): 60–65.

Coleman, Kathleen. 1990. "Fatal Charades: Roman Executions Staged as Mythological Enactments." *Journal of Roman Studies* 80: 44–73.

Conybeare, F. C. 1898. "The Testament of Solomon." *Jewish Quarterly Review* 11 (October): 1–45.

Cowley, Robert, and Geoffrey Parker, eds. 1996. *The Reader's Companion to Military History.* Boston: Houghton Mifflin.

Creveld, Martin van. 1991. "The Gulf Crisis and the Rules of War." *MHQ: Quarterly Journal of Military History* 3, no. 4 (summer): 23–27.

Croddy, Eric. 2002. *Chemical and Biological Warfare.* New York: Springer-Verlag.

Crosby, Alfred W. 2002. *Throwing Fire: Projectile Technology Through History.* Cambridge: Cambridge University Press.

Derbes, V. J. 1966. "De Mussis and the Great Plague of 1348: A Forgotten Episode of Bacteriological War." *JAMA* 196: 59–62.

Dirlmeier, Franz. 1966. *Die Giftpfeile des Odysseus (zu Odyssee 1, 252–266).* Heidelberg: Carl Winter.

Drummond, Andrew J. 1989. "Ammianus Marcellinus and the Roman Rules of War of the Fourth Century AD" MA Thesis, University of Kansas.

Eitzen, E. M., Jr., and E. T. Takafuji. 1997. "Historical Overview of Biological Warfare." Chapter 18 in *Textbook of Military Medicine: Medical Aspects of Chemical and Biological Warfare.* Washington, DC: U.S. Dept. of the Army.

Faraone, Christopher. 1992. *Talismans and Trojan Horses.* New York: Oxford University Press.

Fenn, Elizabeth. 2000. "Biological Warfare in Eighteenth-Century North America: Beyond Jeffery Amherst." *Journal of American History* 86 (March): 1552–80.

Finnegan, William. 2001. "The Poison Keeper." *New Yorker*, January 15: 58–64.

Forbes, R. J. 1964. *Bitumen and Petroleum in Antiquity*. 2nd ed. Leiden: Brill.

Forest, David. 2002. "Burial Ground: Fear and Loathing at Yucca Mountain." *On Earth* (summer): 20–21.

Frank, J. H., and K. Kanamitsu. 1987. "Paederus, Sensu Lato (Coleoptera: Staphylinidae): Natural History and Medical Importance." *Journal of Medical Entomology* 24, no. 2 (March): 155–91.

Frontline Report. 1997. PBS television transcript of "A Whale of a Business: The Story of Navy Dolphins." November 11.

Gantz, Timothy. 1993. *Early Greek Myth: A Guide to Literary and Artistic Sources*. 2 vols. Baltimore: Johns Hopkins University Press.

Goldstein, Laurie. 2001. "Islamic Scholars Call September 11 Attacks a Distortion of Islam." *New York Times*, September 30.

Grafton, Anthony. 1992. *New Worlds, Ancient Texts*. Cambridge: Harvard University Press.

Grmek, Mirko. 1979. "Les Ruses de Guerre Biologiques dans L'Antiquité." *Revue des Études Grecques* 92: 139–63.

Hanson, Victor. 1989. *The Western Way of War: Infantry Battle in Classical Greece*. New York: Knopf.

Harris, Diane. 1995. *The Treasures of the Parthenon and Erechtheion*. Oxford: Clarendon.

Harris, Robert, and Jeremy Paxman. 1982. *A Higher Form of Killing: The Secret Story of Chemical and Biological Warfare*. New York: Hill and Wang.

Harrison, S. J. 1994. "Yew and Bow: Vergil *Georgics* 2.448." *Harvard Studies in Classical Philology* 96: 201–202.

Hashmi, Sohail. Forthcoming. "Islamic Ethics and Weapons of Mass Destruction: An Argument for Nonproliferation." In *Ethics and*

Weapons of Mass Destruction: Religious and Secular Perspectives, ed. Sohail H. Hashmi and Steven P. Lee. Cambridge: Cambridge University Press.

Healy, John. 1999. *Pliny the Elder on Science and Technology.* Oxford: Oxford University Press.

Howard, M., G. J. Andreopoulos, and M. R. Shulman, eds. 1994. *The Laws of War: Constraints on Warfare in the Western World.* New Haven: Yale University Press

Hutchinson, Paul. 2002. "Warnings for the Year 11,997." www.abcnews.com.

Jennison, George. 1971. *Noah's Cargo: Some Curious Chapters of Natural History.* New York: Blom.

Johnston, Sarah Iles. 2002. "The *Testament of Solomon* from Late Antiquity to the Renaissance." In *The Metamorphosis of Magic,* ed. J. Bremmer and J. Veenstra. Leuven: Peeters, pp. 35–49.

Kahn, Joseph. 2002. "Shouting the Pain from Japan's Germ Attacks." *New York Times,* November 23.

Kautilya. 1951. *Arthashastra.* 4th ed. Trans. R. Shamasastry. Mysore: Sri Raghuveer Press.

Kautilya. 1992. *Arthashastra.* Trans. L. N. Rangarajan. Delhi: Penguin Classics.

Kelley, Matt. 2002. "Records Show U.S. Sent Germs to Iraq." *Newsday* (October 1), Associated Press.

Kokatnur, Vaman R. 1948. "Chemical Warfare in Ancient India." *Journal of Chemical Education* 25: 268–72.

Krentz, Peter. 2002. "Fighting by the Rules: The Invention of the Hoplite Agon." *Hesperia* 71: 23–39.

Leary, Warren. 2002. "Scientific Panel Urges Incinerating Obsolete Chemical Arms." *New York Times,* December 4.

Lesho, Emil; David Dorsey; and David Bunner. 1998. "Feces, Dead Horses, and Fleas: Evolution of the Hostile Use of Biological Agents." *Western Journal of Medicine* 168: 512–16.

Lockwood, Jeffrey A. 1987. "Entomological Warfare: The History of the Use of Insects as Weapons of War." *Bulletin of the Entomological Society of America* (summer): 76–82.

McNeill, William H. 1976. *Plagues and Peoples*. New York: Doubleday.

Majno, Guido. 1991 [1975]. *The Healing Hand: Man and Wound in the Ancient World*. Cambridge: Harvard University Press.

Martin, Emmanuel. 2001. "Hadzabe: The Last Archers of Africa." *Primitive Archer* 10, no. 1: 1–8

Maskiell, Michelle, and Adrienne Mayor. 2001. "Killer Khilats: Poisoned Robes of Honor in India., Parts 1 and 2." *Folklore* [London] 112: 23–45, 163–82.

Mayor, Adrienne. 1997a. "Dirty Tricks in Ancient Warfare." *MHQ: Quarterly Journal of Military History* 10 (Autumn): 32–37.

———. 1997b. "Fiery Finery." *Archaeology* (March–April): 54–58.

———. 1995a. "Mad Honey." *Archaeology* (November–December): 32–40.

———. 1995b. "The Nessus Shirt in the New World: Smallpox Blankets in History and Legend." *Journal of American Folklore* 108: 54–77.

Meckler, Laura. 2002. "Mental Impact of Bioterror Studied." Associated Press report on the Biosecurity Conference, Las Vegas, NV, November 20.

Meek, James. 2002. "Live Rats Driven by Remote Control." *The Guardian*, May 2.

Miller, Greg, and Warren Vieth. 2003. "Showdown with Iraq: U.S. Would Move to Safeguard Oil." *Los Angeles Times*, January 25, A9.

Miller, Judith; Stephen Engelberg; and William Broad. 2001. *Germs: Biological Weapons and America's Secret War*. New York: Simon and Schuster.

Miller, Judith. 2002a. "Iraq Said to Try to Buy Antidote Against Nerve Gas." *New York Times*, November 12.

———. 2002b. "CIA Hunts Iraq Tie to Soviet Smallpox." *New York Times*, December 3.

———. 1998. "Biological Weapons, Literally Older than Methuselah." *New York Times*, September 20.

Moon, Tom. 2000. *This Grim and Savage Game: OSS and the Beginning of U.S. Covert Operations in World War II*. New York: Da Capo Press.

Morgan, David. 1990. *The Mongols*. Oxford: Blackwell.

Nardin, Terry, ed. 1996. *The Ethics of War and Peace: Religious and Secular Perspectives*. Princeton: Princeton University Press.

"Nerve Gas Discovered at Old Arsenal Near Denver." 2000. Associated Press story, *Chronicle* (Bozeman, MT), November 18.

Neufeld, Edward. 1980. "Insects as Warfare Agents in the Ancient Near East." *Orientalia* 49: 30–57.

New Oxford Annotated Bible with the Apocrypha. 1973. Ed. H. G. May and B. M. Metzger. New York: Oxford University Press.

Ober, Josiah. 1994. "The Rules of War in Classical Greece." In *The Laws of War: Constraints on Warfare in the Western World*, ed. M. Howard, G. J. Andreopoulos, and M. R. Shulman. New Haven: Yale University Press, pp. 12–26, 227–30.

Onion, Amanda. 2002. "The No-Doze Soldier: Military Seeking Radical Ways of Stumping Need for Sleep." December 18, ABCNews.com.

Oxford Classical Dictionary. 1996. 3rd ed., ed. Simon Hornblower and Antony Spawforth. Oxford: Oxford University Press.

Pala, Christopher. 2003. "Anthrax Island." *New York Times Magazine*, January 12, 36–39.

Partington, J.R. 1999 [1960]. *A History of Greek Fire and Gunpowder*. Introduction by Bert S. Hall. Baltimore: Johns Hopkins University Press.

Paxman, J., and R. Harris. 1982. *A Higher Form of Killing: The Secret Story of Chemical and Biological Warfare*. New York: Hill and Wang.

Penzer, Norman. 1952. *Poison-Damsels and Other Essays in Folklore and Anthropology*. London: Sawyer.

Perry, Tony. 2001. "Relegating Napalm to Its Place in History." *Los Angeles Times*, April 1.

Pethokoukis, James M. 2002. "A Curse to Last 10,000 Years." Posted on www.news.yahoo.com, July 27.

Phelps, Tony. 1981. *Poisonous Snakes*. Dorset: Blandford.

Piller, Charles. 2003. "Biodefense Lab on the Defensive." *New York Times*, February 12.

"Poisoned Island." 1999. *The Economist*, July 10, p. 38.

Pollon, Christopher. 2002. "Danger! Do NOT Dig Here." *Archaeology* (May–June): 8.

Poupard, James, and Miller, Linda. 1992. "History of Biological Warfare: Catapults to Capsomeres." *Annals of the New York Academy of Sciences* 666: 9–20.

Rahman, Shaikh Azizur. 2002. "India Defence Looks to Ancient Text." BBC News, May 14.

Reinach, A. J. 1909. "La flèche en Gaule, ses poisons et ses contrepoisons." *Anthropologie* 20: 51–80, 189–206.

Revkin, Andrew C. 2002. "Bees Learning Smell of Bombs with Backing from Pentagon." *New York Times,* May 13.

Robertson, Andres, and Laura Robertson. 1995. "From Asps to Allegations: Biological Warfare in History." *Military Medicine* 160: 369–73.

Robertson, Hamish. 2002. "How San Hunters Use Beetles to Poison Their Arrows." Iziko Museums, Biodiversity Explorer Web site, Cape Town, South Africa, www.museums.org.za.

Robinson, Julian Perry. 2002. Paper presented at the Biotechnology, Weapons and Humanity Conference, sponsored by the International Committee of the Red Cross, Montreux, Switzerland, September 23–24.

Roland, Alex. 1990. "Greek Fire." *MHQ: The Quarterly Journal of Military History* 2 (spring): 16–19

Rolle, Renate. 1989. *The World of the Scythians.* Trans. F. G. Walls. Berkeley: University of California Press.

Rose, H. J. 1959. *A Handbook of Greek Mythology.* New York: E. P. Dutton.

Rudenko, Sergei. 1970. *The Frozen Tombs of Siberia.* Berkeley and Los Angeles: University of California Press.

"Sailors Sprayed with Nerve Gas in Test, Pentagon Says." 2002. *New York Times,* May 24.

Salazar, Christine F. 2000. *The Treatment of War Wounds in Graeco-Roman Antiquity.* Leiden: Brill.

Sansone, David. 1980. "Plutarch, Alexander, and the Discovery of Naphtha." *Greek, Roman and Byzantine Studies* 21: 63–74.

Sasson, Jack M., ed. 2000. *Civilizations of the Ancient Near East.* Peabody, MA: Hendrickson.

Scarborough, John. 1979. Nicander's *Toxicology*: Spiders, Scorpions,

Insects, and Myriapods, Parts I and II." *Pharmacy in History* 21, nos. 1 and 2: 3–35, 73–92.

———. 1977. "Nicander's *Toxicology*. Snakes." *Pharmacy in History* 19, no. 1: 3–23.

Schultz, Harald. 1962. "Brazil's Big-Lipped Indians." *National Geographic* 1, no 121 (January): 130–32.

"The Science of Apartheid." 1998. *Harper's* (September): 19–25.

Scullard, H. H. 1974. *The Elephant in the Greek and Roman World.* Ithaca, NY: Cornell University Press.

Shenon, Philip. 2003. "Iraq Links Germs for Weapons to U.S. and France." *New York Times*, March 16.

Simons, Geoff. 1994. *Iraq: From Sumer to Saddam.* London: St. Martins Press.

Stockholm International Peace Research Institute [SIPRI]. 1975. *Incendiary Weapons.* Cambridge: MIT Press.

———. 1971. *The Rise of CB Weapons: The Problem of Chemical and Biological Warfare.* New York: Humanities Press.

Stoneman, Richard, trans. 1994. *Legends of Alexander the Great.* London: J. M. Dent.

———. 1991. *Greek Alexander Romance.* Harmondsworth: Penguin.

Taylor, Michael. 2001. "Napalm No More: Pentagon Recycles Remaining Stock of Notorious Weapon." *San Francisco Chronicle*, April 4.

Temple, Robert, 1991. *The Genius of China: 3,000 Years of Science, Discovery, and Invention.* London: Prion.

Trauth, Kathleen; Stephen Hora; and Robert Guzowski. 1993. "Expert Judgment on Markers to Deter Human Intrusion into the Waste Isolation Pilot Plant." Sandia National Laboratories report SAND92-1382/UC-721, November.

Tucker, Jonathan. 2001. "Chemical Weapons: Buried in the Back Yard." *Bulletin of Atomic Scientists* 57 (September–October): 51–56.

"Vile Finds." 2003. *Archaeology* (January–February).

Wald, Matthew. 2002. "Nevada States Case Against Waste Dump in Mountain." *New York Times*, December 3.

Wheelis, Mark. 2002. "Biological Warfare at the 1346 Siege of Caffa." *Emerging Infectious Diseases* 8, no. 9 (September): 971–75.

———. 1999. "Biological Warfare before 1914." In *Biological and Toxin Weapons: Research, Development, and Use from the Middle Ages to 1945,* ed. Erhard Geissler and John van Courtland Moon. Oxford: Oxford University Press, pp. 8–34.

"When Killing Just Won't Do." 2003. *Harper's* (February): 17–19.

Wick, Charles Z. 1988. "Soviet Active Measures in the Era of Glasnost." Prepared by Todd Leventhal, for the U.S. House of Representatives, by the U.S. Information Agency, July, Washington, DC.

Williams, Carol. 2003. "Navy Adds Some Bark to Its Bite: San Diego-Trained Sea Lions Help Guard Against Attacks." *Los Angeles Times,* February 12, 2003, A13.

Williams, Peter, and David Wallace. 1989. *Unit 731: Japan's Secret Biological Warfare in World War II.* New York: Free Press.

Zinsser, Hans. 1963 [1934]. *Rats, Lice, and History.* Boston: Little, Brown.

LIST OF ILLUSTRATIONS

MAP 1. Italy, Greece, and the Aegean. (Map by Michele Angel)
MAP 2. The ancient world. (Map by Michele Angel)
MAP 3. Asia Minor, Near East, Mesopotamia, and Parthia. (Map by Michele Angel)

Introduction

FIGURE 1. Heroic hoplite combat, face-to-face fighting between equally matched Greek warriors using conventional weapons of spear and shield, 500–480 BC, amphora. (The J. Paul Getty Museum)

Chapter 1

FIGURE 2. Hercules and the Hydra. Hercules (left) chops off the heads, while his companion (right) cauterizes the necks with torches. Hercules will later dip his arrows in the Hydra's venom; meanwhile, Athena, Greek goddess of war (far right), holds the conventional weapons of a hoplite warrior, eschewed by Hercules. Krater, about 525 BC, attributed to the Kleophrades Painter. (The J. Paul Getty Museum)

FIGURE 3. Hercules shoots the Centaur Nessus with a Hydra-venom arrow, as he carries away Deianeira. It was the Centaur's venom-poisoned blood that ultimately destroyed Hercules himself.

FIGURE 4. Hercules on his funeral pyre entrusting the quiver of Hydra-venom arrows to the young archer, Philoctetes. Red-figure psykter, 475–425 BC. (Private collection, New York)

FIGURE 5. Archer testing shaft and point of arrow; any archer who tipped his projectiles with poison had to avoid all contact with the sharp point. Red-figure wine cup, Athens, 520–510 BC. (Henry Lillie Pierce Fund © Museum of Fine Arts, Boston)

FIGURE 6. On the way to Troy, Philoctetes was abandoned on a desert island after his accident with a poison arrow. This Athenian vase (about 420 BC) shows him with a bandaged foot and the quiver of poison arrows. (Fletcher Fund, The Metropolitan Museum of Art)

Chapter 2

FIGURE 7. Black hellebore (Christmas rose), a toxic plant used to poison arrows and water supplies in antiquity. (Curtis Botanical Magazine, 1787)

FIGURE 8. Poisonous snakes were deeply feared in antiquity, but some ancients were adept in handling snakes and using their venom to make arrow poisons and antidotes. Amphora, detail, Perseus 1991.07.0133. (University of Pennsylvania Museum)

FIGURE 9. Battle between Greek hoplites and Scythian archers. The fallen warrior had decorated his shield with the image of a snake, perhaps to frighten enemies or to magically deflect snake venom arrows. Red-figure kylix. (University of Pennsylvania Museum)

FIGURE 10. Right, Scythian archer shooting poison arrows at Greek hoplites. Red-figure vase. Left, running Scythian archer with bow, arrow, and quiver, red-figure vase, about 500 BC. (© The British Museum)

FIGURE 11. Top, wooden arrow shafts for snake-venom arrows, painted with red and black designs, found in fifth-century BC Scythian tombs. After Rudenko, *Frozen Tombs of Siberia*. Bottom, the venom of the poisonous European adder, *Vipera berus*, may have been used by the Scythians to treat their arrows.

FIGURE 12. The dreaded Purple Snake of India, as described by Aelian and Ctesias, had a distinctive white head. It may have been the poisonous *Azemiops feae,* discovered by scientists in the late 1800s. (Photo © R. W. Murphy)

FIGURE 13. Achilles treating Telephus's poison wound by scraping rust from his spear. Roman bas relief sculpture, found at Herculaneum. (Museo Archeologico Nazionale, Naples)

Chapter 3

FIGURE 14. Women drawing water at a fountain house. During a siege, a city's water supply could be poisoned. Hydria, 520–510 BC. (Toledo Museum of Art, Libbey Endowment, Gift of Edward Drummond Libbey)

Chapter 4

FIGURE 15. It was realized early in human history that contact with corpses of victims of epidemics, or their possessions, could spread disease. Roman skeleton mosaic, Via Appia, Italy.

FIGURE 16. The Greek myth of Pandora's box is one of the earliest expressions of the idea that contagion could be "trapped" in a sealed container. Red-figure amphora 460–450 BC. (The Walters Art Museum, Baltimore)

FIGURE 17. The Ark of the Covenant, a wooden chest that the Israelites were forbidden to touch, brought plague to each Philistine town that it visited in the twelfth century BC. James Tissot, *The Ark Passes over the Jordan*. (© De Brunoff 1904)

FIGURE 18. The Great Plague of AD 165–80 began when a Roman soldier broke open a golden chest in the Temple of Apollo in Babylon, allowing the "spirits of plague" to escape. The "spirits" in this drawing are taken from a Greek vase painting of "spirits" in 460 BC.

FIGURE 19. Woman placing cloth in chest. If the material had belonged to a victim of an epidemic such as smallpox, it could retain virulence for many years. Terracotta pinax from Lokri. (Museo Archeologico Nazionale, Calabria)

Chapter 5

FIGURE 20. King Mithridates VI of Pontus, arch-enemy of Rome, was a toxicologist searching for the most effective poisons and their antidotes. Here, he tests a poison on a prisoner, while his royal pharmacists display aconite and other toxic plants. Painting by Robert Thom. (Courtesy of Pfizer Inc)

FIGURE 21. Jugs of wine could be sent to enemies or left in an abandoned camp. Foes who fell into a drunken stupor were easily wiped out. Amphora, about 400 BC, detail Perseus 1991.07.1066. (University of Pennsylvania Musem)

FIGURE 22. Queen Tomyris of the Massagetae took revenge on King Cyrus of Persia for poisoning her army with wine. *Head of Cyrus Brought to Queen Tomyris,* oil painting by Peter Paul Rubens, about 1622–23. (Juliana Cheney Edwards Collection © Museum of Fine Arts, Boston)

FIGURE 23. The collection of mandrake, the deadly root used by the Carthaginians and by Julius Caesar to poison wine, required special precautions. This medieval manuscript illustrates one ancient method, tying the root to a dog.

FIGURE 24. One could secretly mix poisons, such as mandrake, hellebore, or aconite, into wine and leave it for the enemy to find. Detail of an Attic kylix, about 520 BC. (Smith College Museum of Art, Northampton, Mass.)

FIGURE 25. The witch-priestess Chrysame of Thessaly devised a successful military strategy to defeat the Ionians. She drugged a sacrificial bull to deliver incapacitating intoxicants to the enemy. Priestess leading a cow to sacrifice, Athenian lekythos, 520–510 BC. (Francis Bartlett Donation of 1912 © Museum of Fine Arts, Boston)

Chapter 6

FIGURE 26. Rodents carry flea-borne bubonic plague and other epidemic diseases. (Dover Pictorial Archives)

FIGURE 27. Wasp nests and beehives were hurled at enemies from Neolithic times onward. (Dover Pictorial Archives)

FIGURE 28. A swarm of bees or hornets attacking men. Amphora from Vulci, about 550 BC. (© The British Museum)

FIGURE 29. Scorpions abound in the desert around Hatra, and they were used as live ammunition against Roman besiegers. (Dover Pictorial Archives)

FIGURE 30. Assyrian war dog on a sculptural relief from Birs Nimrud, about 600 BC.

FIGURE 31. The heroic Athenian war dog at the Battle of Marathon (490 BC) during the defeat of the Persians.

FIGURE 32. Indian war elephant, with tower of warriors and mahout.

FIGURE 33. War elephants could cause chaos in enemy ranks, but sometimes trampled their own men in the melee.

FIGURE 34. A squealing pig was an effective weapon against war elephants. Red-figure kylix, about 490 BC, detail. (University of Pennsylvania Museum)

Chapter 7

FIGURE 35. Greek warrior assaulting a city wall with a burning pine-resin torch. Campanian neck-amphora, about 375 BC. (The J. Paul Getty Museum)

FIGURE 36. Noxious substances could be burned to create toxic smoke. Here two men make a smoky fire. Attic vase painting, 510 BC. (Toledo Museum of Art, Libbey Endowment, Gift of Edward Drummond Libbey)

FIGURE 37. This burning petroleum fountain at Baba Gurgur (in modern Iraq) has been worshipped since 600 BC.

FIGURE 38. In antiquity the deposits of seeping, gushing, and flaming oil deposits from Baku to Persia were known as the "lands of the naphtha fountains." Here, Alexander's Greek soldiers watch local people gathering naphtha in Babylonia. (Painting by Bob Lapsley/Aramco Services/PADIA)

FIGURE 39. According to legend, Alexander the Great created a naphtha-spewing iron cavalry, to rout King Porus of India and his war elephants. This illustration is from the Great Il-Khanid *Shahnama* manuscript, AD 1330–40. (Courtesy of the Arthur M. Sackler Museum, Harvard University Art Museums, Gift of Edward W. Forbes)

FIGURE 40. Naphtha grenades. These ceramic pots were filled with volatile naphtha, lit with a fuse, and hurled at the enemy. (Painting by Bob Lapsley/Aramco Services/PADIA)

FIGURE 41. An artist's conception of naval battle with Greek Fire. (Painting by Bob Lapsley/Aramco Services/PADIA)

FIGURE 42. Licinius Lucullus, the Roman general who pursued Mithridates and encountered biochemical attacks in the Near East in the first century BC. (From Harry Thurston Peck, *Harper's Dictionary of Classical Antiquities,* 1898)

FIGURE 43. Hercules struggling to tear off the burning, poisoned tunic. Bronze sculpture by Pierre Puget, 1680. (Jules S. Bache Collection, The Metropolitan Museum of Art)

Afterword

FIGURE 44. The Many-Headed Hydra, a symbol of the proliferating dilemmas of biological warfare. Caeretan hydria, about 525 BC. (The J. Paul Getty Museum)

FIGURE 45. Landscape of Thorns, one of the designs intended to warn future civilizations away from nuclear materials burial sites like Yucca Mountain. (Concept by architect Michael Brill, art by Safdar Abidi, SAND92-1382. Sandia National Laboratories)

Index

Achilles, 25, 47, 53–54, 59, 62, 93, 97
Aconite, 57, 68–69, 150, 223
Aelian, 16, 64, 73, 69, 72, 74, 80–81,
  86–88, 94–95, 135–36, 145, 154,
  171, 173, 182–84, 192, 200
Aeneas the Tactician, 13, 36–37,
  106–7, 154, 181, 190, 211–12,
  220–21, 239
Aeschines, 105
Africa, 15, 68, 73, 76–77, 94, 155,
  160, 162, 179, 184, 191. See also
  South Africa.
Agari, 148, 164
Akamba, 76, 80
Akatharti, 76
Alexander the Great, 13, 16, 17, 63,
  86–91, 96, 97, 99, 106, 108,
  142–43, 189, 193–94, 199–200,
  202, 215–16, 232–33, 235–36, 247
Alyattes, 12, 192, 198
Ambracia, 224
Ambrose, John, 147, 176, 180
Ammianus Marcellinus, 16, 132–34,
  213, 234
Animals, in war, 12, 17, 165–67,
  171–76, 181, 187–205, 244
Anthrax, 124, 127, 252, 253
Antidotes, 68, 90–97, 103, 112, 116,
  149–53, 226
Antigonus Gonatus, 13, 202
Antiochus, 14, 196
Apollo, 48–50, 53–54, 56, 59, 62, 65,
  97, 100, 102, 123–24, 132–38, 173

Apollonius of Damascus, 15, 220
Apollonius of Tyana, 15, 231
Appian, 15, 120, 134, 181, 249, 252,
  258
Aquileia, 212
Aquillius, 14, 99, 109–10, 245
Archaeology, 57, 82–83, 93, 94, 134,
  136, 172, 224, 238–39, 255, 256
Archimedes, 13, 217–18
Aristotle, 73, 142–43, 235;
  Ps–Aristotle, 80–81
Ark of the Covenant, 11, 128–31,
  134, 175
Armenia, 76, 82, 245, 247
Arrian, 215
Arrows, flaming, 208–10, 212, 215,
  221, 233, 239; poison, 11, 13,
  16, 41–97, 134, 136, 163, 244,
  246, 247, 252, 257; Scythian,
  80–83; Indian, 89–91
Arsenic, 213–14, 223, 233, 239
Arthashastra, 13, 33, 91–92, 106,
  111, 126–27, 136, 142, 150, 155,
  203, 208, 223, 232. See also
  Kautilya.
Asbestos, 221, 237
Assyrians, 11, 171–73, 188, 190–91,
  230–31, 259
Athena, 49, 79, 135, 136, 209
Athens, 12, 23, 78, 80, 99, 100, 106,
  114, 115, 120–21, 136, 192, 207,
  209, 215, 219
Avidius Cassius, 133–34

Babylon, Babylonia, 108, 118, 123, 126, 131, 132–34, 139–40, 145–46, 150, 172, 229, 232, 252, 256–57
Baghdad, 17
Baku, 229
Bauer, Aaron, 86, 90
Bees, 176–81, 244. See also Insects.
Belladonna, 72
Berossus, 172
Biological weapons, definitions, 28, 260
Birds, 86, 112, 203–4; *Dikairon*, 73–74
Boeotians, 12, 219
Britain, 94, 157, 196, 199

Caesar, Julius, 14, 108–9, 162, 199
Cairo, 237–39
Calmatives, 26, 167–69, 219
Cambyses, 12, 189–90, 193
Camels, 17, 197–98, 204–5
Carlsbad, New Mexico, 254, 255
Carthage, 13, 33,109, 110, 115, 118, 123, 134, 154–55, 157, 159–60, 196–97, 203, 220, 222. See also Hannibal.
Catapults, 17, 27, 119–20, 136–37, 169, 180, 188–89, 212, 216, 219, 237, 240–41
Cato, 15, 96, 164,
Cedrenus, 121
Celsus, 14, 66, 95
Celts, 157, 162–63. See also Gauls.
Centaurs, 45–47, 66, 97, 102, 113, 155
Chandragupta, King, 13, 88, 91, 142, 164
Characitani, 225
Chemical weapons, definitions, 28, 290
China, 13, 16, 17, 25, 34, 74, 76, 87, 150, 164, 182, 200, 203–4, 208, 213, 222–24, 225, 229, 239, 240, 241
Chrysame, 11, 165–67, 190
Chryse, desert island, 51, 53, 249–50; town near Troy, 138, 173
Churchill, Winston, 103, 168
CIA, 164, 167

Cicero, 14, 37, 217
Cimmerians, 12, 192
Circe, 57–58, 75, 97, 153
Claudius Marcellus, 217–18
Clearchus, 13, 117–18
Cnopus, 165–67
Colchis, 145–46, 153, 201, 207, 229
Collateral damage. See Friendly fire.
Combustible chemicals. See Fire; Napalm; Petroleum; Pitch; Quicklime; Sulphur
Commodus, 15, 126
Constantine, 221, 240
Constantinople, 16, 17, 241
Contagion. See Disease; Plague.
Cornelius Nepos, 188–89
Crimea, 119 (Kaffa), 148, 152
Croddy, Eric, 246
Croesus, 198
Crosby, Alfred, 208, 210, 240
Crusaders, 136, 237–39, 241
Ctesias, 12, 73–74, 231
Cyrus, 12, 108, 157–59, 198; Cyrus the Younger, 145
Cyzicus, 120, 122, 221

Dacians, 67, 76
Dalmatians, 67, 76
Damascus, 237, 241, 246
Darius, 77, 198–99
DARPA, 92, 186–88
Deadly nightshade, 57, 72. See also Belladonna
Defense Advanced Research Projects Agency. See DARPA.
Defense Department, US, 186–87. See also DARPA; Pentagon.
Delium, 12, 219–20, 224
Demetrius Poliorcetes, 13, 212
Deuteronomy, 11, 34
Dio Cassius, 15, 82, 126, 186, 220, 234, 245–46
Diodorus of Sicily, 14, 65, 89, 90, 115, 134, 208, 213, 216
Dioscorides, 14, 41
Disease, 119–43; ancient theories of, 111, 112–18. See also Anthrax; Plague; Smallpox.
Dogs, 12, 190–93, 197
Domitian, 15, 126, 155

Dura–Europos, 224–25

Egypt, 12, 17, 34, 77, 120–21, 123–25, 131, 132, 151, 171–73, 176, 184, 188, 189, 193, 221, 256
Elephants, 13, 14, 17, 88, 171, 188, 193–97, 202–3, 204
Elijah, 11, 227, 229
Empedocles, 12, 113
Ephyra, 56–57, 68, 113
Epidemics. See Plague; Smallpox.
Erythrae, 165–67
Eumenes, 169, 188–89
Euripides, 12, 52, 207–8, 210, 228
Excrement, 81, 213

Faraone, Christopher, 138, 140, 174
Fenton, Col. George, 218
Firdawsi, 17, 235
Fire weapons, 43–44, 48, 207–50; fire delivered by animals, 202–5; fire–pots, 208, 212, 231, 238–39; fire–ships, 27, 214–16, 232; fire tricks, 11, 227
First Sacred War, 100–106
Flame–throwers, 219–20
Florus, 15, 37, 99, 110–11
Friendly fire, and unexpected consequences of biochemical weapons, 39, 45–49, 50–53, 60, 79–80, 118, 130, 140–41, 168–69, 179–80, 193, 196–97, 198, 204, 215, 222, 225–26, 239–40, 252–58. See also "Poisoner poisoned."
Frog, poison, 70–71
Frontinus, 15, 101, 107–8, 115, 161, 203, 215

Galatians, 14, 196
Galen, 15, 63, 132, 140, 152
Gauls, 66, 68, 71, 76, 108–9, 132, 196
Genetic weapons, 26, 125
Geneva Convention, 105, 270
Genghis Khan, 17, 203, 256
Germanic tribes, 14, 37, 108, 110, 115, 116, 200
Glauke, 207, 228–29, 232, 234, 243, 247
Greek Fire, 16, 17, 27, 39, 136, 139, 208, 240–43, 246
Grmek, Mirko, 66, 104–5, 115, 118
Gulf War of 1991, 151, 193, 201, 238; Gulf War syndrome, 60, 151–52
Gunpowder, 17, 213

Hamaxitius, 135, 173
Hamilcar Barca, 13, 203
Hannibal, 13, 14, 23, 154–55, 169, 188–89, 203, 220
Hanson, Victor, 31
Harmatelia, 13, 89–90
Hasdrubal, 13, 119, 197
Hatra, 16, 181–86, 234, 247, 250
Hellebore, 57, 67–68, 101–103, 105, 160, 163, 166, 168
Hemlock, 71–72
Henbane, 69–70
Heptakometes, 153–54
Hercules, 25, 41–49, 53, 56, 58–59, 61–62, 64–66, 78, 80, 97, 102, 109, 121, 138, 208, 216, 234, 247–54, 257
Herod, King, 125
Herodian, 182, 184–86
Herodotus, 12, 36, 57, 77–78, 83, 158–59, 171–72, 198, 231
Himilco, 13, 159–60, 162, 164, 222
Hippocrates, 67, 102, 104
Hippolytus, 224
Hitler, Adolf, 139, 167
Hittites, 11, 122–23, 141, 143, 179
Homer, 11, 32, 50, 54, 63. See also *Iliad*; Odysseus.
Honey, toxic, 14, 73, 145–48, 150, 153–54, 176, 250
Horses, 197–200, 225
Hydra, 41–49, 78–79, 208, 250, 252, 253, 254, 256, 257

Iliad, 32, 49, 59, 63, 124, 138, 249. See also Trojan War.
Incendiaries. See Arrows, flaming; Fire; Naphtha.
India, 13, 14, 17, 25, 33–34, 63, 68–69, 73–74, 76, 86–92, 96, 94, 96, 99, 105–6, 111–12, 126–27, 136, 141–43, 149–50, 155, 156, 164, 193–94, 200, 203–4, 208, 213–14,

221, 222–24, 226, 229, 231–33, 235, 241
Indonesia, 95, 151
Insects, 73–74120, 124, 176–87, 190, 197, 222, 223 . See also Bees; Scorpions.
Intoxicants, 165–69. See also Calmatives; Honey; Wine.
Iraq, 60, 118, 137, 103, 150, 181, 193, 204, 229, 238
Isaura, 108
Ishii, Dr. Shiro, 33, 140, 163–64
Islamic weapons, 17, 33, 35, 131–32, 203, 226, 235–39, 247
Isocrates, 105
Israelites, 11, 34, 128–31, 175, 178–79, 229

Japan, 140, 182, 204. See also Ishii, Dr. Shiro.
Jerusalem, 11, 15, 129–32, 172–73, 252
Joint Non–Lethal Weapons Directorate, 167–68, 218–19. See also Pentagon.
Josephus, 15, 172
Julius Africanus, 16, 227
Julius Capitolinus, 119, 133–34
Justinian, 16, 202

Kaffa, 17, 119–20, 122
Kallinikos, 16, 241–42
Kautilya, 13, 33–34, 91–92, 111, 127, 136, 142, 150–51, 154, 163, 164, 203, 208, 221, 226, 239. See also Arthashastra.
Kelsay, John, 35
Kirrha, 12, 100–108, 135, 163, 168
Kokatnur, Vaman, 164
Koran, 16, 34–35
Krentz, Peter, 30
Kurds, 103–5, 118, 168

Laws of Manu, 13, 33, 91, 105–6, 149, 208
Lelantine War, 36
Lime. See Quicklime.
Livy, 14, 114, 120, 126, 220, 227
Lucan, 15, 96, 214
Lucius Metellus, 108

Lucius Verus, 16, 109, 132–33, 140, 152, 156
Lucretius, 14, 114, 196, 208, 250
Lucullus, 14, 148, 181, 243–51

Machaon, 50, 53
Maharbal, 13, 159, 162
Majno, Guido, 42
Malaria, 113, 115, 118
Maltha, 246–47, 250
Mandrake, 13, 160–62
Mangonels, 237, 241
Marcus Aurelius, 16, 109, 126, 132, 139, 152, 156
Mari, 11, 122, 131
Marius, 14, 116
Massagetae, 12, 157–59.
Mecca, 16, 35, 237, 240
Medea, 108, 153, 207–8, 210, 228–29, 234, 239, 243, 247
Mehmood, Bashiruddin, 131–32
Mice. See Rodents.
Mithridates, 14, 94, 120, 148–50, 152–53, 164, 181, 221, 234, 244–46, 248–50
Mongols, 235. See also Genghis Khan; Kaffa.
Monkeys, 188, 204
Monkshood. See Aconite.
Morgan, David, 204
Muhammad, 16, 35, 235–37, 247
Muslims. See Islamic weapons; Koran; Muhammad.
Myth, Greek, 25, 38, 41–62, 68, 75, 82, 92–93, 97, 102, 109, 121, 128, 168, 207–8, 228, 243, 249–50, 254, 256–58; Indian, 208; Mesopotamian, 182; Scythian, 78

Napalm, 208, 228, 240, 242, 255
Naphtha, 11, 14, 16, 17, 27, 137, 186, 213, 227, 228–43, 246–47, 250; naphtha troops, 237.
Naples Campaign of 1494–95, 143, 163
Nasamonians, 77, 155–56
Nebros, 102–4, 135, 168
Nebucadnezzar, 12, 131
Nehemiah, 230

Nepal, 69, 147
Neufeld, Edward, 30, 177–79
Nicander, 15, 65, 73, 135
Nixon, Richard, 139
Noncombatants, 35, 167–69, 101–3, 217
Nuclear weapons, 242, 253–58

Ober, Josiah, 30, 36
Odysseus, *Odyssey*, 11, 25, 32, 49, 52–53, 56–60, 62, 68, 75, 97, 145, 168
Ovid, 14, 37, 41, 43, 47, 59, 61, 63

Panama, 201, 218
Pandora, 38, 128–29, 139, 256
Paris, 53–54, 59, 62, 63, 97
Parthia, 76, 109, 132–34, 139–40, 181
Partington, James Riddick, 228, 230, 242
Pausanias, 15, 65, 101
Peloponnesian War, 12, 36, 99, 106, 114, 120–21, 210–11, 219, 226
Pentagon, 128, 167, 180, 218–19. See also DARPA.
Penzer, Norman, 143
Persia, 12, 16, 23, 33, 36, 73, 77, 106, 145, 157–59, 174, 182, 189–90, 192, 198–99, 202, 209–10, 221, 224–25, 229
Petroleum, 208, 213, 221, 227, 228–43, 246–47, 250. See also Maltha; Naphtha.
Philistines, 11, 128–31, 134, 175
Philoctetes, 48–54, 56, 59, 61–62, 65, 66, 80, 82, 85, 95, 97, 134, 249–50, 252, 257–58
Phoenicians, 13, 215–16, 237, 247
Pigs, 13, 200, 202–3
Pitch or pine resin, 43, 44, 207, 210, 212, 213, 214–15, 219, 221, 223, 224, 225, 226, 233, 240, 242
Plague, 12, 15, 16, 119–43, 252, 253, 255; in Athens, 12; in Babylonia, 16, 132–34, 139–40; bubonic, 17, 119, 129, 175; in Egypt, 11, 123–25, 131, 151, 171–75; man–made, 15, 16, 126–28
Plants, poison. See Poisonous plants.

Plataia, 12, 210–11, 214, 219, 221, 222
Pliny the Elder, 15, 67, 70, 72, 85, 93, 94, 116, 147, 152–54,161, 176–77, 182, 184, 191, 220, 226, 228, 234, 246–48
Plutarch, 15, 81, 115, 116, 225, 228, 234
Poison gas, 13, 27, 29, 103, 167–68, 181, 211, 219, 222–226, 234, 255. See also Smoke.
Poison Maidens, 17, 141–43
"Poisoner poisoned" motif, 60, 140–41. See also Friendly Fire.
Poisonous plants, 56–57, 64, 67–73, 86, 89, 111, 127, 213
Polyaenus, 15, 37, 38, 101, 109, 117, 156–57, 165, 191, 202, 222, 224
Polybius, 35
Pompey, 14, 148, 152–54, 176, 250
Pontus, 14, 221, 245, 246. See also Honey; Mithridates.
Porus, 13, 88, 142, 193–94, 200, 235
Preston, Robert, 127, 141
Procopius, 203
Projectile weapons, 32, 35–36, 41–62, 234. See also Arrows; Catapults.
Psychological warfare, 80, 88, 91, 127, 186
Psylli, 15, 70–71, 94–95, 142, 164
Ptah, 171–73, 188
Publius Servilius, 108
Pungee sticks, 81
Punic Wars, 13, 14, 109
Purple snake, 86–88, 89
Pyrrus, 13, 195, 200, 202

Quicklime, 225–28, 231, 235, 239, 241, 242
Quintus Curtius, 89, 215
Quintus of Smyrna, 16, 53, 61, 65, 85

Rabies, 68, 135–36
Rape, as bio–weapon, 26, 125–26
Rats. See Rodents.
Reinach, A. J., 66
Rhodes, 13, 212
Rhododendron, 72–73, 146–47
Rocky Mountain Arsenal, Colorado, 255
Rodents, 135, 171–76, 187–88

Roland, Alex, 242
Rolle, Renate, 82–83
Rufus of Ephesus, 15, 93
Rules of war. See War, rules of.
Russia, 17, 141, 154, 168, 254, 255

Saddam Hussein, 118, 137, 238, 150
Saltpeter, 213–14, 233, 239, 242. See also Gunpowder.
Samosata, 246–47, 250
Sand, burning, 216–17, 247
Scorched earth tactics, 106, 138, 237–38
Scorpions, 16, 176, 182–86, 234
Scythians, 12, 44, 72, 77–86, 89, 148, 164, 192, 198–99. See also Massagetae; Soanes
Sea urchin, 74
Second Lateran Council, 17, 242
Seleuceia, 133–34
Seneca, 15, 228, 234
Sennacherib, 11, 171–73, 175, 189
Septimius Severus, 16, 181–86, 234
Sertorius, 14, 225, 226
Shamans, 71, 81, 123, 135, 148, 164–65, 180
Shukra, 213–14
Sicily, 12, 13, 99, 113–15, 123, 215, 217, 222. See also Syracuse.
Siegecraft, 30, 35, 100–102, 106–7, 185–86, 203–4, 210–12, 215–17, 221, 224. See also Catapults.
Silius Italicus, 15, 63, 77, 212
Smallpox, 26, 121, 124, 127, 132, 136, 140–41, 152, 252
Smell. See Stench weapons.
Smoke, poison, 111, 127, 180, 208, 222–26, 235
Snakes, venomous, 14, 17, 48–51, 63–66, 75–97, 148, 151, 164, 169, 188–89; snake charmers, 15, 94–96, 143. See also Hydra.
Soanes, 76, 81, 201
Solomon, 11, 129–32; Testament of, 16, 130–32
Solon, 101
Sophocles, 12, 47, 52–53, 59, 121
Sound weapons, 200–201
South Africa, 104–5, 118, 125, 164

South America, 71, 75, 177, 223
Spain, 14, 69, 72, 108, 155, 175, 203, 225
Sparta, 12, 23, 106, 114, 210–11, 214, 219, 222
Stench weapons, 26, 81, 201, 226, 269
Stingray, 74–75
Strabo, 14, 30, 76, 81, 91, 89, 99, 153, 173, 175, 201
Strychnine, 72, 166
Sulphur, 211–13, 214, 215, 219, 221, 223, 225, 226–28, 235, 239, 241, 242
Sun Tzu, 12, 34, 208
Susruta Samhita, 14, 112
Swamps, 112–18
Syracuse, 13, 27, 99, 134, 136, 215, 217–18

Ta'if, 236–37, 247
Tacitus, 15, 37, 111, 116, 200, 212
Tamerlane, 17, 204
Telegonus, 57, 75
Telemachus, 56
Telephus, 47, 62, 82, 93
Temple, Robert, 213
Temples and bioweapons, 57, 130–36, 139–41, 252, 255; of Apollo, 16, 119, 173; of Jerusalem, 11, 12, 15, 129–32
Theophrastus, 13, 80–81, 226
Thucydides, 12, 23, 30, 36, 99, 106, 115, 120–21, 210–11, 219
Tiberius, 110–11
Tigranocerta, 14, 245, 250
Titus, 15, 126, 132
Tomyris, Queen, 12, 36, 157–59
Toxic, origin of word, 41. Toxic arrows, see Poison arrows.
Trojan Horse, 32, 55, 61, 101, 159, 235
Trojan War, 11, 23, 25, 32, 42, 44, 47, 49–56, 111, 124, 125–26, 252
Tyre, 13, 215–17, 219, 232, 237
Varro, 14, 114
Vegetius, 16, 37, 114, 213
Venom, see Insects; Scorpion; Sea urchin; Snake; Stingray.

Vietnam War, 81, 180, 186, 193,
    228–29
Vinegar, 214, 220, 221–22
Virgil, 14, 55, 111
Vitruvius, 220
Vozrozhdeniye Island, 253, 255

War, rules of, 11, 29, 33–38, 105–6,
    109, 110, 138–39, 208, 216, 235,
    242, 261–62, 270,
Water, diverting; 107–9; poisoning of,
    12, 14, 99–107, 109–13;
    unhealthy in swamps, 112–18.
Wheelis, Mark, 29, 168–69
Wine, as weapon, 154 (mead),
    155–59; poisoning of, 56, 159–64

World War I, 29, 103, 105, 180, 192,
    252
World War II, 33, 60, 69, 104,
    125,140, 151, 163–64, 167, 182,
    193, 197, 252, 255

Xenophon, 13, 112, 115, 145–48, 153
Xerxes, 106, 209
Yew, 72
Yucca Mountain, Nevada, 254–58,
    293

Yusef, Hamza, 35

Zinsser, William, 173–74